Ways of Being Alive

Baptiste Morizot

Ways of Being Alive

Translated by Andrew Brown

polity

Originally published in French as *Manières d'être vivant*. Afterword by Alain Damasio
© Actes Sud, France, 2020

This English edition © Polity Press, 2022

Cover artwork by Julien Thomas Salaud, Stellar Cave 4, Installation made of nails, string and black light for
the Hertzliya Museum of Contemporary Art, 2015 © ADAGP, Paris and DACS, London 2021

This work received the French Voices Award for excellence in publication and translation. French Voices
is a program created and funded by the French Embassy in the United States and FACE Foundation.
French Voices logo designed by Serge Bloch.

Internal star illustrations: PeterPencil/iStock

Excerpt from *The Overstory: A Novel* by Richard Powers, copyright © 2018 Richard Powers. Reprinted by
permission of Vintage Canada, a division of Penguin Random House Canada Limited. All rights reserved /
Excerpt from *The Overstory* by Richard Powers published by Vintage. Copyright © Richard Powers 2018.
Reprinted by permission of The Random House Group Limited / Excerpt from *The Overstory* by Richard
Powers. Copyright © Richard Powers. Reproduced by permission of the author c/o Rogers, Coleridge &
White Ltd., 20 Powis Mews, London W11 1JN / Excerpt from *The Overstory* by Richard Powers. Copyright
© Richard Powers. Reproduced by permission of W. W. Norton.

Polity Press
65 Bridge Street
Cambridge CB2 1UR, UK

Polity Press
101 Station Landing
Suite 300
Medford, MA 02155, USA

ISBN-13: 978-1-5095-4720-3

ISBN-13: 978-1-5095-4721-0 (paperback)

A catalogue record for this book is available from the British Library.

Library of Congress Cataloging-in-Publication Data
Names: Morizot, Baptiste, author. | Brown, Andrew (Literary translator) translator.
Title: Ways of being alive / Baptiste Morizot ; translated by Andrew Brown.
Other titles: Manières d'être vivant. English
Description: Medford, MA : Polity Press, 2021. | "Originally published in French as Manières d'être vivant.
Afterword by Alain Damasio. Actes Sud, France, 2020." | Includes bibliographical references. | Summary:
"A powerful plea for a new understanding of our relationships with other animals and of ourselves"--
Provided by publisher.
Identifiers: LCCN 2021015849 (print) | LCCN 2021015850 (ebook) | ISBN 9781509547203 (hardback) |
ISBN 9781509547210 (paperback) | ISBN 9781509547227 (epub)
Subjects: LCSH: Environmental ethics. | Human ecology. | Human-animal relationships--Moral and ethical
aspects. | Philosophical anthropology. | Life. | Human beings.
Classification: LCC GE42 .M6913 2021 (print) | LCC GE42 (ebook) | DDC 179/.1--dc23
LC record available at https://lccn.loc.gov/2021015849
LC ebook record available at https://lccn.loc.gov/2021015850

Typeset in 11 on 14 pt Fournier MT
by Cheshire Typesetting Ltd, Cuddington, Cheshire
Printed and bound in Great Britain by TJ Books Ltd, Padstow, Cornwall

For further information on Polity, visit our website:
politybooks.com

Contents

Those who think the most deeply
love what is most alive.

Friedrich Hölderlin,
'Socrates and Alcibiades' (1799)

Foreword

Creative Fire

Something has gone terribly wrong with the way we live on Earth. In small steps, over the course of centuries, we have turned the teeming planet into a mausoleum. We didn't mean to. We were looking for safety, understanding, certainty, a way to simplify and control, a way to manage the chances and hazards of existence. But along the way, we somehow came to believe that we alone, of all the millions of flavours of being in this ever-unfolding experiment of life, are the only ones able to speak, to think, to speculate, to want, and to feel.

We have walled ourselves off and made ourselves exceptional. We've alienated ourselves from the rest of creation, and in doing so we have stripped ourselves of truth and meaning. Far from finding understanding, we have blinded ourselves to our larger purpose. Way short of making ourselves safe, we have put our very existence in peril. We live as if the planet is our wholly-owned subsidiary, when in fact things are exactly the other way around.

Baptiste Morizot has diagnosed this disease with poetic precision:

> by dint of no longer paying attention to the living world, to other species, to environments, to the ecological dynamics that weave everyone together, we are creating from scratch a mute and absurd cosmos . . .

In extinguishing our own capacity for awe and attention, our own powers to engage in the widest theatres of being, we are also launching a new mass extinction.

Morizot has an answer to this culture of annihilation: we must turn our alienation back into a spirit of alien kinship. For a long time, we've devoted ourselves to dispensing with the need for presence. Western modernity has been predicated on 'four centuries of devices that relieve us from having to pay attention to alterities'. But what if those alterities were themselves the key to our existence and the cure for our self-inflicted slide into absurdity? What if the noisy parliament of living things was not something to simplify, monetize, and eliminate, but rather was the source of work and purpose sufficient to keep us forever decoding it? 'After all,' Morizot writes, 'there are meanings everywhere in the living world: they do not need to be projected, but to be found . . .'.

Many brilliant minds are right now engaged in the adventure of building a new-old culture, a culture of interdependence, reciprocity, and interbeing. Morizot is among the most lyrical of these pioneers. His philosophy is bracing, and his proposed solution to human exceptionalism is fiercely articulate. But this book goes well beyond philosophy. It is one of the most developed explorations I've seen of just what a 'landing back on Planet Earth' (to use Bruno Latour's formulation) would look like. It's a detailed dive into the complex, intractable challenges of returning to the community of living things. More than that, it's a systematic account of the constant negotiation such work will involve. But it is also a deeply poetic love song for the ecstasy such hard and endless diplomacy brings. We must, as Robin Wall Kimmerer observes, learn how to become indigenous again. Morizot describes in beautiful detail just what that might look like and just how we might rejoin the work of composing the world in common with other creatures.

The view from the heights of this book is vertiginous and exhilarating. Morizot explores life at all gauges, from the cell to the entire biosphere. He peers through the longest lens of time, backwards across billions of years and forwards into an endlessly unfolding future. His words reawaken consciousness to all its possibilities. For Morizot, 'the best analogy for understanding the evolutionary nature of the biosphere is that of a poetic fire: a *creative fire*'. This book is itself an instance of life's poetry. It spreads the fire of creation. It is at once an adventure story, a personal odyssey, the deepest kind of philosophical meditation, a naturalist's field guide to tracks and scat and chatter, an epic poem, a search for collective purpose, and a how-to manual for the restoration of the mind and soul.

Read these words and be shaken. Let them chill and quicken you, like a night of sleeping out under the stars on a mountainside on a cold winter's night filled with wild calls. Morizot's story will return you to the sharp, painful, complex, ineffable thrill of being alive on Planet Earth. In the howls of his beloved wolves, he hears the world talking in several million different and unfolding tongues, saying:

'I'm here, come, don't come, find me, run away, answer me, I'm your brother, your female lover, a stranger, I am death, I'm afraid, I'm lost, where are you? Which direction should I run in, towards which ridge, on what summit? . . . There's a party to be had, we're about to set off, the ceremony is well under way and I'm a fragment. Anyone there? I look forward. Joy! O joy!'

Richard Powers,
January 2022

ix

Introduction

The ecological crisis as a crisis of sensibility

The world depends on so many different species, each a nutty
experiment.

Richard Powers, *The Overstory*

We're on the Col de la Bataille, it's the end of summer, it's cold, the
strong northerly winds are crashing into the southerly winds. It's a
desolate pass, still in the Palaeolithic era, crossed by a small asphalt
road that's often closed. But it's not a desert: it's a hub of winged
life. Indeed, this is where many birds, countless species of them, pass
through on their long migratory journey to Africa. It's a mythical
doorway opening up to the other side of the world. We're here to
count the birds. Equipped with a handheld counter, the sort used to
count the people entering nightclubs and theatres, we click away
frantically in a kind of joyful trance for every swallow that passes;
and there are thousands of them, and tens of thousands. My companion counts 3,547 in three hours: barn swallows, house martins,
crag martins. They arrive from the north, in clusters, in swarms, and
hunker down in the beech forest under the pass, waiting for signs
that we cannot interpret. They assess the wind, the weather, how
many of them there are, all sorts of other things, and they replenish
their tiny reserves of fat during their halt; at one precise moment,
for reasons that elude us, an entire swoop of swallows plunges into
a breach in time, so they can get across the pass at just the right
moment. The sky is dotted with birds. Once they've passed the
wall of wind that picks them up from the south, they're on the other

side, they've made it, they've got through one door; there will be others. Lower down, glued to the ground, the creeping migration of sparrows takes place: they flit from tree to tree, imperceptibly, as if they were walking, but as they go from tree to tree they're going to the end of the world. Some blue tits need to pass under the wave of wind; they cross the road over the pass on foot, it takes them a minute of stubborn effort to travel the asphalt, without doubting their ability but without hurrying either, on a journey that will take them to North Africa. How can a whole continent of courage be contained in eleven grams of life? The birds of prey are there too, the osprey, the secret king of the rivers, who has inventively transformed his talons into powerful paws like those of a fishing bear, and is now transformed into the pure embodiment of action: a pair of wings plunging down from the sky, grafted onto a pair of inexhaustible hands. Kestrels and hobbies pass through the swarm, predators in the company of prey, just as lions travel with gazelles. This is just one threshold in the long procession from one end of the terrestrial globe to the other: the migration of all that's left of the dinosaurs, still full of life even though some people naively think they're extinct when they've simply transformed into sparrows. The procession includes pipits, wagtails, hedge sparrows, giant vultures and microscopic canaries, wrens, various finches, wallcreepers and royal kites, like Gallic tribes flaunting their colours, each with its customs, its language, its pride without ego and without mirror – each with its own demands. And each of these life forms has its own unique perspective on this shared world, and has mastered the art of reading signs that nobody else can understand.

Swallows, for example, must feed throughout their flight; they have an expert grasp of the climates and the times of day when swarms of insects will cross their path, so they can feed on the wing, without changing course, without stopping, without slowing down.

Suddenly, the noise of an engine distracts our attention. Below, on the road, a single file of vintage cars is climbing up the pass. It's one of those meetings for car collectors who come out on Sundays to show off their pimped up old jalopies on the mountain roads. They stop at the pass. They get out of their cars for a minute or two to take some acrobatic selfies, trying to cram bonnet, smile and landscape into their screen. They're endearing, and happy to be here. And then they leave. My companion, standing next to me, comes up with an image that paralyses us in the terrible wind: 'They didn't notice', she says. 'They didn't notice that they were standing in the middle of something like the liveliest, most cosmopolitan, most colourful port in the Mediterranean, where countless peoples are bound for Africa'.[1] Peoples battling against the elements, weaving in and out of the streams of energy, exulting in the sunlight, coasting along on the force of the wind.

And indeed, we humans are social primates obsessed with our fellows (something we're very good at), so all that those vintage-car enthusiasts saw was a desolate pass, an empty setting, a silent landscape, a bit of wallpaper for their computer screens. But I feel no recrimination towards them as I realize this. They're neither better nor worse than ourselves. How many times have we seen nothing of the lively interweavings happening in a certain place? Probably every day. It's our cultural heritage, our socialization that has made us this way; there are causes behind it. But that's no reason not to fight against it. I do not reproach this blindness, but I feel a certain sadness over it, its extent and its innocent violence. It's a major challenge for us as a society to learn again how to see the world as populated by entities that are *far more* marvellous than car collections and museum galleries. And to recognize that they require a transformation in our ways of living and cohabiting.

A crisis of sensibility

From this experience, we can draw an idea. The ecological crisis we are going through is indeed a crisis for human societies: it endangers future generations, the very bases of our subsistence, and the quality of our existence in polluted environments. It's also a crisis for living beings, in the form of the sixth extinction of species, the destruction of wildlife, and the weakening of ecological dynamics as well as of the evolutionary potential of the biosphere, due to climate change. But it is also a crisis for something else, more discreet, and perhaps more fundamental. This blind spot – for such is my hypothesis – is that the current ecological crisis, more than a crisis in human societies *on the one hand*, or in living beings *on the other*, is a crisis in our *relations* with living beings.

First and foremost, it's a spectacular crisis in our productive relations with living environments, visible in the extractivist and financialized frenzy of the dominant political economy. But it's also a crisis in our collective and existential relations, in our connections and affiliations with living beings, forcing on us the question of their *importance*, the way they are of our world, or *outside* of our perceptual, affective, and political world.

This crisis is difficult to name and understand. However, each of us has a precise sense of what underlies it: we must alter our relationships with living beings.

The contemporary enthusiasm aroused by political experiments with new ways of inhabiting and entering into relationships with living beings, the rise of alternative forms of collective life, the taste for agroecologies and subversive sciences which re-describe living nature in another way, rich in communications and meanings – these are all indistinct and yet powerful signals of this turning point in the present conjuncture.

One aspect of this crisis is noticed less often, however, due to the discreet and subdued hum of its political dimension, of its possibilities of politicization. This involves thinking of it as a crisis of sensibility.

The crisis in our relationships with living beings is a crisis of sensibility because the relationships we have grown accustomed to maintaining with living beings are relationships with 'nature'. As the Brazilian anthropologist Eduardo Viveiros de Castro explains, we are the heirs of Western modernity, and so we think that we maintain relationships of a 'natural' type with the whole world of non-human living beings, because any other relationship with them is impossible. There are two types of potential relations in the modern cosmos: either natural, or socio-political, and the socio-political relations are reserved exclusively for humans. Consequently, this implies that we consider living beings primarily as a backdrop, as a reserve of resources available for production, as a place of healing, or as a prop for emotional and symbolic projection. To be merely a backdrop and a prop for projection is to have lost one's own ontological consistency. Something loses its ontological consistency when we lose the faculty of paying attention to it as a full being, as something which *counts* in collective life. When the living world falls outside the field of collective and political attention, outside the field of what is deemed important, then a crisis of sensibility is triggered.

By 'crisis of sensibility' I mean an impoverishment of what we can feel, perceive, and understand of living beings, and the relations we can weave with them – a reduction in the range of affects, percepts, concepts and practices connecting us to them. We have a multitude of words, types of relationships and types of affects to describe relationships between humans, between collectives and between institutions, with technical objects or with works of art, but far fewer words for our relations to living beings. This impoverishment of the scope of our sensibility towards living beings, of the forms of attention and of the qualities of openness towards them, is both an effect and one of the causes of the ecological crisis we face.

A first symptom of this crisis of sensibility, perhaps the most spectacular, is expressed in the notion of the 'extinction of the experience of nature'[2] proposed by the writer and lepidopterist Robert Pyle: the disappearance of the daily relationships we can experience with living beings. One recent study shows that a North American child aged between four and ten years old is able to recognize and distinguish more than a thousand brand logos at a glance, but cannot identify the leaves of ten plants from his or her region.[3] The ability to distinguish between the different forms and styles of existence of other living beings is overwhelmingly being redirected towards manufactured products, and this problem is compounded by a very low sensitivity to the beings that inhabit the Earth with us. To react to the extinction of experience, to the crisis of sensibility, is to enrich the range of what we can feel and understand of the multiplicity of living beings, and the relations we can weave with them.

There is a discreet but deep connection between the enormous contemporary disappearance of field birds, documented by scientific studies, and the ability of a human ear to make sense of urban bird song. When a Koyukon Native American hears the cry of a crow in Alaska, the sound works its way into him and, through the cluster of memories, simultaneously brings back to his mind the identity of the bird, the myths that tell of its customs, the common filiations between bird and human and their immemorial alliances in mythical time.[4] There are crows everywhere in our cities, their calls reach our ears every day, and yet we hear nothing, because they have been turned into beasts in our imaginations: into 'nature'. There is something sad about the fact that the ten different bird songs that we hear every day do not reach our brains other than as *white noise*, or at best evoke a bird's name, empty of meaning – it's like those ancient languages that no one speaks any more, and whose treasures are invisible.

The violence of our belief in 'Nature' is manifested in the fact that the songs of birds, crickets and locusts, songs in which we are immersed every summer as soon as we move away from the city centre, are experienced in the mythology of modern people as a *restful silence*. But, for whoever seeks to translate them, to release them from being just white noise, they comprise myriads of geopolitical messages, territorial negotiations, serenades of intimidation, games, collective pleasures, challenges laid down, wordless negotiations. The smallest flowery meadow is a caravanserai – cosmopolitan, multilingual, multispecies, and buzzing with activity. It's a spaceship on the edge of the universe, where hundreds of different life forms meet and establish a modus vivendi, communicating through sound. On spring nights, we hear the laser songs of nightingales echoing through this spaceship, fighting without violence, competing in beauty to attract their female companions who have followed them in their migration and wander at night through the woods in search of their males; we are surprised by the barking of the deer, the guttural rumbling of intergalactic beasts, howling the despair of desire.

What we call the 'countryside' on a summer evening is the noisiest, most colourful souk, populated by many species, stirring with industrious energy; it's a non-human Times Square on a Monday morning – and the moderns are crazy enough, their metaphysics is complacent enough, to see in it a resourceful silence, a cosmic solitude, a peaceful space. A place empty of real presences, and silent.

Leaving the city, then, does not mean moving away from noise and nuisance into a pastoral idyll; it isn't a matter of going to live in the countryside, it's about going to live *in a minority*. As soon as nature is denaturalized – no longer a continuous flat area, a one-room stage setting, a background against which human tribulations are played out – and as soon as living beings are translated back into *beings* and no longer seen as *things*, then the cosmopolitanism of many species becomes overwhelming, almost unbreathable, overwhelming for the mind: human beings have become a minority. This is healthy for the moderns, who have adopted the bad habit of transforming all their 'others' into minorities.

From a certain point of view, it is true that we have lost a certain sensibility: massive urbanization, i.e. the fact of not living on a daily basis in contact with many different life forms, has deprived us of the powers of tracking – and I mean tracking in a philosophically enriched sense, as sensibility and openness to the signs of other life forms. This art of reading has been lost: we 'can't see a thing', and the challenge lies in reconstructing paths of sensibility, in order to start learning to see again. If we do not see anything in 'nature', it is not only because of our lack of ecological, ethological and evolutionary knowledge, but because we live in a cosmology in which there is supposedly nothing to see, in other words nothing to *translate*: no meaning to interpret.[5] The whole philosophical issue ultimately lies in making it clear and obvious that there is indeed something to see, and rich meanings to translate, in the living environments that surround us. But we need merely take this one step further for the whole landscape to be recomposed. Hence the first text in this collection, which takes the reader on an expedition tracking a pack of wolves through the snows of the Vercors – something between an ethological thriller and an account of a first contact with alien life forms.

The idea of a 'loss' of sensibility is, however, ambiguous in its very formulation. The misunderstanding in this idea amounts to the fact that it seems to harbour something like a nostalgic primitivism, which is irrelevant in this case. Things weren't necessarily better before, and it's not about going back to ways of living naked in the woods. The point is to *invent* these ways of life.

Animals as intercessors

Another symptom of the crisis of sensibility, now almost invisible as we have so fully naturalized it, is evident in the category to which we confine animals. Apart from the question of the way we treat cattle (which are not the whole animal realm, nor even typical of it), the great invisible violence of our civilization towards animals is to have made them into figures for children: to be interested in animals isn't serious, it's sentimentality. It's for 'animal lovers'. It's regressive. Our relationships with the nature of animals and the animal kingdom are infantilized, primitivized. It's insulting to animals, and it's insulting to children.

Our range of sensibility towards animals is reduced to something elastic and amorphous – an abstract and vague beauty, or an infantile figure, or an object of moral compassion. The ethnography of the relationship between humans and living beings among the Tuvans of the Far North, as described by Charles Stépanoff, or the Runa of the Amazon Basin as discussed by Eduardo Kohn, displays an infinitely richer, more plural, nuanced and intense multiplicity: in these environments, animals inhabit the dreams, imaginations, practices and philosophical systems of the natives.[6]

Our imagination for life forms has shrunk. Our dreams are poor in living beings; they are not populated by wolves acting as guides or bears acting as mentors, nor by nourishing forests, insects, or the pre-human ancestors who have carried us this far. Opening up a space to imagine new places for them in our imaginations – for example in the form of rituals without mysticism – is the purpose of the second text in this collection. Animals are not worthy simply of childish or moral attention: they are cohabitants of the Earth, with whom we share an ascent, the enigma of being alive, and the responsibility for living decent lives together. The mystery of being a body, a body that interprets and lives its life, is shared by all living beings: it's the universal vital condition, and it is this which should summon up the most powerful sense of belonging. The animal is thus a privileged intercessor with the original enigma, that of our way of being alive: it displays an irreducible otherness, and at the same time it is close enough to us for countless parallels and convergences to make their presence felt, with mammals, birds and octopuses, and even insects. These are the creatures who make it possible to reconstruct paths of sensibility to living beings in general, precisely because of their borderline position, their intimate otherness towards us. They allow us to sense, in small steps, our affiliations to plants and bacteria, which lie further back in our common genealogy: relatives so foreign that it is less easy to feel alive in the same way as they do. It requires the equivalent of ferrymen or smugglers: animals are intercessors with this kind of power.

And yet we inherit a conception of the world that has downgraded the animal; this is clearly visible in our language, which crystallizes our mental reflexes. All those expressions – 'to treat someone like an animal', 'they behaved like mere animals' – the whole ladder of contempt, the whole vertical metaphor of the overcoming of an inferior animal nature within us, can be found even in the most everyday corners of our ethics, of our self-representation. It's incredible. And yet these expressions rest on a metaphysical misunderstanding. Hence the third text in this collection, which tracks our inner animal nature through the history of a Western morality that enjoins us to tame our wild impulses.

These complicated relationships with animal life partly originate in the stranglehold of a dualist philosophical anthropology, which runs from Judeo-Christianity to Freudianism. This Western conception thinks of animal nature as an interior bestiality that humans must overcome in order to 'civilize' themselves or, on the contrary, as a purer primal nature from which they replenish themselves, thereby finding a more authentic wildness, freed from social norms. These two imaginaries seem opposed, while nothing could be less true: the latter is merely the reverse of the former, constructed as a symmetrical and opposite reaction. However, we know that reactive creations simply perpetuate the *Weltanschauung* of the enemy that is forcing us to react: in this case, the hierarchical dualism that contrasts humans with animals.

Such dualisms always claim to map the totality of the possible, whereas they are never more than the obverse and the reverse of the *same* coin, and everything outside that coin is obscured, denied, forbidden to thought itself.

What this demands of us is quite mind-blowing. The outside of each term of a dualism is never its opposite term; it is the outside of the dualism itself. Leaving behind all that is Civilized is not to throw oneself into the Wild, any more than leaving Progress implies giving in to Collapse: it means leaving the opposition *between* the two. It means breaking open the world thought of as their binary and undivided reign. It means entering a world that is not organized, structured, rendered fully intelligible on the basis of these categories. The challenge is to cut like the blade of a sword between the two blocks of dualisms, to emerge *on the other side* of the world they claim to enclose, and see what lies behind. It's an art of dodging: we have to fly like a butterfly to avoid being captured by the twin monoliths of Nature and Culture, falling from the Charybdis that is Man with a capital M into the Scylla of the Homogenized Animal, the cult of wild nature as opposed to the cult of the necessary improvement of nature when it needs repair work. We must dance between the ropes, dodging the dualism of animal nature as both inferior bestiality *and* as superior purity. We must open up a hitherto unexplored space: that of worlds to be invented once we have passed to the other side. We must glimpse them, show them: take a deep breath of fresh air.

In my opinion, then, these two formulations of the problem of the relationship between human and animal nature are false and toxic: animals are not more bestial than us, nor are they freer. They do not embody unbridled and ferocious wildness (this is the animal tamers' myth), nor do they embody some purer innocence (this is its reactive reverse side). They are not superior to human beings in authenticity or inferior in elevation: what they mainly embody is *other ways of being alive*.

It is the 'other' that is essential. It expresses a whole quiet logic of difference against a background of common ascent. It's a quiet grammatical revolution that's happening – the revolution that sees the addition of one little word flourishing in all those everyday sentences: 'human beings and animals', 'the difference from animals', 'what an animal does not have' . . .

The one little word is 'other'. 'The differences between humans and *other* animals.' 'What that *other* animal doesn't have.' 'What humans have in common with *other* animals.'

Imagine all the possible sentences and add the word *other*. A very small adjective, so elegant in its cartographic reconfiguration of the world: it alone reframes both *a logic of difference and a common belonging*. It traces bridges and open borders between the beings encountered in experience. Nobody will lose anything in the process. It certainly does not allow us to make any in-depth progress when it comes to similarities and differences. It simply makes it possible to naturalize an adequate logic, to avoid a gross error in biological taxonomy, to incorporate (as a civilization) a mental map with far-reaching political repercussions, and to internalize (as individuals) one more quiet truth, one that will join the roundness of the Earth, heliocentrism, evolutionism, the toxicity of neoliberalism, and the idea that democracy is the worst political model . . . except for all the others.

If we extend this argument, we can in my opinion defend the idea that there is a political effect in the transformation of our relationship with the animal nature of human beings. Our relationship with the animal within us is correlated with our relationship with the living world outside of us. Changing one changes the other. Perhaps this is a psychosocial key to Western modernity, this inability to feel alive, to love ourselves as living beings. If we can accept our identity as living beings, reconnect with our animal nature conceived neither as a primality to be overcome, nor as a purer form of wildness, but as a rich heritage to be welcomed and modulated, we can accept our common destiny with the rest of living beings. If we can accept that humans are not driven by the need for spiritual domination over their animal nature, but by being able to live intelligently with the forces of the living beings within us, we can change our fundamental relationship with the forces of the living world outside of us. This would entail, for example, no longer postulating that 'Nature' is deficient and needs to be improved through rational organization, but regaining *confidence in the dynamics of living beings* – confidence in those ecological and evolutionary dynamics with which we must negotiate different forms of modus vivendi, in part to influence them, and sometimes to modulate them for our needs, but within the horizon of a cohabitation attentive to the 'adjusted consideration'[7] we need to show towards the other life forms that inhabit the Earth with us.

The point is to see the countless forms of animal nature and our countless relationships to them on cultural and political levels as an adult topic. Animal nature is a big question: the enigma of being a human grows clearer, more liveable, and more alive, in the light of the countless animal life forms that face us as enigmas. And the quintessential political enigma of living together in a world of otherness finds other implications, and other resources, in those life forms.

The ecological crisis as a crisis of political attention

But it is clear that openness and sensibility towards living beings, these arts of attention in their own right, are often relegated to the status of bourgeois, aesthetic, or conservative issues by those who campaign for other possible worlds. They are in fact powerfully political matters.

These arts of attention are political, for the discreet and pre-institutional essence of the political sphere is played out in the shifting thresholds that dictate what deserves our attention. The question of feminism has highlighted these shifts in recent decades, and the issue of gender difference has suddenly become a political landmark attracting considerable attention. The question of alienated labour, the question of the condition of all those who do not have the means of production but sell their labour power, is a question that was naturalized in early capitalism, and became – with Marx and after him – an object of the most searching collective attention. The tectonic shifts in the art of the attention of a human collective are highlighted by one eloquent symptom: this is the feeling of the *tolerable* and the *intolerable*.

A king by divine right is no longer tolerable today: the unconscious device of the tolerable and the intolerable is a delicate machine, incorporated in each of us, shaped by social and cultural flows. The point is that our current relationships with living beings are becoming intolerable. The idea of the disappearance of field birds, European insects, and more broadly the life forms around us, through inaction, eco-fragmentation and extractivism (the obsessive stage of the extractive industry which considers everything as a mere resource), must become as intolerable as the divine right of kings. We need to pave the way for encounters that will bring living beings into the political space of what deserves attention, i.e. calls for us to be attentive and considerate to it. Affiliations provide access to an expanded form of self. I remember a passenger on a train looking out anxiously at a rainy spring sky. When he revealed the reason for his concern, I was dumbstruck: he wasn't concerned that the bad weather would ruin his vacation. He announced to me as if he were talking about a relative of his: 'I don't like rainy springs, they're bad for bats. There are a lot less insects. Mothers can't feed their young any more.' An expanded self that other living beings can move into means a few more worries, admittedly, but it is also strangely emancipatory. It is only in this way that the basic value system is transformed, and not because everyone has been made to feel guilty and terrified by the announcement of apocalypses affecting beings who do not exist in their cosmos as *beings*.

The arts of political attention will have changed once we experience the plunder of ocean life, or the pollinator crisis, as being every bit as intolerable as the divine right of kings. The contempt of a sector of industrial agriculture for soil fauna should be as intolerable as a ban on abortion.

We could thus defend the idea that, to a certain extent, in democratic societies crisscrossed by massive flows of information, politics comes after culture, in the sense of representations of desirable life, of the thresholds of the tolerable and the intolerable. Consequently, if we are to change politics, we cannot be content merely with becoming activists, struggling, organizing things differently, raising the alarm, leveraging as much as possible those who are closest to power, and inventing other ways of living; we must also transform the attention we pay to what matters. Hence the fourth text in this collection, an investigation carried out in the open air in contact with wolves, sheep, shepherds, night skies and meadows, which attempts to sketch the outlines of a policy of interdependence. It's a long-term job, but it deserves to be done, because we still have a few millennia to live together on this planet with its cosmopolitan life.

In what direction should we open up this field of our collective political attention? The problem of our systemic ecological crisis, if it is to be understood in its most structural dimension, is a problem of habitat. It is our way of living that is in crisis. And the main reason is its constitutive blindness to the fact that to inhabit is always to cohabit, to live among other life forms; the habitat of a living being is entirely made up from the interweaving of other living beings. The fact is that one of the major causes of the current extinction of biodiversity is eco-fragmentation. This is the invisible fragmentation of the habitats of other living beings, a process which destroys them without our realizing it; we have made our roads, our cities, our industries out of the discreet and familiar paths that ensure their existence, their lasting prosperity as populations.

The significance of eco-fragmentation in extinction has philosophical implications that are not always noted: this fragmentation does not directly originate from productivist and extractivist greed (although this is the contemporary and many-faceted aspect of the destruction of habitats, one which requires us to engage in the bitterest struggles against it). It originates first of all from our blindness to the fact that other living beings *inhabit*: the crisis in our way of inhabiting amounts to denying others the status of inhabitants. So we need to *repopulate*, in the philosophical sense of making visible the fact that the myriad life forms that constitute our nurturing environment have always been, not a backdrop for our human tribulations, but fully-fledged inhabitants of the world. And this is because they *make* that world by their presence. The microfauna of soils literally make the forests and fields. The forests and the plant life of the oceans create the breathable atmosphere that nurtures us. Pollinators literally make what we innocently call 'spring' as if it were a gift from the universe, or the sun: no, it is *their* humming, invisible and planetary, which each year, at the end of winter, summons into the world the flowers, the fruits, the gifts of the earth, and their immemorial return. Pollinators, bees, birds, are not placed like furniture on the natural and unchanging scenery of the seasons: they make spring *live*. Without them, we might have snow melts when the sunshine increases around March, but they would take place in a desert: we would not have the cherry blossoms, nor any other blossom, nor any effect from the cross-fertilization which forms the basis of the life cycle of angiosperms (all the flowering plants on the planet, which form more than nine tenths of earth's plant biodiversity). We would have only an endless winter. A type of being that *makes* spring 'with its own hands', so to speak, isn't just part of the decor, a mere resource. It is an inhabitant, one that enters the political field of the powers with which we will have to negotiate the forms of our common life.

Lack of political attention to living beings

Part of what modernity calls 'progress' describes four centuries of devices that relieve us from having to pay attention to alterities, to other life forms, or to ecosystems.

The conceptual character we are targeting here is someone we could call the 'average modern' (we all are to a certain extent this kind of person in the cultural area which claims to be modern).

Let's observe a typical colonial phenomenon, since this is often where the strangeness of your 'average modern' is best revealed. For a Western colonist, when he arrives in the jungles of Africa or the monsoon rice fields of Asia, civilizing the area where he settles traditionally means making it possible to live there in complete ignorance of its non-human cohabitants. It means suppressing, controlling and channelling the wild animals, insects, rains and floods. Being at home is being able to live without paying attention. However, for the natives, it's the complete opposite: being at home implies a vibratory vigilance, an attention to the interweaving of other life forms which enrich existence, even if it is necessary to compose with them – which is often demanding, sometimes complicated. Coming to an agreement is a costly business in diplomacy between humans, and it is the same with other living beings.

Many of the techniques and representations of the modern world serve this purpose, and that is their function: to dispense with attention, that is to say to be able to operate everywhere, in any place, despite one's ignorance, quite carelessly, i.e. without knowing a place and its inhabitants. It's a disconnection from what in the living world around us calls for a generous openness, an interweaving with pollinators, plants, ecological dynamics and climates. It's a practical metaphysics, whose secret but powerful function is interchangeability: everything must be interchangeable, all places, all techniques, all practices, all skills, all beings, honey bees, apple varieties and wheat strains. It's a matter of being at home everywhere, homogenizing the conditions of existence so you don't need to know the ethology of others and the ecology of a place, in other words the habits and customs of the peoples of living beings who inhabit and constitute it. In this way, the 'average modern' can devote himself to what is 'essential' in his own eyes: the relationships between fellow human beings – relationships of power, accumulation, prestige, love and family, against the backdrop of an inanimate setting made up of the ten million other species which just happen to be our relatives.

This is a highly ambiguous phenomenon, because on certain points it has produced comfortable and beneficial effects. We can't dumbly and radically preach the opposite, in order to move from triumphant modernity to contrite anti-modernity. But we need to draw the right distinctions: there are beings to whom we must learn to pay attention anew. For currently, the comfort of modernity is being reversed: by dint of no longer paying attention to the living world, to other species, to environments, to the ecological dynamics that weave everyone together, we are creating from scratch a mute and absurd cosmos which is very uncomfortable to live in, on an existential, individual and collective scale. Above all, however, we are generating global warming and a biodiversity crisis that concretely threaten the Earth's capacity to provide human beings with habitable conditions.

The paradox, therefore, is that to a certain degree there is a perceptible comfort in the modern art of freeing ourselves from the attention demanded by the environment and those who inhabit it, but as soon as it exceeds a certain threshold or takes a certain form, it becomes worse than uncomfortable: it makes the world uninhabitable. The problem then becomes: what is this threshold and what are these forms, precisely, seriously speaking? How can we intelligently inherit modernity, drawing the right distinctions in our historical legacies between the emancipations to be cherished and protected, and toxic missteps? This is one of the great questions of our century. It is our compass for navigating a firm course through the swell between two

Manichean positions: on the one hand, anti-modern outbursts that condemn all 'modernity' en bloc, as an idea that has gone wrong, while we still enjoy its products; on the other, hypermodern attitudes that want us to accelerate down the same path of progress, which, as we now know, means heading straight towards the worst of outcomes by defending an odious doctrine of TINA ('There Is No Alternative'), making it possible *not* to reflect on, campaign against, or question what is toxic in our heritage.

Finding a way out

One species has transformed into a material backdrop for its human tribulations the ten million other species that constitute its extended family, its giving environment, its daily cohabitants. More exactly, it is one specific small population of this species that has done so, the bearer of a merely historical and local culture. Making all other living beings invisible is a provincial and late phenomenon, not the product of mankind as a whole. Imagine a people approaching a land populated by myriads of other related peoples, and declaring that they don't really exist, not as much as *they* do, that they are the stage and not the actors (ah yes, it's not a fiction which requires a lot of imagination, it also comprises huge swathes of our history). How did we accomplish this miracle of blindness towards the peoples of the living world? We could hazard here, to exacerbate the strangeness of our heritage, a rapid history of the relations between our civilization and other species, a history which leads to the modern condition: once living beings were debased ontologically, that is to say considered as endowed with a second-order existence, of lesser value and lesser consistency, and thus transformed into 'things', human beings discovered that they alone truly existed in the universe.

It simply took Judeo-Christianity to expel God from 'Nature' (this is the hypothesis of the Egyptologist Jan Assmann), to make Nature profane, then the scientific and industrial revolution to transform the nature that remained (the scholastic *phusis*) into a matter devoid of intelligences or of invisible influences, available to extractivism, for human beings to find themselves as solitary travellers in the cosmos, surrounded by dumb, evil matter. The last act involved killing off the last affiliation: alone in the face of matter, human beings nevertheless remained in vertical contact with God, who sanctified it as his Creation (natural theology). The death of God entails a terrible and perfect loneliness, which we might call the anthropo-narcissistic prison.[8]

This false lucidity about our cosmic solitude put the final seal on the serene exclusion of all non-human beings from the field of the ontologically relevant. It explains the 'prison house' of the philosophy and literature cultivated in the great European and Anglo-American capitals. My choice of this expression is not arbitrary: it is now a prison house or 'closed room' in the sense of Sartre's play[9] – but the prison house is the world itself, the universe, which is populated only by us and the pathological relationships with our fellow humans entailed by the disappearance of our plural, affective and active affiliations with other living beings, animals and environments.

This ubiquitous theme in twentieth-century literature and philosophy, which foregrounds the cosmic solitude of human beings, a solitude elevated to grandeur by existentialism, is intriguingly violent. Under cover of the heroism of Camus's absurdity,[10] under cover of having the courage to face the truth, this violence is a form of blindness that refuses to learn how to see the forms of existence of others, negating their status as cohabitants, postulating that in fact they have no communication skills, no 'native senses', no creative point of view, no aptitudes for finding a modus vivendi, no political promptings. And this is the great cunning, and therefore the hidden violence of Western naturalism, which in fact aims to justify exploiting all of nature as a raw material lying to hand for our project of civilization – it means treating others as matter ruled by biological laws, refusing to see their geopolitical promptings, their vital alliances, and all the ways in which we share with living beings a great diplomatic community in which we can learn anew how to live.

The human subject alone in an absurd universe, surrounded by pure matter lying to hand as a stock of resources, or a sanctuary for humans to recharge their batteries spiritually, is a phantasmal invention of modernity. From this point of view, those great thinkers of emancipation, Sartre and Camus, who have probably infused their ideas deeply into the French tradition, are the objective allies of extractivism and the ecological crisis. It is intriguing to reinterpret these discourses of emancipation as vectors of great violence. Yet it was they who transformed into a basic belief of late humanism the myth that we alone are free subjects in a world of inert and absurd objects, doomed to giving meaning through our consciousness to a living world devoid of it. This myth took away from that world something it had always possessed. The shamanists and animists described by Viveiros de Castro and Descola know very well what this lost state had involved, namely complex social relations of reciprocity, exchange and predation which are not peace-loving or pacific, and do not follow Isaiah's prophecy, but are political in a still enigmatic sense, and call for forms of pacification and conciliation, of mutualist and considerate cohabitation. Hence the epilogue to this collection.

After all, there are meanings everywhere in the living world: they do not need to be projected, but to be found, with the means at our disposal: translation and interpretation. It's all about diplomacy. We need interpreters, intermediaries, in-betweens, to do the job of starting to speak again with living beings, to overcome what we might call Lévi-Strauss's curse: the impossibility of communicating with the other species we share the Earth with. 'For despite the ink spilled by the Judeo-Christian tradition to conceal it, no situation seems more tragic, more offensive to heart and mind, than that of a humanity coexisting and sharing the joys of a planet with other living species yet being unable to communicate with them.'[11]

But this impossibility is a fiction of the moderns, it helps to justify reducing living beings to commodities in order to sustain world economic exchanges. Communication is possible, it has always taken place; it is surrounded by mystery, by inexhaustible enigmas, by untranslatable aspects too, but ultimately by creative misunderstandings. It doesn't have the fluidity of a café conversation, but it is nonetheless rich in meaning.

As an enigma among other enigmas, the human way of being alive only makes sense if it is woven into the countless other ways of being alive that the animals, plants, bacteria and ecosystems all around us demand.

The ever-intact enigma of being a human is richer and more poignant when we share it with other life forms in our great family, when we pay attention to them, when we do justice to their otherness. This interplay of kinship and otherness with other living beings, the common causes they foster in the politics of life, are part of what makes the 'mystery of living', of being a human being, so inexhaustible.

A season among the living

✦

Episode 1: In the fog of the encounter

It's the first day of winter. We set out quite late in the sunshine, feeling as heavy as at the beginning of the season, not yet sharpened by the snow, not yet woven by the white winds. The reason we're here in the South Vercors is that we've had some information, heard rumours: certain clues seem to indicate that wolves have settled here, and that they may have reproduced. Has a new pack been born, inventing its territory along these familiar paths? Connoisseurs of the region have pointed out this valley on the map as a possible hotspot for wolf adventures in winter.

We tarry in the sunshine, moving along on our little all-terrain skis, perfect for tracking, as we follow the convoluted track of a fox and the imprint of its vertical leap in the snowpack as it chases a vole. At break time, sitting on the porch of a cabin, we dip our frozen sausage nibbles into the hot tea. It is tough going working our way up in the half-light of the undergrowth. We move over onto a ski slope so we can advance in the sunlight. The resort is closed for lack of snow, as has often been the case in recent years. Ski lift poles tilt like scaffolds from a barbaric past, or the totems of a forgotten cult. It's like tracking through the 'ruins of capitalism'. We climb up in the cold sunshine; the regular crunch of the skis composes a marching song which sets the pace.

We were planning to sleep in a cave in the valley. But the texture of the snow changes under our skis; our sealskins slip and slide, there's no purchase. We decide to cut to the heart of the valley, taking the steep slope. The first part of our descent in the undergrowth is a state of grace, we glide between the evergreens levitating above the powder, in a silence broken only by the swoosh of the silky wing of the ski blade sending out its foam of snow. And then things get complicated, we get stuck in the undergrowth, we curse the wild rose bushes, we move in ski-boar formation, down dirty ice flows, forcing our way out of the claws of the brambles which knit us into the forest.

When we reach the bottom of the valley, there are no traces of the wolf pack, the snow is deep, the forest cover is still dense, the slope steep, it doesn't look anything like the map. We exhaust ourselves for a few hours peering at the opposite slope trying to find the opening of the cave; it's probably blocked by the snow. The sun is setting behind us. Our animal eye – the skin on the back of our necks and hands – senses it declining, in all its perfect slowness. Then there quietly rises the muted anguish of spending a night in the blizzard. We fall back on plan B: an unguarded hut on the plateau, behind the Tête du Faisan.

Orientation is difficult; you have to train your mind to be in several places on the map simultaneously, so as not to risk misinterpreting the landmarks. We finally arrive at the cabin, already occupied by the usual wildlife of mountain dwellers. On the way, traces of the whole guild of ungulates, mustelids and foxes, but not a single wolf print. With nothing to show for our day's efforts, we're empty-handed despite the landscapes we have devoured. In the language of a Siberian hunting people, the word for 'luck' means 'silence of the forest'. Tomorrow we'll make less noise.

We cook in the unguarded refuge, everyone shares their food, we are gently urged to taste all the Savoyard fondues, all the sausage dishes with white wine and onion, with the five different kinds of spirits that they've hoisted up in their rucksacks. We can't say no, we're welded to strangers against the stove; we're just delighted it's so cold outside, that we're close to being far away from the rest of the world, and at ten in the evening the two of us go for a walk, in the immaculate snow, to knock back the white wine.

We advance awkwardly along a small trail of snow piled up at the side by the passage of snowshoes, heading north. A fat moon creates sharp outlines, clouds and horizons as clear as a print, as if a Japanese painter were refining the line of trees behind us with a calligraphy brush as soon as we turn our backs. We're talking about sociology, or something of the kind, bundled up in down jackets and hats, two slightly tottering tipsy friends, grey on white, really quite merry.

And this is when it pierces the night. A perfect wolf howl, right next to us. We stand still as if struck by lightning, each pulls off his companion's cap, we grab each other by the shoulders. Then, a wide-open silence, like when you wait for the response at Mass. So I answer. I howl the way I've learned to, to match the attitude, the shape, the particular curl of their native tongue. I mime it as best I can, like a mediaeval traveller on his way to the Levant who has learned to pronounce by heart a phrase of diplomatic greeting in the language of the mythical people of the Cynocephali, those wild humans with dogs' heads reputed to inhabit the great steppes north of Lake Baikal, as told in Marco Polo's *Book of The Marvels of the World*. But without understanding a single word of it.

Silence again, an almost loving silence, waiting for an answer to our attention. And he sings. A magnificent cry, very monotonous, almost too perfect. So I answer: one has to stay courteous, but how are we to escape this charade? Again he sings out, carefully modulating, louder this time, very close, just behind a ridge thirty metres from us. Then a second wolf replies, further to the south: a deeper, more solid howl, lower too, and we reply together, the hidden wolf and myself. A third wolf responds, over there to the southeast. But not very far away, a few hundred metres at most. The dialogue continues over a few more exchanges, he continues to reply with good grace.

So I make a 'hush' sign with my finger to my lips; let's try and arouse his curiosity. Often wolves come to see who's been howling, even if they know or suspect that it's not a fellow wolf. In the silence, hands clinging to each other's shoulders, we wait, scrutinizing with all the warmth of our eyes the ridge where he is bound to emerge. He howls again, pleadingly, and I bite my lip to stop myself replying. There is something solid about our waiting, the ridge pulsates, a single spruce tree inhabits it, and we can't see the profile of a single figure. I then remember the first time I saw a wolf, it was a black wolf on a crest, it was his profile against the blue air that made him stand out, while his colour in the dusk made him merge with the sage bushes of Lamar Valley in Montana. But here we're two hours by car from Lyon, on the Vercors plateau, a familiar mountainside where you don't expect mythological encounters.

We run back to the cabin, the other travellers have come out onto the threshold. They've heard. I call out into the wind, a long, modu-lated, almost languid cry. And there, in front of us, a hundred metres away, in the dark, a whole polyphony answers: together, all this year's cubs, the whole litter that was born at the end of spring. They sing in curlicues, excited, anxious, high-pitched, joyful, uncontrolled, with-out the perfect economy of adult singing, yapping, trilling, yelping, and all in rhythm. The echo confirms their number (and at the same time we smile at the disproportion: actually, the scientific dimension of this kind of experience is not its ultimate purpose, it often serves as a canvas for encounters of another type, another magnitude).

Once again I answer, we are all as silent as if we were hunting or in a temple, and the pack retorts again. This time it's the cubs and a few adults, impossible to count. Then we all howl in chorus; no answer. Again, we sometimes hear the distant howl of an adult probably looking for the group, but the latter now falls silent. The wind turns and makes it difficult to determine the origin of the distant songs that sometimes reach us. The wolves gathered in front of us are no longer answering. The human beings, on the other hand, are in a state of silent exaltation: the howls gently took everyone outside of themselves, in an ancient wonder of bewilderment and gratitude. Standing by the stove, the mountain experts, who had previously been discussing the shape of snowflakes or the merits of their skis, stammer like children and, by a strange alchemy that I still don't understand, people thank each other, as if we'd all given each other something, and then they laugh as they realize that none of us is the author of the gift. I suspect that this gratitude, one which cannot discover its source, which searches in vain for its recipient, is an unfortunate legacy of the monotheisms of our tradition, which have confined the idea of giving to that which is given voluntarily by an intentional God. So that the true daily gifts, the water which quenches thirst, the sun transformed into a fruit for our flesh, the beauty of the swift and of the light translated into landscapes by our immemorial eyes, are things for which we no longer know who to thank. (If you extricate the gift from the idea of intention, all immanent blessings become possible.)

In this shared emotion, there is something like reverent respect, curiosity and excitement. Welsh philosopher Martyn Evans defines 'wonder' as an 'altered, overwhelmingly heightened attention to something that we immediately recognize as important – something the emergence of which engages our imaginations before our understanding, but which we will probably want to understand more fully over time'.[1]

When we hear the song, we feel that we belong to this story, to this destiny shared by the living on Earth. And we sense that this heightened attention to something tinged with importance in its very mystery is an animal emotion. It is one of the first emotions, the one that filled the first animal faced with a strange and unknown form, emerging from a wood, or leaping out of the water it was lapping. The ability to be suffused by this emotion seems to be part of the equipment needed to tame the unknown, to invent a new source of food, a new nest, a routine.

Just imagine the conundrum that evolution had to face. Perhaps some six hundred million years ago, evolution used the brain to develop the first emotions, so as to allow animals more refined answers to the questions of the environment. The original reflex arcs work very fast, but they don't make it possible to synthesize several contradictory pieces of information, even though that is life itself. A doe is on the edge of a precipice with its fawn, when a wolf appears. If the doe had only a flight reflex, an automatic reaction, she might jump; but she has a whole parliament of emotions to synthesize the fear of the wolf with the risk of the void, attachment to her offspring and her zest for life; she has as her guide the salt of lived experience, namely ambiguous emotions.

Among these emotions, it was necessary to invent one whose aim was to *weigh up* novelty, faced with the constant twofold risk of paranoia (any novelty is a danger to be avoided) and indifference (nothing new is interesting since I already know how to live). It was necessary to invent a burning curiosity for something even though I don't yet know if I'm interested in it. It is this emotion that connects us to the new and the strange, and allows us to metabolize them.

Evolution causes living beings to vary all the time. All of today's mammals come from an ancestor who, over fifty million years ago, looked like a mouse. So, from that point on, each line of mammals had to invent its odd diet and eccentric habits (from anteater to human, from whale to wolf). Each line has had to struggle to invent everything in the face of the environment in which it has settled. Consequently, the heightened attention to something new imbued with significance, something that transports us and to which we must invent a relevant response, is a vital emotion, widespread in evolution. It is the emotion that is designed to react with the most finely adjusted attention to novelty, so that it can take anything new seriously and integrate it by bending the space-time of life in a different way. Thus it can give the unprecedented, discreet event that occurs its enigmatic status, and find its rightful place every time, without considering it a priori as a danger to be avoided by reflex, or as negligible background noise. We share this emotion with all living beings that are 'neophiles', that is, curious about the new – and all living beings are neophiles at some point in their lives, since we are all born innocent. And while life is parsimonious in meanings, it is not stingy with new experiences: each living thing has had to encounter everything, and to consider everything. This emotion is part of the animal ascent of human animals, a shared past.

In human beings it is tinged with a twofold dimension – and I don't know if this is shared by other living beings: the dazzle of reality that amazes us is simultaneously experienced as improbable and as perfect. One day, for the first time, you come across a seahorse. Your emotional reaction is ancient, it's not constructed intellectually, it's independent of any kind of knowledge and older than all of them. It's like desire, tenderness for an infant, compassion for a vulnerable person. It's an animal emotion, and within us it rises up to the surface of time. Biologist E. O. Wilson is amazed at these kinds of emotions: 'The truth is that we never conquered the world, never understood it; we only think we have control. We do not even know why we respond in a certain way to other organisms, and need them in diverse ways, so deeply.'[2]

Despite the modern attitude which consists in trivializing the experience of the living world by erecting the sciences of 'Nature' into a machine for destroying miracles, this emotion is intensified when we learn that the maple tree in the street communicates with the lilies in the flower beds, that bees can dance whole maps, that dolphins can hear shapes. It emerges when we look closely at a cat's face, that tawny variation on the theme of the face, a mask so close and so strange which manifests the unplanned perfection of a life form. It is also the emotion of the fascinated raven encountering for the first time a dazzling shard of strangeness. It is our emotion, immersed this night in the song of the pack. In the midst of this emotion, I'm aged twenty once again, and millions of years old.

Episode 2: The barbarian of a beast

We're under the stars, the slush soaking through our down jackets, but no one seems to notice. After the dialogue with the wolves, the mountain people ask me, in every shape and tone of voice, irritated by the poverty of my answers: 'But does the wolf actually know you're human? Do they think you're a wolf? Do they think you're one of the pack? Why do they answer if they know you're human? Why are they howling anyway?' At the first questions, I insist on answering: I don't know, I'm not one of them. If there's anything striking here, it's the enigma of the meaning of that interaction of the exchange of howls. You'd say there had indeed been dialogue, but in what sense of 'dialogue'? What game of perspective, masquerade, metamorphosis? As at a first contact, the point is to speak up even if we don't have a shared language.

In the magnificent monograph *Le Rêve et la forêt* (*The dream and the forest*), dedicated to the Athabascans of North America, a Native American from Nabesna tells Marie-Françoise Guédon, the White anthropologist: 'In the past, animals were people like us and we could talk to each other directly, but things have changed . . . Today they speak to us in dreams or in their own language. But sometimes everything goes back to the way it was before and the wolf will speak to you and you will understand. [. . .] In a way, it's as if both humans and animals found themselves at the beginning of time, when the distance between the two kinds of beings was much smaller than today.'[3]

She adds that for the Nabesnas 'this does not mean that animals are deemed to think or live like human beings: on the contrary. All the mental qualities that we ascribe to them are exercised by animals in their own way . . . It's as a wolf, in all its reality as wolf, that the wolf communicates with the human being; it's up to his human interlocutor to place himself mentally in a different reality, a continuum including both the human being and the wolf.'[4] It seems to me that there is in these last words a good guide for further investigation, the elements of a method for an ethology 'chimera-ized' by animism, an approach that would accept the influence of non-Western ways of relating to living beings.

Hence, there are certain conjectures that can be cobbled together, sufficiently cautious and reasonable to help us move forward a little on this question of the meaning of our interaction.

Admittedly, while howling as best I can for that wolf behind the crest, trying my hand at his art, I know I don't know what he's thinking. Does he know that I'm a human? At one point he knows it since he falls silent, but did he hear it, or did he see it when he came to meet me? (The next day, we read from his tracks that he came to spy on us, taking a detour around the ridge.) He listens to me and then responds. There's a hint of bewilderment in his answers. He finally falls silent. Howling with wolves in Ontario, or in the Var, I had already discovered that they answered me a few times, then fell silent, while their own exchanges with fellow wolves are often much longer. Do they think I'm a wolf *only* at the start of the interaction, until they finally realize it's all a masquerade, and shut up?

In the case of this wolf of the Vercors who tried to make the exchange last, it seems he thought, at least to begin with, that I was 'speaking wolf', that the dialogue had meaning, since he made it last. Maybe he was continuing it out of perplexity, to make me talk, to determine if this dialogue actually made sense or not. This path leads to some intriguing conclusions. It reconnects with a central figure in the problem of translating between foreigners: the figure that I call the 'barbarian'.

The barbarian in the etymological sense is the one who, to the ear of the Greeks, goes 'barbabar', the person who speaks in unintelligible rumblings – the person who can't speak the *real* language. But, more precisely, the barbarian is not a character, but the name of a *moment* in the encounter: this is the moment when we don't as yet know if the person facing us speaks like us, or is just making random noises. For the Greeks, the wild beasts don't speak, but that's the point: the barbarian is not a wild beast, but occupies the liminal zone between the beast and the human being, that zone of indistinctness: barbarians vocalize, they even seem to address sentences to us, but they're unintelligible, and *it's not yet clear* if barbarians can speak. It's this uncertainty that comprises the barbarian. When we take the time to understand them better, learning their language that we first took for noise, when we see that they can discourse quite skilfully, or produce poetry, we'll give them a different name: foreigner, Persian or Scythian, but not barbarian. 'Barbarian', then, is the transitory name for someone at that moment of suspense when we're not sure they are speaking as we do: we ask the question of ourselves, and then we ask them.

Now it seems to me that a careful interpretation of the situation would at least recognize that this wolf who answers me literally takes me for a barbarian, that is to say one of those beings of whom he *still* doesn't know whether they can actually speak or not, that is to say can speak his language. He's the one wondering if I'm a barbarian. He howls, I reply, I seem to speak, but he's perplexed, maybe these are just random gurglings: he answers to make sure, he talks for a few moments to know if I can hold a dialogue, if it all makes sense, or if it's an unfortunate misunderstanding.

The thing is, I'm a Hellenized barbarian, I'm putting everything into it, I'm miming his own language as best I can, albeit without understanding any of it, I've almost got the accent right. The powerful experience is that of being a barbarian with the ears of a wild animal. I am the barbarian of a beast.

Because he has his doubts.

He really tries to communicate, he repeats himself. For a few seconds I seem like a wolf to his ear. It's a werewolf dialogue. For a few moments, it's all about being a being of metamorphosis, a non-separate being, both wolf and human, of the kind that populated the time of myth at the origin of our time, before the separation. When communication was fluid.

And then the masquerade grows stale, back to the curse of Babel, I'm just a barbarian who would like to talk to you.

This is not to say that wolves are endowed with words 'as we are': I don't know what that means. But all the same, there are philosophical implications to this dialogue. The philologist Barbara Cassin writes about translation in these terms: 'You need at least two languages to speak one and to know it's a language you're speaking, because it takes two languages to translate.'[5] And this is an argument that we can transpose to what's happening here: you need at least two languages to have one and know that you have a language, since it's through the other that our language emerges, with its quirks and its commonplaces. If there's any possibility of being a barbarian for a wolf, it's because there's an attempt at translation, and therefore there is, one way or another, something like two languages. More simply: if there's misunderstanding and an effort on his part to overcome it, if there's a barbarian somewhere, then it means that there's language here.

For once, it is he who speaks and the human who just jabbers: and like a hospitable sovereign welcoming a stranger, he makes an effort to ask his question several times, to know if I too am *someone*, a being with whom communication is possible.

Episode 3: Millions of years folded into a song

But what was the meaning of *his* song, his first howl?

This behaviour is called a grouping howl. It happens when, after spending the day leading their own individual lives, at nightfall or shortly thereafter, the wolves of a pack seek to reunite to begin their collective life. I have observed these rituals several times with a thermal imager on the Canjuers plateau in summer: every evening, around 10:15 pm (the 'golden hour'), we start by hearing a few howls scattered across the landscape. From different crests, we see individuals emerging alone, or sometimes in pairs. Guided by the howls, they come together, converge like the tributaries of a river, and end up where the cubs of the year have gathered. And then it's party time. Another type of howl emerges: this time it's collective, and the wolves who utter it are together, side by side. This is called a 'chorus howl'. It's often a ceremony preparing for a collective activity, for example setting off on a hunt: after it, one of the leaders starts out in one direction and the pack follows him; the tone changes. They're about to take action, they're coordinated, silent, and determined.

And the mesmerized mind returns to this question, one that obsesses us when we're faced with something organized in living beings: *what's it for?* Why did this line of evolution invent this original way of communicating? The form this question has taken since Darwin is: what is the evolutionary function for which the howl was selected? Some say it's to create social bonds. To find each other in the fog. To scare off potential adversaries. But is this really the right question? If we have a prehensile thumb, a beating heart, eyes that can see colours, or a chorus howl, is this due to a precise, defined, unique function? Does each living heritage have a fate imposed on it in the form of a selected function?

To understand the philosophical stakes at issue here, we must distinguish between the function and the use of a biological trait.[6] In evolutionary biology, we call the 'function' of an organ, from among all its effects, the function swayed by natural selection, the one that seems to explain its properties (its form, its functioning). This is Karen Neander's 'selected effect theory': the function of an organ is its effect which has been subjected to natural selection.[7] For example, the function of the heart is haemodynamics, i.e. the circulation of oxygenated blood through all the organs, and not the production of a rhythmic noise (a side effect that is not selected for, even if it can be useful for rocking babies to sleep).

But this argument fails to bring out the complexity of history, and the subversive freedom of living beings. First, the question arises: the function of an organ may well be its selected effect, but selected *when?* This characteristic may be millions of years old, it may have gone through different successive phases of selection that were heterogeneous, even contradictory: which one is the right one, or the real one? The running dinosaurs had feathers millions of years before they could fly. They were used to regulate their temperature and for display. Shall we say that the function of feathers is flight? Often, in fact, we are content to note the organ's dominant use *today*, and we project this into the past as its *truth*.

This is because behavioural biology is still haunted by adaptationism: the idea that every organ exists precisely for *one* function put in place by natural selection, the function that the organ is evidently fulfilling today. But a living thing is not intelligible in the way that an engineer's technical invention would be, in which each device is there because it has a unique, exact and ahistorical function. In fact, faced with the immemorial intertwining that is a body shaped by evolution, the question 'what's it for?', reduced to a mere search for the Function, is not exactly the right question.

First, each living thing inherits traits whose form and function can certainly be explained by natural selection, but this latter has, in the past, affected *many* successive functions. Second, as a result, a wealth of possibilities stir in this heritage. The individual consequently has a certain margin of freedom to reinvent the uses it may serve. It is because it has known several functions in the past that the wolf's howl is rich in complex harmonics, with multiple properties, which make it available for inventive new uses, such as assuring the wolf about the barbarity of a human interlocutor, for example.

What I call 'uses' are *hic et nunc* ways, in individual life, to hijack and use atavistic characteristics by taking advantage of their inherited properties, but for purposes *other than those* for which they were selected.

Consequently, the 'truth' of a biological trait is not a unique function determined by the demand for optimal performance: it is the historical and zigzagging range of functions it has known over the past few million years, the range of its possible uses now, and the range of the inventions that it is laying the path for tomorrow, which form the truth of an organ or behaviour. And not just the question 'what's it for?'[8]

Evolution may well have shaped a howl for you, a howl meant to help you find your friends in the fog or to scare your enemies (functions as 'selected effects'), but it has no say in the daily use you will make of it. And a war cry is a great opportunity for you to hijack it so you can express aloud the joy of those spring nights that sing inside you, or serenade someone, or stave off boredom. The beauty of the thing is that, among these subverted uses, some can be recruited again by selection so as to *become* functions on an evolutionary scale, and to transform the material, heritable, properties of behaviour. Imagine a wolf hijacking the martial howl inherited from his fathers to sing a serenade; the females, by one of these contingencies of life, begin to see it as an interesting criterion for choosing their lover, the father of their children. The ability to sing as a virtuoso will pass through the sieve of sexual selection, and the wolf species will evolve towards a song whose properties will be more and more adapted to the art of charming the ear of a she-wolf.

Consequently, there is not one single function behind the wolf's howl: it stores in its properties the history of the different functions it has known (in the sense of its effects under the pressure of selection), and it's available every day to be subverted and put to a multitude of radical new uses.

This is the elegant way evolution has woven for each creature a past made of precise and structured heritages that seem to determine us (our bodies and, in them, our behavioural matrices); but, unlike the Fates, evolution did not erect the fabric of these legacies into a destiny. The freedom of the living being is that every organ is astir with countless functions, and that every organ is therefore available for inventive new uses.

The conceptual nuance that I am proposing here between function and use aims to pave the way for a philosophy of the living world which accepts biological heritages without transforming them into determinism: on the contrary, they are the condition for inventiveness, novelty and freedom. One example is the black heron of Africa (*Egretta ardesiaca*) which is nowadays subverting the use of its long feathers: this bird has settled into a new environment where the waters are muddy, sometimes because of human activities. By rounding her wings when she is on the prowl, forming a perfect parasol under which she can gaze, she makes a circular shadow on the surface of the water, which attracts fish who are seeking the shade of a water lily to hide from the birds. Past functions (the feather was selected for thermoregulation, display, and flight) doubtless tell us something about the properties of the bodily and behavioural paraphernalia that belong to each individual (feathers are shimmering, breathing, load-bearing) but, as is usual with life, everyone does what they want with what evolution has made of these features; every creature subverts, hijacks and invents from the wealth of its heritage.

The layered multiplicity of the functions of a wolf's howl, therefore, makes it mysterious at first glance, and contributes to the experience of wonder when we hear it. It is this multiplicity that allows our imagination and then our thoughts to engage in a rich and paradoxical process of drawing inferences.[9]

The howl seems perfectly adjusted to make wonderful things, but without our being able to list them all or prioritize them. The message conveyed by the howl does not exhaust itself in a utilitarian translation ('come!'), or in a closed functionalist argument ('the howl of the wolf is used to help find his fellows at night'). This last is the weapon that obtuse evolutionists use to conceal the boundless stirring of history lurking in every organ and every type of behaviour.

Imagine that, on another planet, you come across an entity as elegant and complex as a sailboat, moving along independently. Each of its elements is perfectly designed and shaped. Each of its parts seems to inherit a history of countless different uses, and yet it seems desperately functional, but for ends which we actually cannot grasp, and which are open to all possibilities: this is what all living beings resemble – swifts, orchids, cicadas – if not flattened into their own mere history.

When the first feathers appeared on a clumsy dinosaur lumbering across the ground, who could have predicted that he would open with them, a few million years hence, a new dimension of being: living in the sky, life in three dimensions, the art of dancing very high up there in the chains of gravity?

It is in this first sense that the characters of living beings (organs and types of behaviour) are untranslatable. This does not mean that it is impossible to translate them, but on the contrary that one can never stop translating them, re-translating them differently, doing justice to their intimate otherness, to their compacted historicity, to their inventive new uses, all of which sets them up as so many knots and riddles.

Instead of looking for some ultimate use in the wolf's howling, instead of prioritizing its functions, let's investigate its 'why' differently: let's observe the uses that wolves make of howls, and the effects they produce with them. We can thus draw a landscape of plural usages, which like any landscape is the fruit of a rich and ancient history.

As for the 'howling chorus', for example, it has been observed that the packs which respond to another pack remain where they are, even sending an emissary to investigate the howler – whereas the packs that do not respond when they hear howling nearby silently walk away (this is called spacing). This is a phenomenon that needs to be appreciated without us concluding that this is *the* function, even if we sense that we are here witnessing a mutual signalling that might be called geopolitical.

It has also been observed that packs respond more readily if they are gathered round the remains of their prey, or if there are cubs in their ranks: this seems to indicate that howling in a chorus is one way of holding a position.

During the breeding season, when aggressive hormones are at their highest, packs respond more frequently: so this looks like an explicit, affirmed form of territorial behaviour, which seems to say 'We're here, come and get us!' But, conversely, wolf specialists have occasionally observed packs avoiding a physical encounter after having held a dialogue of howls: the howling is then a method for limiting the risks of physical confrontation between packs, a geopolitical technique for avoiding conflict more than a method for marking out territory, since the howling seems relatively independent of geographical boundaries.

We also know that wolves howl more often in the fog, to find each other by ear.

The litany of observations allows us to sketch the landscape of the uses of one particular animal power, howling, without drawing any conclusions about the precise point on which evolution has determined this howling to play a single role: history is too old to favour single roles, and the immemorial cobbling together that makes living bodies is rich in countless cases of uses being hijacked for some other end.

To shed light on some of the oddities of chorus howling, we can move up to a higher degree of generality. According to the hypotheses of behavioural ecology, in the living world, the types of communication evolve in divergent ways depending on the situation. For the exchanges that take place between allies and relatives, communication will evolve towards messages that are clear and honest. But for exchanges between individuals or groups in potential conflict, the form of communications will evolve differently: towards signals more to the advantage of the sender than of the receiver. Consequently, ambiguous messages, capable of deceiving, will be favoured by evolution when they are intended for belligerents.

Unlike the subtle and information-laden vocalizations from one member of the wolf pack to others (yelping, barking, yapping . . .), the howling is blind; the wolves do not know who can hear, it's a bottle with a message sent out to sea, and so it's wise, from the evolutionary point of view, not to give away too much information. When the juveniles are lonely, without adults, they often emit low-intensity howls to begin with, until a member of the pack whose voice they recognize answers them, and then they sing louder: this is the 'poker howl', which allows you to avoid the risk of being overheard by potentially malicious outsiders.

When the packs meet visually, there is often attack and pursuit, presumably because the information about the size and bellicose capabilities of the opposing pack is given in visual terms. Such behaviour is much rarer when they meet through howls. Maybe it's because wolves limit the wealth of information present in their howling. When they howl together, the wolves harmonize rather than singing on the same note in chorus, thus creating the illusion that there are more wolves than there really are. Despite all the protocols in place, it is almost impossible to count wolves by ear: the multiplicity of harmonies, and the different modulations, often lead the listener to *overestimate* the number of wolves. The relative rarity of confrontations *after* an exchange of howls between packs suggests that uncertainty about the other group makes each pack more cautious. This is called 'the Beau Geste hypothesis': the polyphony of each song is a way of making the other pack believe that there are more wolves than is actually the case, as in the anecdote in Percival Christopher's novel *Beau Geste* where two lonely soldiers in a fort set up armed, dummy soldiers on the battlements to make their attackers believe that there's a countless host of defenders.[10]

In light of this analysis, one might conjecture that the mysterious, elusive, supernatural character of the chorus howl could be the side effect, to our human ear, of a geopolitical phenomenon of lupine counter-intelligence (in the sense of 'intelligence service'). The mystery is ethological: it is maintained by the wolves themselves. The chorus howl is an opaque, metamorphic, spectral song, which deliberately does not provide an unknown pack with too much usable information on the composition and size of the pack. To seem larger, more powerful, and more elusive. To be surrounded by a halo of uncertainty. To lengthen the pack's shadow.

All these empirical observations are gathered in a kind of bible, open on my desk: the synthesis of all contemporary knowledge on the wolf, edited by researchers who have dedicated their lives to it, L. David Mech and Luigi Boitani, and entitled *Wolves: Behavior, Ecology, Conservation*. It's a small written grimoire, a book of spells overloaded with microscopic knowledge and humility. The reader finds nuances of this order: male wolves give voice through an octave, passing to a deep bass with an emphasis on the *o*, while females produce a modulated nasal baritone with an emphasis on the *u*. We learn that howling consists of a fundamental frequency lying between 150 and 780 hertz and including up to twelve harmonics.

When I lift this book, and its mass of infinitesimal and deliberately unusable information, it weighs between my fingers as moving proof of our empathetic obsession with other life forms, of our diplomatic quality: thousands of pages, entire lives dedicated to gaining a somewhat better understanding of other ways of being alive. Treatises of natural history, and certain biology books, turn into something other than scientific summae. They are charged with an unnoticed political significance. Diplomatic grimoires, which – in a deceptively naturalistic tone that deceives the authors themselves and acts as an alibi for their shady passions – clumsily compile ways of understanding how the cohabitants of the Earth live and weave their lives into ours. Hence the adjusted consideration we need to pay them.

They are also charged with a new emotional tone: a desperation to understand these alien kin, to gain access to them. This resembles the obsession with which a transparent lover observes the loved one, beautifully focused on a task, busy with life, inaccessible . . . In a word, it is an unrequited interspecies love.

Episode 4: All of language unseparated

What kinship is there, and what otherness, between wolf howling and human language? For us, the wolf is 'alien kin'. All living beings, in fact, are for us both alien and kin, familiar aliens; in the old French sense, the word *'familier'* means that they are part of the extended family, but their otherness is in certain respects undeniable, like that of civilizations from another planet. When we're in the vicinity of an animal, sometimes the intuition emerges that we may be able to have access to the strangeness of another way of being alive than ours, that of a wolf, for example, without reducing this strangeness. This is what I call, conceptually, the theme of 'alien kin'. This is a way of trying to formulate the impression that animals other than me are part of the family but, simultaneously, they are extraterrestrials. I'm aware of mobilizing here a particular imaginary, that of the most radical otherness, but the challenge is to do justice to their different way of existing. And simultaneously they are so 'familiar': by this I mean our 'common ascent' – this is Darwin's indisputable thesis in *The Origin of Species* – and the feeling of self-evidence that we get from other animals. Faced with another living being, we must hold together the two ideas: this relative is also an alien. This is a daily paradox for us to experience, rather than a problem to solve.

We should contrive to sense what a familiar alien is, or in any case try to find ways to talk about alien kin. To 'dialogue' with a wolf, in other words. The point is to resist the temptation to let the analogy of a 'dialogue' contaminate what it claims to illuminate: as always with alien kin, human analogies serve as heuristic methods, tools to discover things, but we must not transpose en bloc *all* the rules of deduction from the original word to the phenomenon we are trying to illuminate, as in a metaphor. The fact that there is something like a 'dialogue' with the wolf does not imply, for example, the sharing of elaborate information, as in the way language is typically used in human dialogues.

We must indeed recognize that there is a certain poverty in the 'information' conveyed by the howl: that is, it does not deliver any complex information, simply because there are no sentences, i.e. no predication. Predication is the linguistic and logical phenomenon which starts with sentences and allows you to assign a property to a subject: 'the sky is blue', 'you are a liar'. With predication comes truth and falsity, the possibility of error and lies, because there now appears the possibility of asserting something about something. When the language consists of uttering just one word ('Blue!') and not a sentence, there is no lie and no possible error, any more than there is truth, because nothing is being asserted of anything.

There is nevertheless something like an assertion in the wolf's cry, a constative dimension, but it lies more in the situation of enunciation than in predication in the proper sense. It is indexical: if there is a cry and you hear it, it means I'm here, and therefore the deduction induces in all those who hear me the fact that the cry means 'I'm here'.

This is a way of talking before we get to the stage of predication: all these wolf 'sentences' are not actually sentences, and are therefore beyond the true and the false, or below them, like the expression 'I-love-you' according to Barthes, who sees it as 'only one word', with hyphens: it is 'always true', it's an 'action'. 'There is no referent other than its utterance':[11] this is a perfect formula to describe the wolf's howling.

In addition to this constative dimension, there is, in the cry of the wolf, a real incentive dimension (it powerfully encourages those who hear it to behave in certain ways), but also a performative dimension.

The performative, theorized for example by the philosopher John Austin, is a strange function of human language, specific to a certain category of verbs – those which describe an action and simultaneously accomplish it. 'I now declare you husband and wife', or 'I advise you to run away', or 'I order you to come'. But the performative dimension of the wolf's howl isn't the same as that of human language, not exactly, since we are here in a world of aliens, and yet it *is* the same, since these aliens are our relatives. In his performative howl the wolf says: 'We are a pack', and 'Let's be a pack' – and the pack *is*. He makes and remakes the pack by the howling that connects each wolf, isolated in the distance, with the inner world of all the others.

The howl reveals to the other wolves, in a radius of ten kilometres, my person, my emotional state, my desire, my fatigue, my fear, like the voice of a friend on the phone, after years of silence, makes him fully present in the room, with his inimitable style of living.

The grouping howl thus merges several functions of human speech: informative, incentive, performative. There is all of language, without language, in this howl. It is simultaneously a talking-of (I'm here), a talking-to (find me) and a talking-doing. It formulates, in a single unseparated song: 'I'm here, where are you? Let's be a pack'; but it also *makes* the pack by saying these things. It says in the same sound 'I'm looking for you' and 'find me', since loneliness is a lack that must be filled by calling out.

And the wolf probably also calls (to) himself, he recalls himself to existence in the silence of the night. Like a traveller walking alone through a nocturnal landscape, no longer even able to make out his own hands, almost doubting his own existence, begins to speak out loud to himself. To call himself by name. His voice lifts him into existence, as if he were pulling himself out of nothingness by his own hair, by the force of the word.

The great originality of wolf song, if we are to understand its 'alien kin' way of making sense, is that it is sung without a specific addressee, it is sung blindly, it is sung for all: it is sung without knowing who will hear it. What happens to speech when it is not sure of its destiny? Imagine that you are howling at night without knowing who can hear. Imagine what you would say if you couldn't know who will hear your voice, your message, your presence, in a radius of sometimes fifteen kilometres: friend, enemy, prey, rival . . .? This results in the song having a whole series of properties, as we have seen. In particular, it means that if we want to do justice to the sense of howling, in its content, in a perspectivist frame (which takes into account every point of view), we have to hear everything he says to *all* those who can hear him at the same time. In one unseparated song, there is an address to all those who are woven into a relationship with the singer (a relationship of predation, conflict, love, mistrust, commensalism, play, fraternity, or geopolitics). The point is to include in the howling its meaning for the crow who welcomes the possibility of fresh carrion to share, its meaning for the dogs, those hostile and loving descendants, the meaning for the commensal fox who will seek to join the feast if the hunt is successful, the meaning for the roe deer curling up in the undergrowth, and so on.

The song of the wolf is a bouquet of affordances: the material sound works for each listener as a specific *affordance*, it calls up a range of possible actions.[12] Its semantic meaning is secondary to its meaning as a 'performance' in Barbara Cassin's sense: what it *does* to everyone who hears it. It is the range of affordances in the song that is its secret meaning, its native meaning: all its affordances for all those in the web of relationships of which it is, as song, a nodal point.

Howling, like any animal voice, shares with poetry the unseparated use of the functions of language; the magmatic concatenation of meanings and affordances; the straightforward expression of a complex of emotions and desires; the utterance of a completely new and irresistible way of living.

And it would take the resources of poetry to unravel the tapestry of what the wolf potentially says, simultaneously, in the same howl, in front of us, just behind the crest: those affordances that the song contains and that constitute the animal equivalent of meaning for us.

And these affordances differ for each witness, but each is *in* the song, in the relationship between song and living beings:

'I'm here, come, don't come, find me, run away, answer me, I'm your brother, your female lover, a stranger, I am death, I'm afraid, I'm lost, where are you? Which direction should I run in, towards which ridge, on what summit? It's night. Pierce the fog with a sounding star, so that I can follow it! And which of you is within earshot? Friend? (*Sotto voce.*) Enemy? Let's make a pack! We are a pack. Go! Let those who love me follow me! Are you there? I am incomplete, I am yours, I am the ill-fated. (*Allegro.*) There's a party to be had, we're about to set off, the ceremony is well under way and I'm a fragment. Anyone there? I look forward. Joy! O joy!' (*Someone has replied.*)

A single howl.

Episode 5: Following the tracks left by song

The next morning we are on our skis at sunrise, filled with the excitement of the tracking session ahead. Everything we have heard overnight has left its traces, nothing exists without leaving traces, and we will be able to forge this rare connection between the pawprints, their wealth of information, and the interaction we had in vivo with the wolves. The only time this kind of connection was granted me was in a tracking sequence last winter, in the Alps near Digne.

We were leaving one morning in January towards a pass where the opposite slope was crossed by a track, just under the ridge. We were chatting happily, in the way snow alone can incite us to do, and, when we reached the pass, there were pawprints. Extremely fresh, perfectly shaped, without the characteristic erosion of a track on which time has passed. A wolf. We followed him for a while, his pawprints halted on the ridge, with the L-shaped trace he characteristically leaves when he stops to examine things. By adopting the wolf's position, we realized that the place he was examining was precisely the road that we had taken to climb to the pass, on the opposite slope, some five minutes ago. But after this inspection, the wolf bounded away, and the tracks betrayed something like haste, or fear. He was coming back down to the track just under the ridge, out of our sight. But instead of staying there, he was heading further down into a thicket, clearly frightened, fleeing down the track between the trees. We had passed that way the evening before: not a trace. In the hamlet, we were almost alone; no one had gone out before us that morning. No dog could have arrived by that route, and anyway no dog would have scared the wolf like that. The hypothesis sprang up in our minds: what he had examined, what had scared him, was the pack with skis and snowshoes coming up to the pass laughing – it was us. He was right in front of us.

Following the fleeing wolf, we quickly came across the trace of a second wolf. Their pawprints mingled. They were trotting along at quite a pace, running fast, and the track bypassed the hamlet from which we had come: they were speeding up as soon as it became possible. They were there, they were fleeing in front of us. In the tracks, it was our own reflection refracted in their behaviour that we could contemplate. We followed them reacting to our noisy arrival.

There followed a frenzied hunt following their tracks, where some of our friends almost got lost. The trail of pawprints went deep into the undergrowth, and we saw a first individual leaving the path to explore another possible escape route. Then, some fifty metres further, a second, then a third: the sizes of their pawprints made it possible to distinguish individuals. There were at least four of them in this single trace, a polymorphic animal entirely hidden in a single line of pawprints, like different meanings in a single word.

We followed them with all the ardour of wolves, skiing over the thick snow, then smashing the twigs of the conifers in the undergrowth as we shouldered our way through, calling to each other: 'Have you got them? I've lost them! They're over there! I've found them! They've regrouped, they're going up to the ridge! They're right in front!' The pace was exhausting, one by one the trackers stopped under a tree, on a stump, gasping for air, their lungs burned by the icy air, cheerful but empty, while above, the most eager wolves continued to follow the traces.

When we arrived at the top of the ridge overlooking the hamlet, we were sure we would see them opposite: the landscape was empty of trees, they were at our mercy, finally we would be able to cast the free net of our gaze over them, finally we would capture the dense beauty of these ghosts without grasping it. And, of course, they weren't there.

A few minutes later, we found their trace on the opposite slope: they had bounded down the slope at full speed, and climbed the next slope, crossed a new pass, and disappeared behind it, in the time it had taken us to climb no further than the first hillside.

Desperate, delighted, breathless and full of zest like the winds here, we laughed on the ridge, in the undergrowth, with our reddened faces, torn jackets, ski poles and skis hung in the trees, panting friends deposited like Tom Thumb's pebbles along the track of our pursuit, calling enviously to us from the depths of the woods: 'So can you see them?' No they're already far away, ghosts. We see ourselves only in the mirror formed by the footsteps of others.

We don't have the same body, space isn't the same for them as for us, like those vultures who are able to cover a hundred kilometres in *four* wing beats and a few minutes; wolves have hearts of another magnitude, the air passes through their lungs like a mythological forge that is not granted to us. They can run over a hundred kilometres a day, for several days in a row, on almost impossible slopes. Wolves don't like the zigzags of our long-distance hiking trails: they are pitiless towards trackers, they love pure ascents, vertical kilometres, chamois trails that go straight from the spring to the pass. We had missed them, we had never been so close to them.

Back to this morning in the Vercors, after the exchange of howls: this time we were going to be able to follow the traces and rediscover the sequence of the past where they had dialogued with us. We go in search of the first singer, the one who had taken us by surprise behind the low hill. We find him very quickly: I am perplexed at the smallness of his tracks, seven centimetres excluding the claws. But its stride cannot lie: ninety centimetres long at least, it can't be a fox. It's a cub born this year. From the developmental point of view, wolves grow very quickly; their silhouette lengthens from the first months like slender flowers, giving them long, tapering legs from their first winter onwards, so they can follow the pack in the snow. And then their paws will expand and grow from year to year. Yesterday evening, however, I was convinced that it was a young adult, because the howling sounded deep, but on reflection it was too monotonous, not modulated enough, without the characteristic bass notes: probably, when alone, this year's cub has a more constructed, less excited and yelping howl than when he is howling together with the other youngsters around him. We isolate an L-shaped trace, a pause, the place where he issued his first howl. He's definitely looking at the way we have come. He's about fifty metres away from our night position, thirty metres as the crow flies. We follow him. And his pawprints lead in our direction. But not to the ridge where we were waiting for him; he is taking a detour, he goes towards the edge of the forest, and skirts it under the trees. On the ridge, shifted to the left, there's a big vertical rock, and just behind this rock, we can clearly see the trace where the wolf halted.

And when you crouch in his tracks, you can clearly understand the situation: he was on the lookout behind the rock, observing us, his muzzle alone protruding, like my nose now, and when we mimic his position, we can clearly see the small valley below where we waited for him at night: he had indeed come to meet us, but he cunningly bypassed the place where we were waiting, he spied on us spying on him, he came to suss out what kind of thing we were, after having held converse with us. And then his traces disappear into a hidden valley and leave in the direction of other howls, towards real wolves this time.

Then we followed our first singer, the snow was starting to fall, a light wind was ripping apart the fabrics of fog hanging from the spruce needles, the young wolf plunged into a steep undergrowth. We were struggling to follow in the snow transformed by the changes in temperature (the spruce forest traps the nocturnal thermal currents rising from the earth, which produce a cooling in the soil overnight, so that, in the microclimate of the undergrowth, the snow freezes less easily and stays softer than elsewhere).

We finally find a trace, hard to read, blurred, bigger than that of the cub, emerging out of the wood and entering a small bottleneck pass. We glide along this imprint in the thick, soft snow, our skis parallel to the path, a single trail, where we can see the tracks of just one animal, its hind foot exactly placed in the track of the forefoot, in what is called a 'perfect cover', characteristic of the wolf. And suddenly it explodes like a grenade and radiates outwards: one then two then three then four tracks spring from the single trace, like a delta with many arms opening downstream of a river, as if the animal had multiplied within itself; four individuals at least diverge at the level of the valley and dash along the slope, meet and separate again as far as the eye can see in the snow.

At the top of the valley, we isolate a first individual; its trace is massive, twelve centimetres wide and long, probably the breeding male, the father, it's at the centre of the trail. We are excited because a hypothesis that we have long supported is about to be put to the test by life itself: the idea that when they arrive at a pass, when a new landscape presents itself to their noses and eyes, wolves, like humans, stop to explore the new horizon.

At the pass, there is a rock with the marking of a human trail, a stroke of yellow paint, at the key point, the place which governs the passage and affords an optimal view of the valley in front. And at the foot of this rock where every human being stops, along the magnificent straight trail of the father wolf, there is the characteristic L-shaped trace: he stopped, he inhaled the bouquet of scents weaving the memories of the animals that inhabit this forested mountain slope in front of him, scents which rise along the anabatic winds and offer themselves to his sense of smell with its inconceivable sensitivity.

Awkwardly we try to take a photo from the exact point where his muzzle would have been, with our knees in the tracks of his powerful forelegs, to see for once the valley as he will have sniffed it: translating, translating the untranslatable, the impossible and necessary task of the poetry translator, because we need to pierce the barrier of the meanings of others, and the irreducible otherness of life forms is as thin as a titmouse's fluff.

The second trace is that of a subadult, a teenager, almost as massive as that of the father (about ten centimetres). The third is probably the mother's (eleven centimetres long but a little more slender): in her traces are those of this year's cub, probably our first singer who found the family in the undergrowth without our noticing. The tracks bound off along the slope. Those of the breeding male, the leader, come closest to the hut where we howled. We find the area from which the pack answered us, it's a ballet of illegible, untranslatable traces, but we can clearly see the hut less than a hundred metres from us; they saw us as in full daylight, because the night was clear, we were in front of their eyes, and yet they answered twice; it's still a mystery. There is an amazing wealth of interwoven traces in the rising fog.

We follow their weave for a long time, counting between seven and nine individuals at the very least, a real Palaeolithic clan, still with the strange feeling that they are at home, that they exude a form of sovereignty over their territory that you don't sense in most other animals – I can't explain it, it might just be a feeling, but I think it has an eco-ethological foundation.

By tracking them for several kilometres, we have been able to read some intriguing behaviour in their footsteps: for example a scene of dominance, called 'active submission' by ethologists. What we see in the snow speaks volumes: the female advances with a stride of over a metre, and in parallel to her the subadult has a stride of similar size; suddenly he forks towards the female and his stride changes to ten centimetres long, with the paws tucked inward, while the female stride does not shrink. The two traces join up, there's a halt, we imagine them licking their chops, in a strange ritual as clear to them and obscure to us as one of those convoluted handshakes that teenagers invent. We can see in the traces that the youngest wolf is 'acting childish', he plays his role as a consummate actor: evolution has hijacked these signs that call for care and tenderness in adults, and given them a whole range of meanings, sometimes love between adults, sometimes submission. Here it's something like a bodily renewal of one's vows as a vassal: 'I place myself under your protection and accept your authority.' And then the trace resumes, a single trace this time, with a single track, the subadult following in the footsteps of the captain – probably his mother.

Can we translate the untranslatable?

On several occasions, we have followed the twisting and turning departures of the patrollers, who seem to duplicate themselves as they leave the single track in the snow. And, in comparison, we have seen the attempts at an exploratory patrol made by one of the wolf cubs, not a very smart one: he starts off spiking away from the pack's shared trajectory, goes for a few metres, then his stride slows down, as if frightened; instead of branching off to get back into the current, he retraces his steps, perhaps going backwards, in any case showing he's abandoned the attempt. We see the traces of the mother who also comes a metre or two out of the group towards him, as if to reassure him and bring him back into the group.

A little further on, the traces became clearer again: the wolves had left the howling area as a group and made a single clean track, in a straight line through the snow of the undergrowth. We followed this track for several hundred metres; a single set of prints was visible, going in a straight line, with at least five or six individuals in it, which meant they were perfectly placing their two paws (front then rear) in the same pawprint, without the slightest error: ten paws one after the other placed in one and the same trace with the delicacy of a goldsmith.

But in some valleys, when the texture of the snow was changing, something fascinating took shape: indeed, when the snow became shallower, we could see, between the regular pawprints of the pack, every sixty centimetres, small cub pawprints which seemed to spring from the single, polycephalous animal we were following. The wolf cubs lengthen their stride to place their paws in the pawprints of the adults when the snow is deep but, each time the snow becomes shallow, the traces of the juveniles reappeared *between* those of the older ones, they relax and go at their own pace, they stop striving to keep up with the pack.

And then a few metres further on, as soon as the snow becomes deep again, they lengthen their stride and we see just a single trace for the whole family. Here we have confirmation that one origin of this strange habit of all running in the same trace amounts to a collective improvement of running in the snow: there is a characteristic exhaustion when you push your foot in and then pull it out with each step, in weather conditions like these. So the first wolf makes the effort for all the others, who enjoy the road opened and stabilized by the scout. While I was voicing this conjecture aloud, with the traces in front of me, I turned around and followed the prints of my skis the way I had come, and a few metres behind, I saw that my friend had placed his skis exactly in the traces of mine, and we smiled.

But if things were that simple, we wouldn't be dealing with the living world. A single function does not translate the real meaning of a form of behaviour, as we have seen. The logic of the noisy

interleaving of functions and uses that lie behind a certain characteristic, which we explored above in the case of the howl, applies to
everything. For example, it has long been believed and repeated, as
the zoology textbooks say, that the ability of each wolf to place its
hind paw exactly in the track of its front paw came from an adaptation
to running through the winter snow: this limits the energy wasted. I
believed it too, until a certain experience gave new meaning to this
simplistic tale. It was the experience of having to walk in silence
so as not to be heard by other animals, in order to approach them
more closely. The need for stealth is shared by all mammals, and it is
with analogous bodies and with common vital issues in view that we
human beings encounter it. When we try to walk silently, we quickly
realize that it is just when we look up to probe the undergrowth that,
inevitably, we step onto a branch, whose cracking makes the birds
rise, the jay cry, and the attentive creatures flee. That's when we
lose sight of where we've put our foot down. But the great drama of
the four-legged beasts is that they are required to be stealthy, while
being structurally incapable of ever seeing where they place their rear
feet. The solution invented by their evolutionary lineage is obvious:
the body just needs to learn to always position the rear foot exactly
where it had placed the front foot, quite safely, even behind them. In
the light of this hypothesis, we can understand why the lynx and the
lioness, as they pad towards their prey, muzzle pointed at their target,
all antennae deployed, delicately and blindly place their feet exactly
in the print of their hands. Running in the snow, and being stealthy:
both functions, both uses are present in this wolf behaviour, both
must have experienced the pressures of selection or apprenticeship,
with perhaps others of which we are still unaware, and combined
here with the anatomical constraints of running. It is in this millen-
nial interweaving of meanings, of adjustments to the world, and of

constraints, that reside the hidden secrets of each living characteristic that we inherit. And these open up the most wonderful inventions, to help us face the problems of living which will emerge tomorrow. The art historian Edgar Wind, in his work on the 'pagan mysteries' (the secret meanings hidden in the paintings of the Renaissance), shows that layers of meaning accumulate in each picture, meanings that are sometimes contradictory, divergent, and complex – but it is these which give it its artistic richness, its ability to glow with meaning, its inexhaustible character. He writes: 'A great symbol is the opposite of the sphinx: it has even more life once the riddle has been solved.'[13]

The same is true of the meanings in the living world: once we have found one, once we have solved a riddle, it is not disenchanted, but more alive, because a little light makes it possible for us to see the potential interplay between this elucidated meaning and all the others which are astir around it.

Episode 6: Being part of a gang – whatever the species

The blizzard started to push us forward, bringing a very dense fog along with it; the tracks of the wolves were leading us into the forest far from our way home. We had to abandon them, saying goodbye, struggling on our skis to the pass where we were parked.

After a few kilometres the snow started to fall, and we arrived at the valley we'd been in the day before. Perpendicular to our route, we came across the trail of the pack, which was at most a few hours old: they had passed the same morning, trotting along as if in a parade, a sovereign clan, first along a single line, then in a delta-like explosion of individuals crossing the human path. Again, I sensed the similarity to a feudal dynasty – but why? The traces have a characteristic tone here: an expansive, demonstrative message, almost show-off, very relaxed, rolling along mechanically, not hiding for a moment. Not all the feverish traces of the chamois, or the vigilant track of the deer hugging shelter, no: in full sunshine, in the middle, nonchalant, curious, exploratory, clearly directed by a group that reassures and provides confidence. There's something ethological, beyond the human, in the effect that a gang makes: something we've all felt, sometimes from within, in a bar with friends, and often from outside, when we're out on the street, a 'look who's in town' kind of effect. The gang effect is a piece of animal ascent shared by several species, those which have ventured into this original form of social life. It is an existential convergence. From the inside: in a gang we're stronger, more confident, less inhibited, less personal, more acephalous and at the same time bigger loudmouths; from the outside: a gang is a bit scary, it has a membrane that surrounds it, it comprises its own territory. Two individuals and a gang are quite different ethological phenomena when you meet them on a pavement or in the forest. A gang is autonomous, like a school of fish, it's metamorphic, it's dangerous, it assumes a shape and then shifts shape, it's turned inward, it can neglect the outside, and yet it has antennae and eyes in the back of its head, you can't take it by surprise, it's not in danger on the surface of its skin in the way that loners are. It's turned in, less attentive to the outside, and yet more expansive towards the outside, more affirmative, more exploratory, more joyful, louder, more at home. It's an effect of this order that is sometimes produced by the prints of a wolf pack. How are we to read in these traces a being-in-the-world, a tonality of existence?

Tracking is not a form of reading, as I believed and wrote for a long time. It's analogous, as reading is a hijacking of the original tracking, of the perceptual and mental gesture of interpreting continuous sequences of signs in the mud that make a story. But reading is a very particular form of tracking, produced by the strictly intentional dimension of the written message and its powerful semantic and symbolic charge. Tracking is much more ambiguous and suspended than reading: it's a form of translating. It translates signs emitted by a living being who is simultaneously alien and kin. It translates 'untranslatables'. The concept of 'untranslatable' is very elegant because it expresses the impossibility of translating, in the sense that we will never have the 'true' meaning. This makes it possible to formulate a rule of simple honesty, though one that does not mean we can stop trying to translate. On the contrary, an untranslatable is something that we must continue to translate indefinitely. It's a concept proposed by the philosopher Barbara Cassin to describe those words which idiomatically belong so deeply to a language that any attempt to translate them into a single word will fail: for example, the *saudade* of the Brazilians, the German *Dasein*, the English 'spleen' . . . Faced with these untranslatables, we are not doomed to silence; we must translate, but translating then amounts to retranslating yet again, multiplying our attempts to do justice to the original. I believe the same can be said of what we are discussing here: when faced with the different behaviours and life forms of other living beings, we are doomed to translate untranslatable things. The meaning is still in suspense, we run after it, we keep re-translating, we're always afraid of misunderstanding it, but a misunderstanding is sometimes creative – and though admittedly the perfect dictionary of other life forms does not exist, we still have to live, and live together.

It was time to head home, the fog was hiding all the paths and slopes. At one point in the blizzard, chilled with cold, pushing my ski poles like an automaton as I made my way towards the world of cities, I followed a path where human beings had passed on snowshoes, as well as deer and other untranslatable animals. This trail was bound to take us home and, on this very trail, there were the fresh tracks of a six-month-old wolf cub.

He had left the pack at the pass and, being a smart chap, he was exploring this path along the side of the valley; it was our path, the only one we had left, with the hope that it would indeed take us back to our warm home. I could hardly make out any more his little wolf's paws in the fog, as if he were guiding us. After a few hundred metres, we realized that it was probably a female. Her urine had fallen between her legs, towards the back of her hind legs and not forward as in young males, or on the side as with the leader. (Note that, in wolves, only the leading male lifts his paw to urinate, while in dogs, *all* males do so, which suggests that all tame dogs, even when they are alone, even yappy little mutts, are convinced in their heart of hearts that they are alpha males.)

The animal we were following in the fog was a smart female wolf child who had left the pack at the top of the previous pass and was exploring this side of the mountain by herself. Several times she left the path, patrolled for a few metres to one side to smell or to see something, and we were overcome by a slight sadness at the thought of losing her; she left us, and then invariably came back to the trail, which we followed by skiing in the trace of her pawprints, filled with joy at finding her again. It's the same kind of patrol you see when following a pack: they're all pursuing a single track, and then a curious individual will regularly leave to sketch out an arabesque on the right or left, then fall back into line.

Here, the line was formed by this path, with the human traces and the traces of deer, and I had the strange feeling that we all belonged to the same big multispecies pack, a gang led by the wolf child in the fog. She was a scout, advancing along a shared path. It was a beautiful day.

Episode 7: The art of living variants

It's a month later, January. We're back almost in the same place, in the fog, on snow hard as a rock. We're tracking the same wolf territory, but on the other side of the Vercors, to the west of Mont Aiguille. We're looking for the pack. There are four of us on Nordic touring skis. We have a feeling that they have reason to pass along this wild little mountain side. We go back up into the forest, on old forest tracks, dotted with a fresh troop of young conifer shoots, tracks long since forgotten. We almost get lost; the geography of animals isn't indicated on the map.

The track disappears steeply down the course of a mountain torrent. I take off my boots, feeling desperate: for hours we have seen nothing, found nothing, and there's no way of getting through. It's cold, and the hospitality leaves much to be desired. I slide down to the bed of the torrent, in the hope of finding the start of a forest track on the opposite side, only to find myself stuck in an avalanche corridor. I turn around annoyed, and wave to the gang: 'U-turn. We're giving up, it's not possible.'

And there, as I drag my feet back to where I'd been a minute before, between the traces of my boots, there's a perfect print, in dia-mond shape – so, a wolf. Then another. Then the traces of the whole pack: nine individuals who came down into the inaccessible torrent, nonchalantly crossing the avalanche flow. We're at the bottom of the bush, there are no human trails anywhere. The wolves went down to quench their thirst: we can see where they pierced the thin layer of frost on the stream, with their snouts, to lap up the water, taking turns, in the same well. I howl into the valley, my song bounding down the stream, in case they are still within earshot, to let them know that we're in the neighbourhood. A couple of black peaks echo my howl.

We chase after the pack. They make us go through the usual roller coasters. They go straight up the ridge along muddy and impassable slopes, they descend straight down some almost vertical ice corridors, and here we go again . . . Their trajectories are, for our bodies, almost impossible. We curse them: 'They have no respect, just no respect for trackers!' we keep saying, cursing and laughing. From the top of a ridge, we can see a snow slide under our feet: the snow has been continuously crushed and washed away, they descended by sledding down on their hindquarters. Finally, they bring us back to a forest track.

They follow it for a few hundred yards, then they leave it and launch out again into an impossible canyon . . . We continue to follow them, magnetized, struggling down the slope, with tense smiles, and they finally lead us to a human track.

These two fragments of forest tracks were not on our maps, they were forgotten. What is fascinating is that the pack has its own logic of movement. Their trajectory does not wander, it cuts smooth as a knife blade. They are going somewhere, you can feel it, it's evident from the inside (this will be confirmed at the end of the path). They know their territory much better than we do, they know it as a forester knows it.

They know a priori where they want to go, and then they plan the optimal trajectory. I have the map in front of me, and I can't find the minimum trajectory.

At this point, I learn something strange: when you're lost in the forest, it gives you a curious sense of being saved when you find traces of wolves because, if the wolves have been there, that indicates that the path leads to something and will optimally overlap with human tracks and bring you back to 'civilization'. At one point, one of us scouts up a stream to look for a practicable track higher up. At the same moment, I see that the wolves have passed right by us, and I find myself saying to my friend: 'It's no use you going up there: if the wolves have passed this way, it means there isn't a more practical trail higher up.' We exchange glances, in silence. We sense the zoocephalic strangeness of the argument: taking wolves as our guides in the forest. I think of a tale told by the Tanaina, Native Americans of Alaska, which I had previously viewed as a bit of folklore: this tale advises the walker lost in the forest to call to the wolf for help to find his way.[14] Compared with 'Peter and the Wolf' and 'Little Red Riding Hood', this is a fairly pure inversion of the theme of our fables about being 'lost in the forest': what is a great danger here is salvation over there. Perhaps this Native American tale originates partly in the confidence one may feel on the ground for the wolf's choices when it comes to orientation: he's a better compass than the official map, and we tend to believe, with the help of experience, that by following the wolf we will quickly come across a track forgotten by the cartographers, a perfect path for reaching a key point of the territory, a shortcut to optimize a beautiful trajectory outside the forest, towards a crossroads, a hub in the landscape, which the pack will reach to mark it with their coat of arms.

And indeed, after a long chase through the undergrowth, the pack brings us back, from lost track to deserted path, onto the main central path which all the hikers use, at the bottom of the valley. We can hear the skiers before we see them. We are following the wolves, camouflaged by the edge of the wood. We emerge on the human path by adopting the point of view of the wolf. We see for a moment the route along which humans pass through the wolves' eyes, hidden as they are at the edge of the wood. We feel that they have examined the place cautiously ('is the path clear?'), then moved straight onto the track in question, and trotted up along it.

And yet we'd been along this track the day before, without seeing their traces. Hundreds of crossings by skiers and dogs made their pawprints almost illegible. But as usual, once we've spotted them, they start to appear everywhere, they rise up in the landscape, and we still follow them along the traces left by the skis, which the wolves in turn take (the skis pack the snow for them), slaloming, exploring, sniffing the edges of the path. What is fascinating in this case is the dramatic change in their track. We had been following them continuously for at least a kilometre in the bush and there was no territorial marking, no urine traces, no scratching. And then, no sooner has the pack come out onto the path with its busy swarm of humans, dogs, foxes and others, than a flag stands out prominently every fifty metres: urine, excrement, scratching. At every bridge there's a marking, at the beginning and the end, as at every crossroads. So it's necessarily in reply to the presence of other species (humans, dogs, and so on), it's inevitably a geopolitical arrangement.

The interesting thing is that this is not a monospecific dialogue. Next to the wolf markings, we can distinguish the markings of foxes, dogs and mustelids. We don't know yet what that means, but these are coats of arms and flags: there's a kind of silent dialogue with other species. The dimension of geopolitical signalling is explicit. Meaning escapes us completely, but this must have a meaning: there *is* interspecies communication.

How should we understand this use of the metaphor of the coat of arms and the flag to describe the territorial marking of carnivores, and of wolves in particular? Concretely speaking, wolves have glands around their anus and between their toes, rich in a potion with which they coat their excrement, or that they rub into the earth (scraping). This potion contains a wide range of information for a wolf's muzzle: it reveals the identity of the one who made the mark, the pack to which he belongs, his current diet, his sexual availability, and even his emotional state (his degree of stress for example). It's in this sense that it acts as a coat of arms, or a biometric passport erected into a coat of arms. But the marking is also a conventional territorial limit. It does not physically stop anyone passing but constitutes a boundary stone which, aligned with the others, comprises a border of odours, one that other packs will respect or sometimes cross, depending on their mood and their plans. It's in this sense that it constitutes a flag.

This kind of expression is often criticized for being an anthropomorphic metaphor, and yet I would like to show here that this usage is epistemologically defensible, that it even constitutes the method of an ethology finally capable of doing justice to the intimate otherness of life forms different from ours.

It's what I call a perspectivist ethology. Anthropologist Eduardo Viveiros de Castro, in *The Relative Native*, notes in passing the links between perspectivism and ethology.[15] Perspectivism, like the 'cosmovision' of certain animist peoples, postulates that the visible and the invisible are relative to the capacities of the one who perceives (here we must understand 'visible and invisible' in the broad sense of perceptible and imperceptible, accessible and inaccessible). Strictly speaking, each animal does not see or configure the world from its mind, but from its body: its perspective on the world is based on its body with its own powers of feeling and doing. This is the great idea of perspectivism. Now this body is provided with its unique powers and perspectives by an original effect of ecoevolution.

Everyone's point of view, then, is not 'in the body' (like a mind) but the body itself, nothing other than the body – a body thick with ancestral characteristics all combined together, which are always reinterpreting the present afresh. For example the conversion of the dropping coated with pheromones, now hijacked into a geopolitical signal, is a magnificent reinterpretation on the part of the carnivore's body of the excretory function it inherits from its mammalian ancestor. Combined with another ancestral feature, a subtle and discriminating sense of smell, it invents a mode of life previously unimaginable; it opens up to wolves a whole dimension of being: the geopolitics of odours.

Amazonian perspectivism cannot be reduced to an ethology of perspectives, in Viveiros de Castro's own words, but it is a powerful tool for comparative ethology. To say that droppings are coats of arms and flags is not an anthropomorphic metaphor, but an analogy of perspectivist ethology.

We need to clarify exactly what this kind of formula means, and the type of operation of mind and body that it implies. It means: the dropping is seen by the relevant animals in pretty much the same way that we see coats of arms and flags. Here again, we mustn't understand 'see' in a sensory sense: perspective is a visual metaphor for talking about something more fundamental – a way of experiencing, of conferring meaning. It means wolves experience the dropping in a similar way to our experience of the coat of arms; it means something similar, it activates analogous things, it is taken up in analogous uses. This is not a metaphor, because there is no original domain (the human world, with its coats of arms), and no derived domain (the wolf world, with its droppings). It's an ethology of 'seeing as', working with analogies without a derived domain or original domain, but where each form only takes on meaning as a variation from the other.[16] These are variants which are not defined in relation to an original, but compared to other variants, by their deviation from other variations. Philosophically speaking, a variant is a fascinating thing. It's a typical evolutionary argument, acrobatic like life itself: territoriality *in itself* does not exist, there is admittedly an ancestor common to wolves and humans, but its territoriality was already a variant which wolves and humans inherit, but as variants of the variant. The origin is *not* the original, there is no original, pattern, or model: just variations, flows of variations that have family resemblances, due to their common source or their evolutionary convergence.

Merleau-Ponty has a similar intuition, although he does not clearly see the crucial evolutionary background, when he speaks of the Inuit transformation masks of the Inua (in which an animal face opens onto a human face). He writes that these masks offer an 'extraordinary representation of the animal as a variant of mankind and of humanity as a variant of animal life'.[17] Each life form is a variant of the others, but there is no pattern, only variations.

Thus, at the origin of the territoriality of humans and wolves, there is no essence of territoriality, but 'the disparate coexistence of other things'.[18] Territoriality, then, is an idea that we create by analogy, combining countless modes of being territorial, it is a certain range of ways of relating to lived space; it has no model anywhere, but it can happily have origins, each time hijacked and subverted in every form of life.

As territoriality is pre-individual, we have no proper words to express it. So we use the similarity of relationship with territorial devices to circumscribe it: wolves see and interact with the dropping *more or less as* we see and interact with devices such as flags and coats of arms.

Handling the analogies of perspectivist ethology simultaneously frees us from simplistic anthropomorphism ('droppings *are* coats of arms'), from the crass naturalization of the human ('human coats of arms *are nothing but* droppings') and ethological reductionism ('droppings are nothing but stimuli that are triggered by operant conditioning').

Using this type of analogy is therefore fair game epistemologically, as long as we remember that the comparison bears precisely on the *relationship* us/coats of arms and them/droppings, and not on the ontological nature of each of them in turn.

It is right to remember, finally, that the analogy serves essentially to bring out what is common against a background of *difference*: the differences in the uses they make of droppings in comparison with those we make of the coat of arms. The concept here is not a Procrustean bed where we tidy up disparate things by pruning the differences of each of them, but a yardstick with which we endeavour to see where the compared element always exceeds the limits of the measuring device – how, and by how much.[19]

This kind of perspectivist analogy is fair game in practical terms, finally, because, from the perspective of interspecies diplomacy, the act of naming is more a matter of pragmatic use than of scientific accuracy: its aim is to make it possible for us to gain access to the world of the other, to interact with the other, to imagine devices for facilitating dialogue.

Episode 8: Translating them in the spring

It's the equinox, the weather is beautiful. We're back in the Vercors. Spring skiing is, in sensorial terms, the richest form of skiing: the snow explodes with light, it's made of crystal, tablecloths and streams, the sky roars with blue and your skin gently tans, your lips are of clay, they crackle at the corners, and the hardwoods bud together, filled with the desire to go, and thirsty with it. Everywhere, the sparrows strut their stuff.

This time we try to find the cave where we'd wanted to sleep the first time. We compare maps, data, clues: it can't be found, we wander round for an hour, we shovel snow looking for an entrance blocked by a snowfield, but there's nothing, just stupid wet stone. So I look up and, high in the rock wall, three metres from the cliff, the shadowy mouth: it's the cave. We have to climb up to get there. It's not very safe, we risk slipping, but there's snow below, and too much enthusiasm inside us for us to turn around now. When I get to the edge, a hole five feet in diameter, short of breath, I sit in the wet clay, a resurgent flow springs from the back of the cave, and before my very eyes, on the threshold, there's a wolf dropping, then another one a few centimetres away, and the gnawed hairs of wild boars. But how did they get up here? It's inconceivable: we needed all of our primate 'bimania', those opposable thumbs forged by a million years of arboreal life, good for climbing in the branches of the jungles. And the wolves came up as if by magic, with their quadrupedal vigour, their clawed paws, their sense of balance. What for?

The cave is cold, it's a horizontal tunnel that plunges deep into the stone, the passage narrows very quickly to the point where you have to get down on all fours, then crawl, and finally twist through bottlenecks, sideways and at an angle, to move forward. After two metres, on the ground I find a first dropping left by a carnivore, probably a wolf, and then, one step further, another dropping, a third, a fourth: it's stunning, I've never found them together in such density. In the ten metres that I crawl through, there are droppings at every step. But what *is* this place?

My first guess is that it's an old lair. The droppings are not fresh, they seem to date from last summer, they could have been preserved by ice. If they had been any older, the spring melt, reinforcing the resurgence, would have swept them away, or at least wrung them out. At every turn I wonder if I might come across the she-wolf, I stop to see if I can hear the screeching cubs at the end of the tunnel, I ask myself: shouldn't we turn around, not disturb them? But a voice inside me keeps telling me that there's no one there: there were no pawprints on the climb, none in the clay, the droppings are old – the wolves are no longer here.

You get this prehistoric emotion of the cave, the feeling of having passed into a parallel dimension, another time, a mythical time governed by other rules: silence, confinement, sensory poverty, echoes – all this gives a solemnity to this physically tiring journey. I scratch my knees on the stones as I crawl, I'm covered in mud, I tear my clothes against the walls that close in on me. The beam of my headlamp barely illuminates that source of mythological shadows, the bottleneck that ends up getting too small for my human body. I wait here for a few minutes, listening for noises, waiting for some revelation, and then I turn around in the silence of the earth.

On the way back, I take a closer look at the droppings: at first glance, we thought they all looked like wolf droppings. In fact, some are fox droppings. Some are impossible to identify. We even wonder about the risk it might be a badger's litter, as some droppings have the particular texture we have seen in the litters of the Jura, but the badger 'putts', he digs holes to collect his excrement – there's nothing of the kind here.

It's a complete mystery: is it really an old lair? There are bones of small mammals dotted around the floor of the cave. Is it a storm shelter which animals can stay in, where each of them has territorially marked the place in response to the pervasive odours left by occupants from the previous storm? It's a puzzle, we don't understand the use of the place, its animal meaning. Its multispecies meaning escapes us. Our emotion is actually of a quite different nature; we have the diffuse feeling that it's a ritual place, a place of worship: the markings with their complex significance for carnivores, the bones that bring to mind the decorated Palaeolithic caves, the initiatory dimension of the inaccessible entrance and the bottleneck tunnel that plunges into the heart of the earth . . . The place doesn't seem usable, due to its uncomfortable nature which doesn't allow you to turn around or to lie down, and it's too small to provide much of a habitat.

Our emotion is that of a place full of meaning, especially because of the unique density of those droppings, dozens of them, everywhere, on the ground, when we know that for wolves they play a complex role, rich in messages, announcements, coats of arms and flags. But this feeling is probably a projection – the sense it has the dimension of a place of worship, at least. As for the ritual dimension, this makes sense, it seems to me: it's a difficult space to access, whose utilitarian dimension is not obvious, and it's dotted with markings; it looks like an animal ritualization, in the sense of suggesting forms of behaviour without any vital use, but endowed with meanings that we can't grasp.

We descend with difficulty, like real rock climbers, dumbfounded by the fact that the wolves manage to climb up here. We're silent, we've come up with endless hypotheses, entertained a whole range of conjectures; finally, we just stay silent, accepting the mystery.

Sleeping up here is out of the question. We'll have to sleep out of doors, on the snowy plateau. We set up camp in a small patch of meadow, under a mountain pine, surrounded by snow, on a small promontory overlooking the plateau.

The night is clear, limpid, a full moon rises above the valley. Everywhere the snow is iridescent with the nocturnal light, but it's not cold. We're soaked with mud, unrecognizable, we've turned into golems. I watch my hands covered with clay, the flesh mingled with the earth, as if embarked on the mythical process by which a fragment of mud became the first human being – but in reverse order.

We have to build a fire, we have no choice. The temperature will go down, and the mud soaked our trousers and socks when we had to crawl in the cave: they must be dried before the mercury sinks below zero. We secure a small hearth, soaking the circle of grass around the fire with snow; then we build a heat deflector with large shards of dead wood, like a ship's bow protecting the hearth, so that it filters the air supply and reflects the heat of the fire to us. Our socks are already smoking in front of the flames, as we wiggle our toes above the embers, laughing as life returns to them, circulates through them (do you always feel ticklish when life returns?).

We talk at length about the cave, its mystery, without coming to any conclusions, without trying to figure it out, just thinking of it in many different ways, following paths of meaning, echoes. While devouring our meal, merry with the hot mulled wine, we are actually waiting for the time to call the lords of this place: the time for reunion, when the wolves who separated during the day howl to each other so they can assemble as a group and begin their nightly operations. It's at this point of their ethogram (the mapping of their specific behaviours) that we hear ourselves inserting our voices in order to dialogue with them again: if we howl at that moment, in the gap where separated individuals await news of their brothers and the pack, they might well answer.

10 pm, we can see as clearly as in broad daylight (the moon). We approach the valley so that it will carry our cries. The silence is as perfect as everything else. I launch a first howl that bounces around the valley and resonates long after I've closed my mouth. We wait,

the wind is frozen here, outside of the shelter, time has grown denser, but the suspense doesn't even have time to exist: after a few seconds, a wolf responds. It's the usual flash of lightning, our emotion is precisely the same, the mixture of the extraordinary and the obvious (but how is it possible for an unknown wild wolf to answer our calls? And simultaneously: why not? We're living beings like him, sharing vocal powers and vital issues).

He's very far away, it's really intense: his howl in the wind seems to come from the west, due west, on the mountain opposite, more than five kilometres away, maybe even on the next ridge. The sound comes to us in the wind, like a spectre, difficult to locate, as if from another world, so far away, yet piercing the curse of distance. His song is long, melodious, questioning, almost lascivious; we almost share the joy of modulating that long plaintive tune, the joy of howling, of cancelling the distance, travelling at the speed of sound, transcending with the body the limits of the body. The joy of hearing and rediscovering ourselves in this nocturnal, desolate, lonely landscape.

We continue to howl, the dialogue lasts, he responds to each of us individually, four times, five times, then we fall silent together. I remember what a singer who has performed in the most refined operas once confessed on the radio: 'singing . . . it's what's still wolfish about me'.

No one else has replied: no news from the pack. No singing from the other isolated individuals. I assume they are far, very far to the east, when we had been thinking that they were at the bottom of the valley, just to the west. But no other song has come from the west, which seemed to us to be the epicentre of the pack. Nevertheless, the female may have chosen a new den; they could be anywhere.

We go to bed, feeling as light as only that resonance makes you feel light: the feeling that we can dialogue with the world, that, despite its strangeness, it hears us, it answers us; that we can, in the space of a few exchanges, tear up the modern myth of the silence of the universe. In fact, if we do the diplomatic work of translation, of intercession, if we move through this border zone where specific shapes become blurry, it's possible to come into contact with all those alien kin.

It is in fact a singular power of the wolf that we too hastily erect into a property of the whole living cosmos: the evolutionary convergence that makes our voice able to mimic his, our way of life resemble his; we are him and we are sufficiently individual and social for the call to make sense in his ear, so that he is prepared to answer it; this is indeed a strangeness, a special meeting point between two otherwise incomparable life forms. Communication is not so easy with garden spiders, common buzzards (although we happily whistle at each other) or beech trees, although we are relentlessly seeking resonant relations with them. This is another point in which the wolf is an intercessor animal: an ambassador of possible resonant relationships with other living beings, our alien kin, those untranslatable animals.

But untranslatable, as we have seen, in the dynamic sense: in the sense that we must never stop retranslating them, again and again, to do justice to what is taking place, to what they are, to the relationship. When he describes the 'savage mind', thought in its 'wild state',[20] common to all humanity, Lévi-Strauss describes it as bifid: it has a 'consuming symbolic ambition' which is combined with its opposite, a 'scrupulous attention directed entirely to the concrete'.[21] This, indeed, is what the infinite retranslation of the meaning of living beings resembles. So we resume our wild palaver on the meaning of howling, we get back to work, we continue to weave sentences and meanings to approach the mythological animal that is any animal, once its million-year-old density has been restored to it, its rustle of sedimented ancestralities, its art of making them play simultaneously on the surface of the present (in a word: living).

What happens if we try to think about evolution as a sedimentary accumulation of animal, sometimes vegetal, and indeed bacterial ascents, in each living body? What I mean by 'sedimentation' of animal ascents (or ancestralities) is not identical to geological sedimentation, where each layer is all the more inaccessible because it was deposited there a long time ago. A living thing is sedimented temporally like a rock, but the difference between the former and the latter is that, in living beings, the layers of the various ancestralities are all simultaneously *available on the surface*, and are combined together despite their different seniority: in the act of writing these lines, the opposable thumb provided by primates three million years ago combines with the pit of the eye which I inherit from an ancestor of the Cambrian (five hundred and forty million years ago), and the two combine with writing, a technique that appeared some six thousand years ago.

Animal ascents are like spectres that haunt you, rising to the surface of the present. Benevolent spectres, who come to help you – which makes you a *panimal*, a total animal, a shapeshifter like the god Pan – when the need arises, to invent a brand new solution to the problem of living. It's the little quadrumanous primate that invented your opposable thumb which rises up through you and comes to the rescue, every time you use your hand to gratefully shake the hand of a friend, to gently hold a pen, or to impatiently swipe left or right in your daily combat with your mobile.

It was the palaeomammal that invented the parental attachment that rises up in you, like a spectre, across millions of years, from inside your body, every time you waxed tender over a little critter ('neotenia', a spontaneous tenderness towards young creatures of all kinds, is a mammal invariant: it's not your human sentimentality that it reveals, but your animal empathy).

It's the colour vision of your furry fruit-eating ancestor, in which evolution has placed the optical resources necessary to detect the subtle ripening of the fruit of the jungle, with its yellow, orange, then carmine hues, which is activating in you each time you enjoy the beauty of a sunset (which is first and foremost, for the animal eye, the ripening of a landscape). Why else would the slightest purple be more attractive than any green?

It's this same ancestor who whispers emotion into your ear, when it buzzes inside of you, because on a cinema screen the ruddy mouth of Laura Harring in David Lynch's *Mulholland Drive* has appeared (red lips, the non-gendered reminiscence of an original fruit). But it's also countless other living ascents in you, a hundred personal reminiscences, which act together in an incandescent alloy to contribute to this emotion, layered with time and polyphonic with its own inner menagerie.

All of us living beings have a thick body of time, made of millions of years, woven from alien kin, and astir with available ascents.

And these ascents are shared. It's the idea that, for a certain segment of their evolutionary history, two life forms have shared the same ecological conditions and the same relationships with other life forms that can be incredibly far apart on the 'tree' of life. This common heritage or evolutionary convergence has meant that sedimented dispositions have been created, similar forms of behaviour and affective tones: shared ways of being alive.

Episode 9: Composing a body for yourself

Let's get back around the fire, sheltered behind the deflector, that night in the Vercors. The riddle that's nagging at us this time is the problem of the distance of howling. It's the first time that we have been fascinated by this phenomenon: we can communicate with the wolves miles away in the depths of forests, in meadows, on scree.

Confronted with the inhuman scope of its response, right over there, on the mountain opposite, we understand the magic specific to the device of howling: it allows one to transcend the horizon. To meet in the densest bush. To compensate for the limits of sight: where sight doesn't reach, sound carries. While sight does not act on what it sees, and the gaze does not alert the distant body on which it rests, the voice can: it touches, literally, from a distance, with its natural magic. It touches the body of a loved one beyond the horizon, pushing invisible air particles against each other, over the ridges, through deep forests, until it makes the delicate and hidden surface of the eardrum become iridescent, in circles of waves, like a stone on a lake. Living beings have this art: playing with the laws of physics.

If sound travels faster than my paws, why not fly on the wings of sound to dialogue with and touch the others, far beyond the distance that my paws can cover?

A group of humans would hardly be capable of such a feat, although peoples of the Amazon Basin, like the Eagles, from the Tupi family, have invented whistled languages for exactly the same reason: to communicate through the density of the jungle, where sight gets entangled in the lianas.

What is fascinating about the howl is that it constitutes an original bodily power which makes a unique lifestyle possible: the form of life invented by wolves in the space opened up by the powers specific to their living body (their weaving of legacies concatenated in a *body*, that great mystery, that strange attractor, from which everything comes).

This very particular form of life invented by the wolves is an alternation between intense sociality, often nocturnal, and a deliberate, sovereign, elective solitude, often during the day (but there are no rules: it's a living thing). And this is so because, despite having run alone, all day long, in the forests, the mountains and the plains, each in the direction we have chosen, we can always *meet* no matter where, when we want, when it suits us.

Not all animals have this power of meeting up that *permits* solitary excursions. Young wild boar, for example, must follow their mother: if they lose sight of her they'll never find her again. Their sociality is forced into constant contact with others by their inability to find one another. When a young male leaves, it's to lead his life alone. He won't come back. He doesn't go back and forth. Herds of deer don't separate much. Herds of chamois are held together by the need to watch out for predators, and the risk of becoming isolated. Explorer species are rarely sociable: either they don't leave each other when they are living as nomads, or they live alone (and they certainly have other bodily oddities, which open up a space for other surprising forms of life).

But wolves are endowed with these three powers of bodies, three ancestralities among a thousand others, of different ages, which here are combined to make a certain form of life possible: first this neophile desire to explore what lies *behind*; then pulsating paws with perfect powers of endurance to eat up the asphalt of the mountain roads and devour whole ridges; finally howling as an instrument for meeting.

A howl is a foghorn, it smashes the wall of distance and murmurs my presence into your ear, while I remain invisible in a distant forest. A howl helps you meet up beyond the visible. 'Our body is wiser than our mind', says Nietzsche[22] – in any case the body is immensely prodigal in opening up possibilities of existence.

In the unseparated approach to living defended here, evolutionary dynamics take on a different guise than just the 'theory of evolution' by variation-selection. They become the sedimentation of devices in the body, produced by a history: what I call ascents. And these ascents enter particular constellations at each moment of the drama that is the life of a lineage or an individual. These constellations of bodily powers will literally invent a space of possibilities, an adventure of existence never seen before: that way of being alive as a wolf, as a tick, as a meadow sage, as a human being. If animal, plant or bacterial ancestrality is the form of the sedimented trait when it is latent and folded into a body, then ascent is the dynamic form assumed by ancestrality when it *rises to the surface of the present* to combine with others, and give the appearance – so strange and yet necessary, so elegant in the way it has been pieced together – of each specific and individual form of life.[23] The poet Novalis has a very liberating way of redescribing what our tradition calls Nature. He writes: 'I call Nature that wonderful community into which our body introduces us.'[24] This is the body he is talking about: thick with time, woven together from alien kin, astir with available ascents.

Endowed with these three bodily powers, wolves have invented this original form of life: they can combine quiet solitude with intense social life and community warmth; the sovereign intoxication of retreat in the mountains, alone on the summit, and the calm disappearance of the ego in the collective, when the pack moves as one body, in the effort, in the hunt; meditative memories when a wolf is isolated in the autumn rain, insensitive to the water running off its fur, lost in wolfish reveries; and the dramatic intensity of discords, political conflicts between dominant males, alliances and sudden seizures of power. But always with the non-negotiable right to retreat *to one's corner*. (This is an invaluable law in big families, and the pack is just a big family.)

The space of possibilities of existence opened up by their bodily powers allows us, then, to better understand the peculiar life form of wolves.

It's a kind of ethnographic exercise by means of traces: they separate by day, isolate themselves, concern themselves with their personal demons, enjoy the sensations, the smells, the inquiries they pursue each in their own way, and thus cultivate the joy of meeting up again in the evening, in a few howls, to launch collective life, its discipline, its cooperation, its attention focused on the signs of others, on their emotions, with a respect for hierarchies, the etiquette of collective life, the social ranks, the dominances to be won again, lost again, won by cunning or undermined, the complex relationships, ambiguous friendships, affection for a cousin whose sister can't stand you, every imaginable kind of drama in the life of an extended family – dramas that may be infinitesimal but define each participant.

A family that works together, collaborates, takes action sometimes as an expedition of explorers, sometimes as a military border patrol; as a Palaeolithic clan of big-game hunters; a multigenerational school that takes care of the little ones, where everyone plays a role in their education; cartographers coming along single file, redrawing borders by using smell, depositing the coats of arms of the pack and the flags of the territory in the form of droppings left to replace those that the bad weather has washed out . . .

And then comes rosy-fanged dawn, and everyone separates, tired of this intense activity, tired of the hierarchy, tired of having to pay attention to each and every one, tired of having to put the collective project ahead of inner nomadic desires, and this smell of a flower that I alone can smell; and then each goes his own way, one towards the crest, one along the river, another deep into the forest.

The most loving or friendly, the most timid, stay together, two, sometimes three, another stays with the babies, the dominant couple retreat to their tent made of a grove overlooking the stream.

But the hotheads, those who suffer the most from the wolf hierarchy, move away, head off to explore – finally free, far from military disciplines and hierarchical obligations – new skies, new springs; they eat first, without following etiquette, sleep with their paws in the air watching the clouds go by, running wherever I want to, and not putting my paw exactly in the pawprint of the runner ahead, who has placed his paw exactly in the leader's pawprint; feeling, breathing everything in, wallowing in things, wallowing in the entire cosmos, intoxicated with the scent of musk and wild mint, and the challenging smell of a lynx who has also left his mark on this same trunk; and on this wooden bridge watching the trout for hours (can you eat it? worth a try); tasting everything, trying everything, doing nothing, wandering around, getting bored, and then the sun sets over there, and you can feel a little bit of loneliness rising up inside you, the desire for a wolf mask to lick, the longing for the excitement of being together, the warm smell of others like a smoke that bathes us, the longing for others; the desire to do, that is, to do *together*, to be one body, a pure river of fangs, sweeping along, an impersonal person like the wind, able to capture everything however much it refuses, resists, struggles, to take the life force of everything that vigorously wants to live, and to incorporate it, to steal it in the form of flesh, one big body able to bring down beasts like the sky, the deer with their forest of antlers, smouldering wild boar-hills; being together, the infernal band, unstoppable, the lady-killers, the bosses, the cousins, the shared laughter of the inner circle that makes you feel warm, the way a friend licks me, just in passing, the same way a human in passing puts his hand on a friend's back to say 'there you are', 'the force is with you', 'here I am'.

Suddenly I feel the warm side of a she-wolf against me while we wait to head off for the hunt, her flank with the weight she leans against my flank, the pure joy as she abandons herself against my coat of wolf, this sign of confidence, this silent sign of the desire for contact, the euphoric sensation of the mere touch of the other's body, innocent, each looking elsewhere, ears pricked up to catch the movements of the pack, of the cubs, to the moon; the loyalty and attachment that this contact expresses without needing to say anything (I'm here, I feel better leaning against you than anywhere else, that says it all already); come on, the hunt's about to start, she gets up, she trots towards the river, she's thirsty, I know her, and I follow her, even if I'm not thirsty, because the hot centre of the world is shifting, it's no longer with me, but in front of me.

As she laps the water in the night, I watch the river upstream, I lose myself in its meanders, they call to me, I want to explore them, but a howl echoes behind us in the clearing where we were with the pack, it's our leader, the female who's guiding us, she's calling us to go hunting, our four ears point erect towards her voice, and we join her, my snout magnetized in front of me by the talkative tail of the she-wolf. There is no vision more familiar: following the furry tip of a beloved tail, the field of vision occupied by the graceful rhythm of the sway of her rump in front, through the surrounding landscapes made evanescent by speed. The silhouette in front of you, that of another trotting wolf – that's the home of the wolf. In me, in front of me, in me, in front of me, thus circulates the centre of the wolf-world, its daily pulsation.

But at dawn, yes, at dawn, at the time when the countryside grows white, I will leave, my muzzle free at last, magnetized by a thousand odours borne by the winds, by their promises, and I will go up this river to its source, finally alone, finally quiet, up to its source.

It's dawn, we're lazing in the duvets. The sky is still cloudless, it hasn't even been cold, we slept the sleep of the blessed.

Episode 10: A season in super-faces

By cobbling together this lifestyle that includes both the solitude of idle wandering and the most tightly meshed collective action, wolves have invented something quite different: the joy of reunion.

This is the crazy, dishevelled, yelping joy that we so often see them demonstrating on the thermal imager when they meet up in the evenings. We have watched them for hours at a time on the Canjuers plateau, our eyes glued to the viewfinder, our bodies as immobile as statues in the night mistral, so as not to make the image wobble, petrified by the intimacy of the scene. Suddenly the father wolf is the first to arrive in the clearing where the young wolves have spent the day. Then it's like the kill in hunting – a chaos of love and fangs pounces on him, pitilessly, they're going to put on a real party for him; six wolf cubs male and female, the big brothers and the big sisters, everyone joins in the ceremony. Crazy races, a licking of chops, mysterious rituals, playful postures.

These sarabandes are, to us, as enigmatic as the etiquette of some distant, elegant kingdom, but the vital heritage that we share with them nonetheless allows us to decipher quite unequivocally the emotional tone of these rituals (all animals are, to varying degrees, born ethologists, artists in deciphering their congeners – and other species too). It's pure joy, which discovers countless displays and adornments to express itself in all its wealth, since living as an animal also means inventing ways of expressing the intense emotions that we share. And if, as wolves, we don't have spoken poetry at our disposal, we will have the poetry of bodily attitudes, vocalizations, flicks of ear and tail. We will have the complex eloquence of our face masks, cunningly wrought by evolution to enrich the possibilities of expression. A carnival deep in the woods.

These types of behaviour have a profound mirroring effect on us, if we wish to investigate human animality without prejudice. These merry reunions are very intimate expressions of their inner emotions, and yet they assume codified forms in what is called the animals' ethogram: the catalogue of behavioural sequences that they share as a species. On closer inspection, this is something that also exists among us humans. The act of spontaneously *hugging* a friend you meet again after months of absence, or a loved one you are about to leave forever, is not universal in human cultures, which may for cultural reasons keep things more distant, but it is very common, and spontaneous in children. It is also found in other social primates, which spontaneously use hugs to express their affection, to reassure, to forge links. I hypothesize that this behaviour is one of the ancestral animal traits of human beings, the legacy of an ancestral social primate whose bodily shape makes it possible to hug face to face, in an upright position (something that being a wolf, a deer or a cat does not allow). This animal ancestral trait is analogous to the bodily games that we see in wolf reunions. It's a mobile, culturally variable element of the human ethogram. My argument is fragile but based on observation: cats do not express affection this way, they rub their cheeks and flanks; worse, they can't really cope with demonstrations of primate affectivity: a hug makes them panic, because being wrapped in the arms of a loved one scares them, whereas it calms us humans down. As an animal ancestral trait hugging someone is not an arbitrary cultural code, or a sovereign and free personal decision, but rather the spontaneous way in which our animal body expresses, activates and realizes love. And tactile contact, such as being hugged, has been shown to confer deep forms of sensory and psychic satisfaction. Now this is the point of my argument: this gesture is not a pure cultural code, and yet it's intimate and deeply meaningful, it accurately expresses higher emotions – while still being animal. This reminds us that some of the intimate manifestations of our highest human affects are in fact deeply and strictly animal, they are dispositions of our bodies, inherited from our evolutionary history. Given this, the human form of animality has nothing to do with bestiality, ferocity, or coarseness. It is made up of ascents, of animal affects that can be modified or subverted, but which continue to be expressed even in our most everyday, most demanding, and most varied forms of behaviour. Animal ascents are everywhere, in all of our behaviours, and manifest themselves in patterns like mosaics, which can be hijacked and repurposed by individual culture and decision, by our intimate styles of drawing on these legacies, but they are there every moment, and that is the animal nature of humans. So what joy it is to be an animal then!

Humanity is only a certain animality; poignant and of sovereign significance for us, of course, but just as the wolf's animality is for him.

In the light of this kind of idea, one conclusion emerges: we are indeed animals, but it's all fine, it's no problem, nothing to worry about. There's no lost dignity in this idea, no ladder of ascent has been stolen from us. Nor is there any restoration to a purer primality either. The question is no longer one of knowing if the human being is an animal like any other, but *in what way*. In what *other* way. What type of animality is humanity?

Now let's return, more attentively than before, to alien kin, to our wolves who dance, bark and spiral round each other to celebrate their reunion. How can you express varied social emotions if you can't speak? Evolution has answered this question in many ways. In the wolf, we have one clue in the expression 'the wolf's lip mask'. This zoological term is used to describe the band of white fur which runs under the wolf's muzzle, along its lips, and down to his throat. This band contrasts with the dark forehead above, which goes from the nose to the top of the skull, which gave its origin to the 'wolf' mask of the carnival. It's intriguing that biologists use the word 'masks' for the lower part (the white lip mask) when popular culture uses 'mask' to refer to the upper dark part (the wolf of the carnival). In short, a wolf's face is two masks. In fact, it's the whole face that is a big compound mask. This mask is a product of evolution: symmetries and ornaments serve to accentuate facial expressions. For example, the two white spots above the wolf's eyes, where human eyebrows are found, are like a mime's makeup: they stylize and accentuate positions of the gaze that convey interest, fear, surprise, submission or majesty.

The wolfish mask is capable of playing countless games: dense anger wrinkles the forehead vertically, like waterspouts, when the wolf needs to mimic ferocity to get a message across. Anger is an unworthy affect when you experience it or force someone else to do so, but it's an interesting tool sometimes when you use it as a mask: in wolves, this mask of thunder helps maintain social cohesion by replaying hierarchies *without* needing to use force. The mask allows you to accentuate imperious glances, expressions that can *act out* dominance and maintain order. Conversely, stillness smooths the whole forehead when it comes to calming down a scared wolf cub.

These are political masks, masks for daily use to ensure the modus vivendi, masks of pacification and sovereignty. See how they accentuate the facial capacity of the biggest wolf to pretend to be a wolf cub that makes you melt with tenderness, and the next moment to play the part of a king in majesty.

The wolf mask works like a mask in Noh theatre, or a tribal dance, but with all the delicate and embodied mobility of a face, its expressiveness both intimate and visceral, its unique way of expressing a self, a flow of affects, the whole inner dramatic dialogue of life. The animal mask is like a landscape that can transform itself right in front of your eyes. Complex emotions set all the facial features vibrating, like a swell emerging from the inland sea. It's a metamorphic mask: it folds and unfolds to convey the animal's inner life in the purest, most radiant, and most artistically expressive way.

Sometimes we are surprised that a dog's gaze can express, according to its master's lexicon, the most unconditional, most authentic love. But this is no magical effect of domestication, no revelation of the fact that other animals are capable of a sincerer sentimentality than ours. Rather, in another paradox, it shows there is an exacerbated expressiveness in the face of other social animals, those who have not embarked on the adventure of human language (they have to compensate). The dog is a direct descendent of the wolf: it has the same powers of expressiveness. The dog can express profound meaning in the metamorphosis of the features around his eyes, deploying significant symmetries. It looks with its whole face. It is ecoevolution, yet again, that has made *Canis lupus* a great master of emotional expression by means of its mask-face, for the purposes of intensifying and ordering its collective life, and making it more fluid. There is an echo of this in the dog, a trait which the latter hijacks, an exapted trait for communicating with *us*.

If biologists have called the wolf's face a 'mask', this is a clue that they dimly sense that it is *more* than a face. It's a face that has been stylized to refine, amplify and enrich the expression of a whole range of emotions and messages. The Western tradition of the hierarchical human/animal dualism has seen their face as something vile, a bestial maw, an under-face. But most animal masks are something different: super-faces. They can manifest with superior skill the art of the human face: expressiveness.

And everywhere these masks were invented by life. There's the mask of the boreal lynx, more expressive than a carnival. There's the mask of the greater African kudu, a mute display of minimalist elegance. There's the mask of the American badger, enough to make any Iroquois with his war paint go green with envy. There's the mask of the commonplace goldfinch of our gardens, which makes any poet despair. These incorporated adornments indicate how we are to do justice to the animal face. Adolf Portmann, the biologist of appearances, notes that the animal face is displayed to other living beings through a whole series of adornments, contrasts, symmetries. He adds, and this lapidary formula points precisely to the essence of the animal super-face in animals, 'the highest degree of individual existence, the possibility of displaying inner states, is at the service of the encounter'.[25]

Thanks to this detour which gives animals their super-face, it's the *human* face that suddenly becomes more intelligible, more sensitive. The eyebrow, for example. The wolf mask is endowed with a furry eyebrow more eloquent than a magpie. So is our face.

By one of these perspectivist analogies, we could dwell for a moment on the mystery of the human eyebrow. Take a closer look: it's a strange smear of hairs stuck in the middle of the face of a hairless primate. The fact that it is still to be found on the face of human beings even though they have lost their fur is puzzling enough. Some have speculated that it was selected to protect the eyes from the sun's rays at noon, but we now know we must beware of unambiguous stories about the origin of any trait.

We could surmise rather that our eyebrow is a survival with the same type of use as that to which wolves, lynxes and other animals put it. Due to the interlaced, layered, hijacked history behind any living feature, we can hypothesize that the stylized line of the eyebrows has *also* been preserved on the human face (by natural or sexual selection), like two brushstrokes, to *accentuate* the expressiveness of our emotions. Countless facial expressions full of meaning imply an artistic use of the play of our eyebrows, from the most spontaneous to the most voluntary expressions. Silent cinema was the last golden age of this animal use of the eyebrow. But any time you can't speak the language of an interlocutor, and need to communicate effectively, watch how the eyebrows are activated and regain the full extent of their expressive function. Any time we talk to an infant, our animal face knows very well what to do: it recalls to the surface the immemorial art of its animal super-face, and we soon start playing our eyebrows the way we play the violin. The care that some people take over their eyebrow line still reveals the expressive importance of this living comma: we can sculpt our animal mask, weaving two creativities.

The eyebrows of every human face are in this sense reminiscent of an animal mask in the present, the active remnant of a super-face. 'Reminiscent' because we have forgotten it, not because we have become something other than an animal. With us, it is aided by language in its expressive vocation. But the spoken word hides as much as it shows, and the animal mask conferred by the human eyebrow is just as important to us today as it was *before* human language: we have not lost the animal mask by becoming human, it is now simply combined with language. The face of Audrey Hepburn is a pure she-wolf's mask: the same ancient art is inherited there, recruited for active service. We have not fallen from the visual glory of the animal world, we belong to it fully.

But the human face is interwoven with the so-called maw of beasts in even more intimate ways that lie deep down in our cultures: their super-faces live within our adornments. Let's go back to the wolf's eye: if we examine it closely, the entire periphery of this eye forms a clear moving area. There's the dark forehead, pierced with white spots around the eyes, and in the middle the pupil of the wolf's eye, sometimes dark, sometimes honey-coloured. Dark, white, dark: this is a fairly common evolutionary invention, because the bio-optical property of this shape is *to accentuate contrast*. It's a powerful shape (a *Gestalt*) which enables the gaze and its expressiveness to stand out more. It was Nikolaas Tinbergen, the founder of ethology, who first demonstrated this in the case of herring gulls: using decoys, he realized that babies reacted more intensely to a rod with a dark/light/dark pattern used to encourage pecking than to the beak of the mother herself (a clear beak with a darker spot). But it seems that this also applies to humans, wolves, and many others.

This basic arrangement is very common in living beings (a bright outline around a dark eye), and is found in the grey warbler as in the Jersey cow; it provides a solution to an evolutionary problem that is deeply perplexing when you start to pay attention to it: how to indicate to others, to your fellows, that it is there, in the eyes, in the gaze, that the expressiveness of the hidden depths inside is most eloquently played out. The living realm, from unicellular bacteria onwards, had to invent the symmetrical body, with its basic anterior-posterior axis. Then, when evolution, a few hundred million years ago, placed the organs of perception and expression on the face, living beings had to figure out how to tell others that *this* was the place to look, that this was the place to interact. Some forms of autism make it transparently clear that there is nothing obvious about seeking to catch someone's eyes to communicate with them: what we find in this case is an attention that circulates indifferently all over the other's body, not stopping at the face. This is because the solar character of the face as it radiates outward has to be indicated, learned, maintained in living beings, since they had to invent expressiveness out of an inert material which has no front or rear, no cap or cape, as it were, no 'head' (in both senses). The martial arts provide us with the ethological lesson that it's somewhere around the other person's eyes that we can see the sequence of events; this is just as true in love – it's what living beings have had to teach themselves.

This has been clearly understood by those artist animals who make up their faces, namely human beings. Some make-up patterns are not pure inventions of the human imagination, arbitrary creations: they are bio-inspired. They accentuate the ethological powers of the human super-face, they further stylize our animal mask.

The two clearest cases are two ways of intensifying the contrast to accentuate the intensity of the gaze. The first technique is eyeliner.

By accentuating the contrast between the pupil and the fundus of the eye, adding a dark feline ring around it, eyeliner mimics the depth of the panther's gaze (from birth, the panther has this black line around the eye). It's exactly the same dark/light/dark structure that the wolf's natural mask uses. Men and women of the theatre paint around their eye with black before going onstage: they have always known that it accentuates expressiveness. But this technique was invented by evolution millions of years before actors came along, in the case of the lineage of the big cats as well as others.

The historical origin of eyeliner lies in the kohl powder that painted the eyes of the Egyptians, both male and female. This lineage is a clue, a detail that reveals a deeper lineage, which we can track as far as our bathrooms. Ancient Egypt was familiar with half-animal, half-human forms (its therianthropic gods, beast-headed, bird-headed, snake-headed, and so on). This ancient culture was also familiar with panther and antelope super-faces: these were the everyday wildlife of the country. And it is from Ancient Egypt that part of our tradition for making up the eyes stems: they would draw around their eyes, as seen on the frescoes, and probably also darken their eyelashes. It is not going too far to conjecture that Egyptian line of kohl (and thus eyeliner) is a bio-inspired technique that deliberately gives the human eye the intensity of the panther's gaze. A technique that captures the same intensification of contrast that evolution has painted on the big cat's face. In a culture where your goddess has the head of a lioness, where animals are not just so many critters but actual deities, taking their face as a model for learning how to heighten your expressiveness makes perfect sense. This is still true these days: even the most obtuse people sense, almost painfully, the aesthetic power of a panther's super-face. Ancient tradition derived beauty lessons from it, in the most living sense: beauty as a way of inhabiting a form. The panther, like the wolf, has an inhabited face, a super-face, because its lineage attempted this adventure of visual expressiveness rather than that of spoken language to solve the problem of expressing the countless sparks hidden within.

The second biomimetic human make-up technique is mascara: it captures the look of the antelope, by emphasizing the length and thickness of the eyelash. This technique for eyelashes most probably stems from Ancient Egypt. One can reasonably surmise that the original mascara was inspired by the endless eyelashes of the African antelope, for example the Queen of Sheba's gazelle, now extinct (*Gazella bilkis*, with endless eyelashes). To appropriate its aesthetic powers (the name 'gazelle' comes from the Arabic word *ghazâl*, which means 'elegant and quick'). The antelope does not evoke a woman because she has long eyelashes: it's quite the opposite, it's the make-up applied to the eyelashes that has reappropriated from the antelope that bodily power which makes the gaze more eloquent and reinterpreted it in a human face (in the morning in front of the mirror, carefully applying mascara: 'Antelope: activated!').

These ideas find their origin in an anthropology of the living, a philosophy of forms of life; to put them to the test, we would need historians of adornment sensitive to comparative ethology, to the aesthetic sense shared between living beings.

Let's go further: the ability to metamorphose into two simultaneous animals by means of the make-up bag is still more striking in its expressive richness, because it also consists in capturing the twofold and indeed contradictory imaginary power of these animals – becoming at one and the same time the fierce prey and the empathetic predator, with all the range of emotions and attitudes in the relationship to the other that this involves; becoming a *panimal*, a total animal, a chimera with the lashes of the antelope and the black eye of the panther, the expressive power of the former and the hypnotic power of the latter. The unconscious emotional and semantic density of these adornments is literally immemorial. There are ancient echoes stirring in them, as ancient as life itself, as eloquent as all contradiction.

This morning in front of the mirror, shall I metamorphose into a panther-antelope, a pantherlope, or not?

Far from assigning them to the feminine gender, we can reopen these two adornments up to the fresh air of their origin: the dialogue that the savannah maintains with itself, through the mouths of prey and predators. We can re-animalize these two adornments: this is not a return to something more primal, more authentic, not even to the past – but a restitution of oneself, an interior enrichment of the whole menagerie of the living past rising to the surface, hospitality for the whole present diversity knocking on the door of the human face, from within, to display and mix bodies, mix powers. Applying make-up: 'activating in oneself the powers of a different body'.[26]

Episode 11: So many ways of being alive

Back to the snows of the Vercors. In the morning, hot coffee, sipped in the sun, eyes on the plateau, but we're not paying attention, we're chatting, chirruping like birds – if a deer passed right under our noses, we wouldn't see him (we're real weekend trackers). Yesterday evening we heard a howl in response, but no sign of the pack.

We hoist our rucksacks onto our backs, and put on our Altai skis, with integrated sealskins, very short, wide and stable, ideal for following animals in the most rugged terrain; the sealskin slows down the glide, adapting to the rhythm of following each track in the snow.

We decide to head east: this is where we hoped to find the pack, but yesterday it was all quiet in this direction, which makes me think there's no one there. We believe that the pack is far away in the opposite direction, in the west, where we heard the howl. The day before, we didn't find any trace at the bottom of the valley coming from the east, which reinforces our hypothesis that there aren't any wolves there. We're taking this direction, however, for orientation purposes: this is the only path that will allow you to descend into the valley so as to go up the other side, slaloming between scree and cliffs.

We hope to find other tracks, deer, foxes, martens. The sky is a very pure blue, it's already hot, the snow is sparkling, it's still hard and brittle from the night, we advance on the ridge waiting for it to soften enough for us to descend: you need a fairly soft texture so that the edges of the skis can bite and allow for tight manoeuvring between the trees. We move forward in the cheerful morning, the crossbills, the tits, the jays utter their daily vociferation, a debauchery of expressive energy on the deserted plateau. We haven't seen a single human.

As I elbow my way through, digging a breach between two trees, a pawprint jumps out at me. It's very discreet, barely marked. Beside it there are very deep traces of wild boar, but the pawprint has barely notched the snow, it didn't sink into it, but merely crushed the superficial crystals, which configures them differently so that the sunlight is reflected in a different style: it reflects the rays back in a very light yellow colour, iridescent, barely noticeable. It's the trace of a canine. We find a series of pawprints all in a line, in a grove where the snow has remained soft thanks to the tree cover, which trapped the thermal rays rising from the ground at night and kept them from vanishing into the atmosphere. It's a wolf. No, there are several, at least three. The track arrives in front of us, as it meets us, and the orientation of the foot is clear: it's heading in exactly the opposite direction from us.

We retrace our steps to follow it. It's sometimes invisible, we lose it on hard snow, several times, and find it later, in the delicate iridescence of a bright snowy patch, in the trace of a claw that has left its mark, in the almost invisible design of the central ball of the foot, with convex edges, very sharp, very wolf-like. We have rarely followed such a fragile, evanescent trail. Its discretion isn't due to its being an old trail, on the contrary, it hasn't been eroded, it's very precise, very fresh; but animals have passed by in the heart of night, when the snow was hard as concrete, and their steps barely leave a mark. In a softer part of the track, we are struck to see that there are not three of them but at least five – six in my opinion (but I will never find confirmation of the sixth). They're running in an unruly way, the snow is solid and it's not necessary to stay in single file. When an obstacle demands it, they split up, the whole clan tapers off like the arms of a river, and meet up again further along. It's here that we can count them. The nucleus of the family. The big male doesn't seem to be here: the biggest trace is much smaller than what we had measured for him.

The track disappears and reappears as if by magic. There are two of us; when one finds a trace, he points it out to the other, in all the excitement of the hunt: 'They're here!' It takes a few moments of dumbfounded blindness for the second person to capture the revealing detail, the slender break, the ghostly form that the first saw in the ground. But once captured, this tiny detail becomes obvious, there's nothing else, it imposes itself on perception like a strong shape on the underlying snow, and with it the whole wolf is reconstituted, with his quiet trot, and the whole pack afterwards. The small notch in the soil secretes in the imagination all the life that has passed this way, connected in a constellation of other clues. The almost invisible details conjure up presences, redrawing the whole trajectory, the pace of the running animals, the river of legs and buttocks, tails up, muzzles flush with the snow, the fine branching out of trajectories, the collective running and at the same time the individual initiative in the choice of paths.

They go west, so we follow them, retracing our steps. The traces are from last night, now it's definite. And as the metres of their track are counted off, it becomes more obvious, and doubt becomes more volatile; we do not dare to say it out loud, the tension mounts in the hunt, we accelerate without paying attention to the other, our attention is more vibrant, our voices deeper; we can sense it, with an ambiguous, dumbstruck emotion: they are coming towards us, towards the place where we howled a few hours earlier. The whole pack's coming our way. The use of tenses gets confused in our minds, which is often the case in tracking: we spontaneously talk in the present ('they're there, here they stop'), because the trace is a presence-absence, a past that percolates into the present, and we must summon back the image of the animal in all its corporeality to follow its absence. It creates the strange impression of an encounter, like a dialogue with spectres, like living on several levels at the same time, crossing the past with the present, raising the past in the interstices of the now, seeing the past moving like a ghost among us.

They're heading straight for our camp. They're coming from the east. Where yesterday no one answered. Complete silence. We concluded that they weren't there, that they were far to the west, on the opposite side, where one wolf did respond.

But they were there. They heard us. They were silent. And they came.

They came, maybe from miles away. At one moment, we look up. Obsessed with following their trail, we had forgotten where we were.

When we look around, the shock paralyses us: we're just below our bivouac from yesterday. The wolf traces are there, under our skis. They mark halts which are oriented very clearly in one direction, and, when we look further, barely thirty paces away, we come to the tree that gave us shelter. They came to us, in silent response to our howls, to our calls. We are filled with a peculiar emotion: we are tracking the wolves towards ourselves. I follow their trail to myself, to my old self, who was laughing up there, talking in the bivouac, nice and warm. From here I see us in the glow of the flames, behind a small secure fire and a heat deflector, drinking the mulled wine, I wrinkle my nose to smell the odour of charcuterie drifting down from this camp, where two cheerful voices are conversing together, my vibrissae bristle, I can taste the smells, my ears twirl then bend towards the sounds falling from this bivouac, collecting every drop, I'm under the full moon, in the night, in silence, with my clan, and up there, some thirty strides away, there are two bipeds uttering their particular vocalizations, chirruping like birds; they're funny, as carefree as wolf cubs, they don't see us, obsessed as they are by their own pack, around the fire, and we stay there for a long time, listening to them babble, how puzzling! The wind turns slightly and sends us their aroma, one of them has this smell that I know well: it is the old self that I was yesterday. He called us, and we have come; I am the whole pack, here I am.

They hadn't answered last night, but they did advance towards us. They did indeed in one sense *answer*, but it is this sense that is fascinating, because they answered without answering in the way we had expected. This is no reflex act in reaction to a stimulus, no instinct that condemns them to howl if it is triggered: their refusal to answer is also an answer, it's an even more active answer, because it's a *restraint*, the opposite virtue of the ferocious excessiveness that we fantasize about in wild animals ('I would prefer not to howl', says Bartleby the Wolf).

Since they came, the fact that they did not answer appears to be a power of existential affirmation: it's not that they didn't answer because we mimed their call poorly, and failed to activate their reflex howl. It's the manifestation in them of a complex inner decision-making faculty. They impose this sense of an act of self-affirmation on their part, especially since they evade our authority. And our human bias as masters of the Earth leads us to take all the more seriously the ontological consistency of another being that refuses our call. As Xenophon sadly puts it: 'Humans are so made that they despise those who submit, and respect those who resist them.' This is a rather comical animist invariant: those who resist always seem to have a little more interiority and existence than the others.

At one point these wolves said something to each other like, 'Hey, let's go and take a look.' Why are we interesting to them? Because we are new? Because we sing, however badly, their song? Because we are in an important place for them (the cave)? Because we have tried to establish communication? If this is the case, it's quite fascinating: it shows that they are receptive to the idea of interspecies contact. They have skills in interspecies diplomacy. They are curious about bipeds engaged in the middle ground between life forms.

So in a sense they have come to our call, but not like a dog that comes when you whistle it. Their *belated* way of responding expresses all the power of their initiative in interaction, their sovereign tact: they comply with the interaction requested by another, but they still impose their own style on it. They have not replied vocally, but they made up a way of responding that was not dictated by our call: they did what they wanted with our request. They thus activated the highest form of dialogue, one where you do indeed respond to the one questioning, but by rejecting the normativity of his question, by doing something else. A bit like when, sitting together on the terrace of a cafe, we ask a friend, rather anxiously, 'What time is it?' and he replies: 'Never mind the time, make the most of me while I'm here!'

This is a dialogue without having to face the constraint always lurking in a question: it's as if the pack is taking over, word for word, the phrase that Nietzsche applies to himself in *Ecce Homo*: 'I am too inquisitive, too incredulous, too high spirited, to be satisfied with such a palpably clumsy solution of things.'[27]

What a strange emotion it is to be the object of the curiosity of an animal which comes to see you from far away, at night, to know who you are, even though he knows that you are not who you say you are, even though he knows that you are neither from the pack nor even a wolf; and yet he's come to investigate. This is an inversion that really gives you food for thought: being the object of an animal's investigation.

Epilogue: The incandescent alloy

Tracking, in the broad sense of an investigative sensitivity towards living beings, is a very clear experience of the way we can access the meanings and communications of other life forms.

The tracker, in fact, can be any practitioner of the living world who is interested in signs, and this includes, in no particular order, walkers escaping from their own selves, foresters pondering the behaviour of trees, peasants and agroecologists investigating the dialogues between roots, voles and raptors (there *is* a link), naturalists who question every living form, local gatherers investigating the dens and habits of tubers, Runa Puma Amazonian hunters who are adepts in sylvan thinking . . . More broadly speaking, a tracker is any human being who activates in himself or herself an enriched style of attention to the living world outside — who considers it worthy of investigation, and rich in meanings. One who postulates that there are things to translate, and who is trying to learn. In this style of attention, we are all the time racking up signs, all the time making connections, noticing shards of strangeness, and imagining stories to make them understandable, to deduce the visible effects of these invisible stories, to seek things out in the field. The bewitching richness of the living landscape, its dizzying cosmos of meanings, its way of immersing you like a wave of sense (and of sense impressions) then emerges like a sperm whale from the depths of the monotonous sea.

This style of attention extends beyond and outside the modern dualism of the faculties, which contrasts sensibility with reasoning. Tracking is a decisive experience for learning to think differently because, when you are outside sniffing out the clues, you don't get rid of reason so as to become more animal (modern dualism, albeit with a reversal of the usual stigma); rather, you are simultaneously more animal *and* more rational, more attuned both to sense impressions and to thought.

The typical exhaustion of a late afternoon's tracking, precisely when we have to shut down our senses because we are exhausted with feeling, thinking, interpreting, summoning up invisible things: this is exactly the symptom that tells us we need, not to withdraw from the supposed alienations of thought into the supposed authenticity of sensibility (in the anti-modern myth), or indeed that we need to cut off deceptive sensation and rise to pure thought (in the Platonic myth which has nourished the modern Galilean sciences), but rather to combine, *in a complete style of attention*, all the components of human openness to the outside. To deploy together all the vibrating antennae of sensation, perception, interpretation, deduction, intuition, imagination. We need the incandescent alloy of a vibratory sensitivity to others in their otherness, a participant perception, an interpretive and imaginative activity of great boldness and caution, a rigorous and wild activity of deduction, a creation of hypotheses that is dishevelled in its heuristics and perfectly reasonable in its conclusions, a general openness to signs, an investigative use of the sensing and walking animal body: with all these elements we can reweave sensitive, powerful connections to living territories. We can overcome the blindness of the moderns and recreate affiliations with the living, by recognizing their wealth of meanings. We can try, although we often get it wrong, to translate them a bit.

This sensibility exists, in the wealth of practices of being alive, only because it is inextricably woven into thought, and today it can be enriched by a knowledge of the non-reductionist life sciences which are emerging everywhere. It is enriched with intelligence in its most rigorous, most Cartesian form of reasoning, a baby that cannot be thrown out with the bathwater of modernity without giving in to complacent irrationalism, but must be reconnected to the most vibrational, the most generous sensibility, expurgated of what has *never* been the essence of science or reasoning but their violent folklore (blind objectification, pure quantification, de-animation). The challenge is to weave this knowledge together with the most poetic sensibility, to imagine the best informed poetry, the sensuality most attentive to the exact texture of the skin of an aspen, the bark of a river, the flow of a cloud, the movement of a forest.

This is why the current taste for animism, thought as a mystical and sensitive connection to nature, opposed to Western rationality conceived as objectifying and alienating, constitutes a problematic position. On the one hand, it tends to reactivate the highly ethnocentric belief that the first peoples do not investigate. That they access the truth of their ecosystems just by listening to the trees and clouds, by a mystical, strictly 'sensitive' and affective perception. This approach paradoxically commits great violence against animism: it forgets that investigation in cultural forms other than ours is not characterized by absence, but by the way it is continuous, immersive and shared by all. It's not that there is no analytical thinking among hunter-gatherers, it's that it can be found there diffusely all the time, woven into the rest. Unlike our tradition where it is officially located in isolated acts of 'research'. Ever since the Greek theorists, mediaeval clerics and up to contemporary professional researchers, we are the only civilization that has separated out and appropriated the field of investigation, by professionalizing the job of the investigator (whom we call a scientist, or an expert), reducing all legitimate knowledge to the product of the activity of a few. This is an appropriation of great violence, which conceals the fact that, as soon as you start to grapple with life, everyone is an investigator. Practitioners from all countries, indigenous Amazonians or farmers from the Creuse area of central France, spend their time investigating, without any official experimental protocols or peer reviews. Some are brilliant and capture countless things unknown to others, they conduct precise, intuitive, imaginative and yet ultimately accurate investigations, resulting in fascinating knowledge, such as we can see in Australian agroecologists and permaculturalists as well as in the Bushmen trackers of the Kalahari. Some of them (as always happens) are more obtuse, they apply recipes, dwell on dogmatic certainties, project meanings that aren't there, reason out of a mere habit of thought, out of superficiality, out of superstition. But investigation is there, it's everywhere, it's the hidden name of life.[28]

Thus it is this diffuse and lived investigation, offered to all, connected to the world of the senses, which we must reactivate towards living beings, and not a romantic and mystical sensibility on the one hand, nor a reductionist scientific reasoning appropriated by experts, which is only a fig-leaf for extractivism (nature must indeed be reified as inanimate matter to justify the remorseless way we exploit it).

On the other hand, this taste for animism thought of as a sensitive connection rather than a rational approach is based on the idea that access to the unseen, to the meanings and communications of other living beings, is lessened by the work of the sciences, by their use of reasoning and language. Now, the infernal paradox of this idea can be summed up in one sentence: today, when opponents of science speak out against the way we reduce the living world to raw material by leveraging their criticism on the way trees communicate and exchange nutrients, they are forgetting something, namely that it is precisely the sciences (the reanimating life sciences) that have generated this emancipatory knowledge with regard to the living. It is in this sense that we glimpse the way certain sciences are also a tool for blowing up naturalism from within. What should be eliminated from the sciences is not the huge range of wonderful knowledge that they provide about the invisible dynamics or the hidden behaviours of living beings, but their modernist folklore of objectification and reduction. This requires wielding the scalpel much more finely than a blunt opposition between Science and Sensitivity does.

To escape this sterile opposition between cold analytical reason, which sets us at a distance from living experience, and an immersive sensibility supposedly liberated from thought, the point is not to wager on the minor trend against the dominant trend, because it is the hierarchical dualism itself that is really dominant, and by indulging in it we perpetuate it. You have to think outside of this dualism: not to wager on one against the other, not to value one attitude that has been *withdrawn* from the other. In my view, this is the main lesson to be drawn from the practical experience of tracking in the field.

This gives access to a broader, unamputated sense of what sensitivity is: the instrument for capturing reality which a human being uses is the weaving together of *all* the powers of the senses and of thought, in the crucible of the body connected to the outside, and not one power being used to the detriment of the others, the one power annihilating the others, reason cutting us off from the truth of the senses, or the senses deluding reason. That one can enjoy the two sensitivities split apart from one another, quite separately, is a fact, as when we read the equation for the force of gravitation instead of watching the sky spinning, or when we enjoy stars like diamonds stuck in black velvet, regardless of their astrophysical nature. But the idea that we are doomed to oscillate between one and the other without bringing them together is a very modern aberration. Everywhere there are practices of thought and the senses which spontaneously mobilize both, and in them lies the key to opening a way to the living territories that are our foundation.

We see the same phenomenon in the permaculturist: she needs to spend her night on the Internet gleaning knowledge, so that the next day she can have an enriched perception of what is happening in her bewitching forest-garden, accessing the invisible, immersed in its design among the strangeness of the living beings in it, which she has learned to translate through dialogue with other permaculturalists, blogs, biology textbooks, the observations of other agriculturalists in the past, articles on the microbiology of soil or the ethology of earthworms.

In some ways, this approach shares the philosophical affect of vitalism: it is indeed life, the fact of being alive, which is the great mystery and the great power around which everything revolves, and not culture, mind, consciousness, ethics, reason . . . But the point here is to give substance to this fascination for life by looking seriously at living beings: by metabolizing the most advanced and open biological knowledge so as to restore its mythical power, subverting it in the process.

It is an attempt to circumvent with a nonchalant shrug the dualisms between science and fiction, poetry and accuracy, sensitivity and reason, to forge a kind of incandescent alloy of all living faculties: the sharpest senses, the most alert body, the wildest imagination, the closest reasoning, the most vibrating sensitivity, both fabulation and knowledge. To prepare for the meeting with the world, and to invent new relationships, rich in adjusted consideration, towards other ways of being alive.

In one sense, the secret experimentation behind this 'season among the living', this whole odyssey of words, comes down to a riddle: how is one to write in the time of myth?

What, after all, is a myth? Lévi-Strauss suggested the reply a native might give: 'If you were to ask an American Indian, he would most likely tell you that it is a story of the time before men and animals became distinct beings.'[29] In Native American cosmologies, this time of myth has never completely passed, it still haunts the present, on its edge, ready to pounce on us as soon as we are inattentive, as soon as we stop trying to cordon off the difference between them and us (once we no longer create defensive structures to conceal the 'original connivance' between forms of life).[30]

A whole mythographic or mythopoietic writing project emerges from these experiences of a more richly variegated form of tracking. Write in the time of myth. Step through that time, for a few suspended moments. In the forest, we play a game: when we come across a bent tree that makes an arch, we tell each other that it's a portal into the time of myth. When we come out on the other side, everything is the same but everything has subtly changed; access to the mysteries is easy, well-stabilized modern categories are no longer valid, we can finally see the animal ancestralities of our bodies on the surface, activated right there, under the skin. We glimpse animals and trees in their true form, that of alien kin. There is a sense of the diplomatic possibilities of a shared living world.

By *interspecies diplomacy* I mean a theory and practice of adjusted consideration. Adjusted consideration begins with an understanding of the form of life of others, one which attempts to do justice to their otherness: thus it involves honing an *adjusted style* to speak about them, to transcribe their vital allure into words – something they themselves can never do. And in a way it's always a failure, we never do them justice, but that's why we must endlessly waffle on, translate and re-translate the untranslatable, try again. You have to be able to talk about them with the language we use to talk about ourselves, to show that they are not physical matter, not 'Nature'; but by bending this language so as to let their strangeness appear. We should be able to read this text the same way as if it started with the words: 'You've just landed on another planet (yours, actually), and you encounter an incredible life form, and you immediately embark on a bit of extraterrestrial ethnography: they don't have reasoned speech, semantic language, the same cognitive forms as you, and you have to emphasize that this is not a deficiency, not a lack.'[31] Like aliens they invent their own scale of values: these are customs that they are describing, thick and woven customs, millions of years thick, woven into the customs of other living beings. And they are inventive because they are thick with time and woven with otherness.

They are customs, an ethos, of *theirs*, quite independent of us: this is the difference with the colonial ethnographic discourse about indigenous life forms, which still values them surreptitiously on the basis of the settlers' scale of values set up as norms (reason against superstition, 'optimized' organization against custom, the energy of achievement against indigenous 'laziness').

They have, above all, a different *body* from ours, and just as the body thick with time and woven of aliens is, here below, for all, the configurator of the possibilities of existence, they embody and activate *other ways of being alive*. We would have to imagine a guide to prodigious bodies, like a naturalist guide, but no longer dedicated to teaching us how to recognize birds or mushrooms, rather giving us access to the enigma of being another body, a thrilling adventure trembling with life – the body of a vulture or an ancient oak, insofar as it opens up an incredible space of possible existences.

The challenge is to restore the fullness of their form of life while retaining its kinship, despite the absence in them of some of our most spectacular attributes, such as human language – but *using* language.

The fabric of the living world is a tapestry of time, but we are in it, immersed in it, never standing in front of it. We are doomed to see and understand it from within, we will never escape it.

This is what makes it possible for us to envisage an *unseparated approach to the living world*: a philosophy that is simultaneously eco-evo-ethophilosophy, that is, sensitive to our horizontal interweaving with the biotic community all around (denaturalized ecology), sensitive to our vertical weaving with the manna of ancestralities plunging into the immemorial realm (demechanized evolution), and attentive to the power of the living world to open up whole dimensions of being – a space for inventive forms of existence (a philosophically enriched ethology).

Denaturalized ecology is open to the political dimensions of interspecies relationships; demechanized evolution works on the sedimentations of available ascents and the exaptive reserve which makes new relationships possible; enriched ethology is an ethology of 'seeing as' built on the *perspectivist analogy* as a method. It embraces the biosemiotic dimension of communications and conventions, the agreements, mores and customs of living beings.

Enriched tracking is the sensitive and practical aspect of an unseparated philosophical approach to living beings – a style of attention. A way of always being on the alert, open to the lavish signs of life thick with time and woven from alien kin, an alertness immersed in the world, always inside and never in front of it. In it, everyone shows their irresistible way of existing by signs, in a roundabout way ('And without the willow, how can you know the beauty of the wind?' said Lao She). And without the soil, how can you know the fabulous existence of living beings?

And it's on Earth that you've landed, of course, good old Earth, and yet it's an alien planet, an exoplanet, as soon as you restore to its inhabitants – bees that dance maps, trees that interact with fungi, bacteria that form an alliance with your digestion – the ontological status they deserve: beings of metamorphosis, alien kin. Thereupon, the realm of the unexplored opens up, vast as the world, and what it demands of us: the exploratory, diplomatic investigation that is designed to do those beings justice. To invent the rules of a 'cosmopoliteness', to share this good old new Earth.

2

The promises of a sponge

✦

At each meal, we make a gesture of major ritual significance. A form of ancestor worship that has so far not been revealed. We dip three fingers into a jar of coarse salt to throw a handful into a cooking pot, as the witch throws a magic substance into the potion. Or, casually grabbing the salt shaker and, like the Zen monk with his gong, shaking it rhythmically three times above the plate, we *add salt*.

It's a daily ritual, whose immemorial protagonists we barely notice: those to whom the ritual renders its discreet worship.

We do indeed need to eat salt every day to maintain our metabolic balance (that is, our osmotic pressure). We can maintain ourselves on dry land 'only because our body harbours a huge amount of salt water'.[1] But how come we are composed of salt water, and doomed to the daily curse of replenishing this interior salinity *from outside*?

Our metabolism works thanks to ion pumps which circulate sodium and potassium based on differences in the concentration and electric charges of the ions. In neurons, these pumps allow communication between cells. That is, all nerve and brain activity needs this salt. To read these lines, your body is activating these sodium pumps. All your alertness depends on them. But why do these constituent pumps work with *sodium*, i.e. salt?

Our need for salt, in fact, is a secret legacy of our long aquatic past: of these few billion years in which our ancestors lived in an ocean environment with high salinity. Thereby, in their exchanges with the environment, they incorporated salt water, to the point of having to regulate their *internal* salinity.

Evolution grasped this opportunity to use the electric forces of the sodium ions, so as to operate the pumps for circulating matter and energy that are the basis of the metabolic activity of the present human organism.

This present need for salt, for salt water intended to saturate living tissue, is the organic memory of the sea that we brought onto land with us in the Palaeozoic, around the end of the Devonian, about three hundred and seventy-five million years ago, when in the process of turning into land animals the tetrapods who are our ancestors[2] came out of the water to explore the dry land. But the sea is still inside us, like a memory in our flesh, embedded in us in the form of the need we have for salt in order to function, that is, to live. Like those ancient aqueducts, now forgotten, which serve as the foundation of a new city.

Salt is necessary for an organism that has been made in the sea, by the sea, that has found the very raw material for its constitution. This salt water in which we bathed constitutes seven tenths of our organism, encapsulated in our tissues.[3] The salt water that runs through our veins is only the concrete persistence of seawater from the primordial oceans, the water that constituted our original, amniotic, constitutive element. A neutral hypothesis to underpin this idea is the following thought experiment: an animal that had evolved *on dry land* right from the *start* would not be constituted by the same *physiological salt requirements*.

When we eat salt, then, we reconstitute in ourselves our native environment: the part of the ocean that we brought with us when we came out of the water. (Reminder: think of the ocean every time we add salt – think of what we owe to it?)

This is even clearer when we remember that, among our direct ancestors, the *first* living animal in the sea was a sponge – let this be clear, so that everyone understands the nature of their own body, that is to say the mystery of being made up essentially of water, and of water that needs to be resalted every day so the body will not perish.

Or, more strictly, present-day sponges, the *Porifera*, forming the basal branch of the metazoa, are probably the life forms closest to what was the common ancestor of all animals. Sea sponges, which seem so inert, are actually animals. We descend in a straight line from a sponge full of seawater. Metaphorically, this is our most constitutive ancestrality from the point of view of our relationship to the water that fills us.

Think about this when you use a natural sponge in the shower: you are rubbing your body with the body of your ancestor (the present-day animal that most closely resembles your ancestor, since of course sponges nowadays have changed a bit since then – they are in fact your cousins). Washing with a natural sponge is another bit of ancestor worship performed in secret and unconsciously: a sensual and silent ritual of connection with the whole animal kingdom, of which the sponge is, as it were, the common ancestor in the palm of our hand.

And the water itself which constitutes us, which fills and activates two-thirds of our body, passed only yesterday through the oceans and clouds, it was storm and streams, and it will return to them tomorrow. Each of us is also an open-air rainwater tank. It's all in the experience of a shower. From there one could almost access the physical sensation of having *been* a sponge. Could this feeling be used to give new meaning to our unquestioned daily ritual of adding salt?

Descending from those we are wiping out

The meaning of this whole story emerges a little more clearly in the light of a drawing that provides many philosophical lessons, which deserve to be examined in detail. This drawing, by cartoonist Dan Piraro, is an elegant way of connecting the question of our evolution to certain contemporary ecological issues.

The key to the whole design is the dead fish's tail which emerges discreetly on the surface on the far right, while at the bottom of the image a similar fish is transformed into a creature that climbs onto dry land, becomes a mammal and then a primate: it gradually transforms itself into the very same human who is emptying out his toxic waste onto the creature that represents *his ancestor*. The spatial round of characters closes in a time loop: the present impacting the past, which is the matrix of the future.

The profound thought experiment which this drawing invites us to share is the rather tautological one of remembering that, although we descend from forms of life that seem very crude to us, these were still the ancestors of what we are. The philosophical lesson that can be extrapolated from this, armed with the most recent tectonic movements in the theoretical biology of evolution (which will be spelled out later), is this: every species, down to the simplest (from the point of view of its differentiated cell types, for example), or the species with the most stereotypical reflexes to our eyes – every

Devolution by Dan Piraro. Bizarro © 2007 Dan Piraro, Distributed by King Features Syndicate, Inc.

current species is potentially the ancestor of life forms with traits *analogous* to those we value most in mankind.

Here we must understand the word 'simple' in the descriptive, not the normative sense: 'simple' does not mean 'less advanced'. All who are alive today are just as evolved as each other; it is a fact, they have evolved for just as long, they have blossomed and realized themselves, they are adjusted to their world, which they enrich.

There are no 'simple' organisms in the evolutionary sense: there are simple organisms in the anatomical sense (unicellular without nucleus, unicellular with nucleus, multicellular, multicellular with differentiated cells, and so on). There are simple organisms in the metabolic sense, and also in a genetic sense, but they are not always the ones you might think, because the sea anemone has just as many genes as we do. Be that as it may, there are no things that are simple and complex in the negative or positive sense, there are only potentials, evolutionary potentials encapsulated in living beings. And the paradox is that the simplest (anatomically speaking) are often the richest in potential, precisely because they have not yet embarked on evolutionary paths that will make them more rigid, with hyper-specialized organs that cannot be diverted into other uses because they have acquired architectures that are so intertwined that their bases cannot change without destroying the rest. The so-called 'complex' animals are slowed down by the cathedrals they comprise; they restrict their own possible evolutionary metamorphoses. The simple beings are the embers whose range of possibilities is often the widest.

The futurology of forms of life

To put it more clearly still, each contemporary life form, from bees to amoebas, from the laurel to the octopus, is potentially the ancestor, if you give it the millions of years needed, of life forms that are more socially gifted, more creative, more considerate of the environment, more gifted with meaningful articulate language, more self-aware, more intelligent in other forms, *than we are*.

This statement may seem shocking but it is actually indisputable *per absurdum*, simply because *we* are the product, through the *same* evolutionary processes that act on *all* living beings, of an ancestor who has been at each stage of its transformation just as 'crude', single-celled and devoid of neurons and then of a cortex as many of the species that today share Earth with us. It is logically irrefutable, liberating to the imagination, and ethically disturbing.

This is a reasonable thesis in speculative biology.

And some life forms are already manifesting these strange superiorities even over what we had set up as 'proper to human beings', for example the memory of hiding birds or, better, the enigmatic hypertrophy in cetaceans, and killer whales in particular, of areas of the brain correlated with richness of emotional social life and the capacity for making connections.[4]

Of course, present life forms are not deficient in anything, they are just as accomplished as we are from an evolutionary point of view. But from the point of view of values that modern human beings highlight among themselves, those which are a cultural product, other living beings are almost always lower down on the scale (if we valued echolocation, or the photosynthetic prodigy of being able to feed on the carbon in the air from the sun, we would be lesser plants, or rather backward bats).

So this is not to say that every form of life has the potential to produce human beings, or even that this is a legitimate final purpose, de facto or de jure. It is simply to recall the overlooked logical implication that each current species, abused and destroyed by certain effects of unsustainable economic activity and the indiscriminate human domination of the environment, is the promise of life forms endowed with what at first glance are intriguing skills.

In biology, we cannot reject the idea that there is a chance, however small, that from each current species, even the most apparently simple, whether comprising endangered or flourishing populations, there may emerge, in a few tens or hundreds of millions of years, forms of life that would be similar to those most valued in the human species, in incredible forms: styles of benevolence and love, self-awareness, faculties of culture, cooperation, forms of ethics, capacities to coexist on the planet in close understanding with other forms of life, and amazing intelligences (in the plural). And 'freedom', or at any rate what is given this name in the human species – and which makes us capable of both the best and the worst.

A speculative biology of humanist virtues

I am not saying, of course, that you have to look like mankind with its works of art and its few ethical beauties to be an admirable living creature: but the humans of our modern tradition are so made that they have been trained to prioritize their strange animal powers (from painting the Sistine Chapel to producing democracy) far above those of other forms of life. It is a question here of turning this argument against itself, of catching humanocentrism out with its own values, so that it can understand what it's doing. Thus, it will be able to realize that its scale is not the only one or the right one. In the meantime, in some cases, we can also play games with its tradition rather than stigmatizing it, if we want to blow it apart from the inside.

The singular power of this parable comes down to the fact that we do not know, that we will not be able to know, what lineage is rich with the greatest promises; and, even when we are convinced that all life is already wonderful and accomplished (an idea that I share), we are forced to recognize, through our humanistic bias, that there is something terrible about considering eliminating a species that will raise even higher the values that we extol.

The situation requires infinite delicacy, then, since in a few million years the population of trees that have the slowest powers of reflection, or the most 'derisory' insects (by the evolutionary reversion of some of their rigidities), could become better ambassadors than we are of the powers that we cherish as the highest in humans (forms of symbolism, the arts, political forms emancipated from the countless forms of violence that still populate our democracies, varied and empathetic ethics, new and conscious forms of consideration for life on Earth).

So if we go back as far as we wish in the ascent of the life form that we are, we are descended from a placental mammal from the Cretaceous analogous to a current rodent, and if we go back even further, from jellyfish, and again, from sponges, and again, proto-plants, paramecia, and finally bacteria: consequently, logically, you are not immune from the possibility that each of those around you will one day beget the *descendants* of ticks as righteous as Martin Luther King, or trees as wise as Gandhi – descendants of amoebas as artistically badass as Beyoncé.

That is, if we take seriously the concept of *evolutionary potential*, then every current form of life, from sponge to octopus, from bee to matsutake mushroom, is *potentially* the ancestor of more interesting species *by humanist and anthropocentric criteria* than we are.

And, of course, symmetrically, we human beings aren't to be left behind, as there are other equally valuable criteria. Can we imagine evolving until we acquire the art which bees deploy to dance out their maps? The art of dolphins to hear the shape of the landscape? The art of the octopus to make decisions with every extremity of its body? The art of the trees to devour the sun, and to release breathable oxygen into the atmosphere, thus making thousands of other life forms possible?

Our place in evolution: contemporary developments in the philosophy of biology

If this possibility is irrefutable from a logical point of view, why has it not had more of an effect on the way we understand our place in the biosphere, when it is already latent in Darwinism? The reason is that, while a whole series of philosophical conceptions linked to the theory of evolution over the last centuries did not deny that this was possible, it *did* deny that it was probable.

Why has this thought experiment become possible right now, in the current theoretical and philosophical context? We need a detailed X-ray of the transformations in the latent philosophy of evolutionism since Darwin to understand this phenomenon. Something major but invisible has changed. We need look no further than recent scientific history to realize that a certain dominant version of the hidden philosophy of evolutionism almost ruled out this idea of the 'promise of simple forms' during the twentieth century. It springs from the erroneous idea that there is a spontaneous tendency to complexity in the evolutionary process: a telos (a final, intended goal) in evolution that opens up a royal road from lowly and simple forms of living beings to complex human perfection (this is a version that we still find, in disguise, or with various qualifications, in the philosophies of the founding biologists of the synthetic theory of evolution, Dobzhansky, Simpson, up to and including Mayr).[5] On this view, the simpler forms are intrinsically former rungs on the ladder up which complexity rises, and not singular adventures which are also able, despite being (for example) single-celled, to do some pretty fascinating things, as when bacteria communicate with one another to trigger a collective effect of virulence or luminescence (this is the 'quorum sensing' recently described by microbiologists).[6]

But a certain counter-narrative then took over in the last quarter of the twentieth century, until the beginning of the twenty-first. It might be called the contingentism associated with Stephen Jay Gould – the idea that evolution is fundamentally contingent, an idea which paradoxically and quite innocently embraced human exceptionalism in evolution. Paradoxically, because Gould's goal was precisely to avoid seeing human beings as 'chosen', and to reject any hierarchy in other forms of life. Gould's ambition was indeed to reject the sovereignty of human beings, to challenge the idea that evolution tended *towards* human beings as a perfect form; but the only theoretical solution he could find that would accomplish this philosophical project and at the same time be in accordance with his scientific conception of evolution involved a paradox. So as not to be the end or the triumph of evolution, humans must have been a *completely* improbable coincidence, an accident, an oddity: this is the idea of the extreme improbability of human beings coming into existence. Gouldism, as a philosophy of biological evolution based on the idea of the radical contingency of the evolutionary process, deduced from this idea that the uniqueness of the human life form (requiring the intriguing conjunction of an opposable thumb, biomechanical and neuronal language faculties, bipedalism, a large brain, the change towards an omnivorous diet, and so on) must be thought of as a *roll of the dice* that was impossible to reproduce – *unique*.

Even those who are not familiar with the work of Gould, a hugely important biologist and polymathic thinker, are still aware of this version of the story of 'our place in evolution', because it has infused our culture since the 1990s: everyone probably knows it in the form of the parable (very 'analogue', very nineties), of 'replaying the tape of life'. In Gould's parable,[7] if we rewound the tape of life and pressed the 'play' button, the tape would play out again but in a *very different* way from what actually took place, because microscopic differences in the initial conditions (let's add them, so as to make the thought experiment more precise) create major differences in the evolution of living systems. As a consequence, current life forms in all their singularity are the product of pure and perfect contingency, of maximum improbability; the human life form, the form of this intriguing animal, is an *irreproducible statistical singularity*.

But the exception of the lottery winner rather than the exception of being a chosen people is still an exception.

Our cosmic solitude among living beings is, strangely enough, preserved in this parable, even though Gould's aim was to deconstruct the idea of any necessity, any final cause in the appearance of human beings. Seeking to dethrone human beings as the outcome of an evolutionary project, he reconstituted them as an exception, but in the form of a pure singularity of chance. Paradoxically, his parable constitutes a conservative force in Gould's avant-garde biology (and we must not be too critical of Gould here, for he also created the concepts which now help us understand that this philosophical implication of the biology of evolution was *false*).

For, in addition to contingency, there are *constraints*: biological constraints on evolution and transformation, which are widely shared by all living beings because of their common ascent and common environmental conditions, and it was Gould who partly helped to bring them to light. It is the rise of another concept in biology which now allows us to view the place of human beings as something other than as an ontological exception, either in 'chosen' terms or as statistical, while still retaining the Gouldian idea of the decisive importance (but not the absoluteness) of contingency in evolution.

The banality of miracles

For some years now, the biology of evolution, fuelled by the idea of constraints, has been developing the concept of convergence,[8] which shows that where we had previously seen nothing but irreducible singularities among the living, there are in fact major convergences. This is the great debate between Stephen Jay Gould and Simon Conway Morris on the Cambrian Explosion, which caused a great stir in palaeontology at the turn of the century.[9] Scientists have shown that photosynthesis, a miraculous aptitude found in bacteria (and later incorporated by plants) to feed on the sun, transforming it into carbon, has been acquired relatively independently more than one hundred and twenty times in evolution. Simon Conway Morris convincingly documents the multiple parallel appearances of the eye, of C_4 type photosynthesis, and even of 'intelligence', in a fascinating chapter on convergences in complex social life forms.[10]

There are of course crucial (and unsettled) terminological debates about what we are talking about when we talk about an 'intelligence' that is supposed to have appeared several times. But in a loose and yet convincing sense, intelligence *has* appeared many times in living beings. It is something like the ability to solve complex problems without necessarily having the usual motor patterns, in the sense of inherited and stereotyped sequences of movements – in other words, by finding solutions which require sequences of connected, coherent and mediated behaviours in order to arrive at a certain end. Birds do not have the same cortex as us, and it was long assumed that they could not have any intelligence. And yet, it is simply that the conformation of their brain structure has taken a different turn from ours; this enables them to perform with brio things that fulfil the minimum definition of intelligence: solving problems with the body-mind.[11] Octopuses separated out from us six hundred million years ago, and yet they developed extraordinary cognitive forms based on a neural and cerebral apparatus of a completely different type from ours.[12] Even trees display unsuspected operations of a 'cognitive' style: they use neurotransmitters, not just in chemical form, but as signalling pathways. One needs to appreciate the extent of this phenomenon: they use *neurotransmitters* despite having no brains or *neurons*.[13] (This shows that we still have a non-functional definition of cognitive processes.)

We are not the single roll of the dice that led to the emergence of intelligence, we are one such form among others, and among other potential forms (but a form, whatever we may say – let's be sensible! – that is particularly distinguished and singular when it comes to certain faculties). The discovery of the complex cognitive forms of other living beings makes it possible to understand that other intelligences are possible.

The paradox is that the idea of convergence has been vigorously defended by a thinker whose metaphysical agenda is after all quite clear: Simon Conway Morris is a Christian, and part of his animosity towards Gould probably stems from the latter's atheism. Hence Conway Morris defends convergence as the proof that biologists have overestimated the place of chance in evolution, and that the cosmic lines of force leading to the emergence of a 'bipedal intelligent life form' would cause evolution to repeat itself in broad outline. Thus, one has the impression of a conflict between two metaphysics of the place of human beings in the living world. In fact, it does not do justice to either of the two biologists to reduce their debate to metaphysical agendas. They are above all honest analysts of the fossil records, and the fact is there, very clear, very evident for anyone prepared to look: convergence is omnipresent.

Contingency and convergence: life

The idea that it was highly unlikely that we or any intelligent life form would appear is therefore now outdated by the very robust documentation of convergences proposed by Conway Morris in particular. The emergence of intelligent life has taken place several times, it is often repeated, and will often be repeated, because intelligence is, for living beings, a 'good trick' on the part of evolution, as the Darwinian Daniel Dennett puts it: a wonderful invention which makes life more liveable and more sustainable. We are no longer Gouldian from the point of view of his parable of the tape of life, or of the absolute contingentism that it conceals. But that does not detract from the relevance of the idea that there is a *relative* contingency to evolution. It is simply a constrained contingency, where good solutions are rediscovered several times, by chance: but by a chance constrained in its expression by the material conditions of evolution.

Accepting the omnipresence of convergence does not therefore force us to take a religious point of view on evolution: we can quite simply endorse a strictly materialist interpretation of convergence (it being understood that we do not know what matter is: it is just that matter does not need the God hypothesis to do wonderful things). Convergences are thus the expression of generative constraints (genetic, developmental and selective).

Schematically put: imagine a Lego game. A randomly functioning blind robot assembles pieces in a room. The constraints on the combinations of parts are such that the potential number of constructions is finite in number, and the laws of gravity are such that the constructions that hold up are also finite in number: in between is the space of possible forms, which repeat themselves frequently. But the robot still displays a certain final purpose in the variations it can create. By analogy: evolutionary convergences do not in the least undermine the Darwinian discovery of chance, in the sense of an absence of final purpose between variation and selection. It is not because the field of possibilities is constrained that its exploration through variations is not independent of environmental conditions.

Do human beings occupy a comfortable place in the coral reef of evolution?

What then is the effect of these theoretical movements on the much more interesting philosophical question of the place of human beings in the living world?

A philosophical interpretation of the implications of this new biology of convergence lies in the sketch I presented above: each species or current population is *potentially* the ancestor of life forms endowed with intelligence, or aptitudes for creation, or love, analogous or superior to those of the primate that we are. We are merely in the vanguard of over-acute forms of intelligence or civilization among living beings (and a painfully imperfect sketch at that).

Behind us, the entire biosphere advances, at its perfectly slow pace, to engage in an all-out experiment with other ventures of living intelligence, of dwelling, culture, communication, benevolence, even justice.

There are already spectacular examples, as in the Capuchin monkeys who insist on receiving an equivalent reward for carrying out the same task as another monkey (the video of this famous experiment shows a monkey throwing the slice of cucumber he has been given at the experimenter, since his companion in the cage next door has been rewarded with a succulent piece of fruit).[14]

Our intelligence is not a hapax of evolution, a unique and infinitely improbable roll of the dice, but one form of intelligence among other forms which are being tried out everywhere, and which *over time* could resemble ours, exceed it, or diverge completely from it into unheard-of forms. Because this is the whole point: it needed some six hundred million years for the *sponge* to become *sapiens* – it takes time and, precisely, this is what species are being deprived of today: the time and space to be able to continue to evolve in heavily anthropized environments.

The philosophical implications of convergentism for the ecological crisis have been rarely noticed, especially when it comes to the place of human beings (their rarity, their singularity) in the blossoming of *future* life. The theoretical debate, captured by the controversy between Gould and Conway Morris, instead focused on the rewound tape metaphor of life, based on the following question: could a being endowed with an intelligence comparable to that of humans appear if we restarted evolution in the past? But the decisive thought experiment lies elsewhere: what happens if we let the evolutionary tape play from *now*, giving space and time to other forms of life around us?

Burning more than a library

There is a metaphor in conservation biology, which says that the sixth extinction amounts to burning the library of evolution.[15] Each population or species is then considered as a genetic memory, a book: all the treasures of ecological knowledge incorporated into organs, sedimented over millions of years. The immemorial ethological arts that each species has set in place to invent wonderful solutions to the problem of living in changing environments – all burnt. The secret of the art of flying, written and transmitted in every bird cell, every butterfly – all burnt. The secret of breathing, safeguarded in each animal; the secret of devouring the sun, folded into the genetic information of chloroplasts; the secret of digesting cellulose thanks to host bacteria in herbivores – all burnt. The secret of synthesizing opioids for one's own pain, the secret of thinking, of forming attachments with small mammals, with relatives and friends . . . All these secrets *partly* encapsulated in each cell, in genetic and epigenetic form, all gone up in smoke.[16]

This library metaphor is correct, but it is insufficient. The sixth, contemporary extinction is not just a matter of burning the library of evolution, and all the works of the *past*; it means burning the poets too. The poets yet to come: that is to say, the possibility for each life form to produce others with as yet unknown aptitudes, vital arts, and powers. We are not just burning what has happened, but everything that could happen. This is what we call the evolutionary potential of each population of living beings, going up in smoke in the furnaces of the extractivist and resource-plundering machine comprised by the political economy of the dominant countries – their blindness to non-human living beings.

Given the urgency of the contemporary biodiversity crisis, what then are the ethical implications of this thought experiment that tries to track down the philosophical meaning of the place of human beings in the new evolutionary biology?

We can say first that each species should not be preserved simply because it is a unique heritage, simply because it has an inalienable right to life founded in an ethics, simply because it is beautiful, simply because it can provide us with new medicines, or simply out of consideration for life; or because it is already a marvel, from the evolutionary point of view (which is true). It is worth preserving for another reason too: because it is the potential ancestor of adventurous life forms that will be marvels, even from the most humanist point of view possible – species more considerate of others and their world than we have as yet contrived to become.

This is all a trick: it's easier to spread our bucket of Roundup weedkiller on critters, cockroaches and other creepie-crawlies, than on the potential ancestors of the jewels of the non-human civilizations of the future, right?

To restore all its elegance to this phenomenon, we need to remember, however, that we will never know which fly or bacteria is a promise of this kind, and which intends to remain a bacterium for millions of years to come, feeling that it is quite perfect enough as it is (and from its own point of view, it's quite right).

In order not to be trapped by analogies, we must however point out the limit of the metaphor of the library, which implies the idea of an irreversible and definitive loss: a biological population, from the evolutionary point of view, should not be thought of only as a monument destroyed by barbarians, or a flammable old book, but as a fire. The original Darwinian power of proliferation is such that if living conditions become favourable again, then one ember, one small population (as long as it is genetically diverse enough), can give birth to a flourishing population, capable of major evolutionary developments towards unheard-of life forms. But for that, it is necessary to cherish the last embers, and not in the whimsical form of zoo specimens, but in the form of living populations, in protected and integrated environments (for the habitat of one life form is only the weaving together of all others), with great connectivity and numbers sufficient to ensure genetic robustness and the ability to change, to adapt to environmental metamorphoses which are inevitably going to come in the wake of global warming.

By its ontological nature, the best analogy for understanding the evolutionary nature of the biosphere is that of a poetic fire: a *creative fire* – this being said without the slightest mysticism, unless of the unassuming form required by the spectacle of evolution outside of us and within us.

By 'fire' I mean that the biosphere may well be reduced, but just an ember, a lifting of selective constraints (emerging niches, milder conditions), will suffice for it to proliferate and spread; by 'creative' I mean that this spread will invent thousands of new shapes. In this regard, then, the risk is more ambiguous than one should admit strategically, for those who believe that the most apocalyptic catastrophism is the best pragmatic line when it comes to shifting the transformation of our societies in a way that will create more sustainable interwoven relations with living beings. But it is not necessary for ecological thought to paint a gloomier picture, we know that credibility is the most valuable virtue for those who would raise the alarm:[17] in fact, past extinctions have *also* produced major and quite magnificent evolutionary developments. The mammals that we love so much (and that we ourselves are) were able to diversify and produce the current flowering only thanks to the extinction of a large proportion of dinosaurs, which had kept the little nocturnal mammal that was our ancestor at the junction between the Cretaceous and the Tertiary confined to microscopic forms and very small niches. So we have to acknowledge that there will be other poets, and the biosphere will recover from the damage done to it. At worst, it will waste hundreds of millions of years of blind design, extraordinary creations that require improbable combinations of evolutionary history, genetic and epigenetic variation, and a pile of blueprints – this memory will disappear. This is already a real tragedy. But the vital problem lies elsewhere: it is our living relationships that will be destroyed – and these relations constitute us, from outside as well as the inside.

And in truth, this is not just one more reason to act differently (we already have many reasons, excellent reasons to protect biodiversity, and we do not act on them – reasons are of limited effectiveness in the current situation).

That is why I would like to do something quite different, not limited to protecting the various species to be added to the list of a WWF report: I would like to restore meaning to the ritual of salting. A ritual without metaphysical depth, with all the simplicity of the pagan mysteries, like those of Eleusis which, when people came seeking meaning, simply displayed the daily wonder of the grain that nourishes and the water that quenches thirst.

Ancestor worship

If we connect these two thought experiments together (the way our daily dose of salt reminds us of our origins as a sponge in the oceans, and the idea of a sketched out design), they create a thread of meaning, a story that could fit into one line; and here we could restore an eco-evolutionary meaning to this ritual that we already perform to our pre-human ancestors whenever we salt our food. A silent, simple ritual, performed deep inside ourselves, without any mysticism – without any other mysticism than that of life itself.

What type of gift deserves our gratitude? The cult of ancestors found in Asian traditions is an interesting inspiration here, because it allows us to change our conception of what we *can* give thanks to. Because it does not allow the characteristic sweet madness of Western tradition, probably inherited from anthropomorphic monotheism, according to which only what has been given to us *voluntarily* is a gift that implies *gratitude*. The Judeo-Christian God, with his intentional, conscious and voluntary nature, transformed the immemorial concept of the daily gift which makes us live (the wild fruit, the water that quenches thirst, the hunted animal), so that something appears as a gift only when it has been given by a *conscious will* (his). By this theological sleight of hand, any gift that is *not* given voluntarily, and does not involve a sacrifice, is not considered a *true* gift, it does not call for gratitude: it is considered as a natural *given*, an available resource, an appropriable effect of the material causality that supposedly governs

'Nature'. It was this mutation that transformed our relationship with 'giving environments'. When later on we stopped believing in God, renouncing the daily blessings thanking him for the bread on the table, we did not know how to channel this gratitude towards what *actually* gives us bread and water: the ecological dynamics and the living flows of evolution that circulate in the biosphere and are the basis of its continuity. We no longer knew who to thank for the joy of being alive, for the mammalian attachment to our loved ones, for the daily joys offered by our body-minds shaped by an immemorial evolution. Reducing the living nature that creates and reshapes us to a mechanistic and absurd matter has deprived of meaning any gratitude towards the living world which nevertheless makes us live.

However, ancestor worship is an anthropological ritual form that has avoided this metaphysical misunderstanding: in the Asian traditions where it is customary, it is irrelevant whether your ancestors had the will or the intention to create you: you still owe them some gratitude for being alive. But here the nature of worship shifts: it is to our *prehuman* ancestors that we owe thanks, because they were much more numerous and much more generous towards us, endowing us with all the bodily, mental, affective and vital powers which make us, than that handful of great-grandparents who bequeathed us a family name, a gold watch, a country house or a piece of land.

Can we imagine a way of worshipping our prehuman ancestors that would make us less forgetful descendants? Simple rituals to thank, without melodrama or exaggerated religiosity, those ancestors who have borne us in their arms this far, who have offered us their evolutionary and ecological powers? What would an ancestral altar for all these ancestors look like? And who are those ancestors? They include the small placental mammal, analogous to a field mouse, surviving the Cretaceous-Tertiary extinction which engulfed the great saurians, to relay to us the miracle of sexed life, of viviparity, of the emotional fullness of parenthood. And the first cell, which, by endo-symbiosis, incorporated within it a bacterium that then became mito-chondria, an organelle that at every moment activates in our bodies the marvellous synthesis of *energy*. And the fur-covered, naked hom-inid who brilliantly discovered fire, and in doing so originated, by filiation as well as by cultural invention, the form of life that we are.

And, by extension, should we not invent rituals of gratitude for the pollinators who each year produce spring and its vegetables, providing food for us; for the life of soils farmed by microfauna, that great headless peasant; for forests that cobble together the breathable cocoon of the atmosphere?

Can we imagine injecting a little of all this meaning into the daily act of salting our food? Throwing a handful of coarse salt into the pan the way the witch adds it to her potion. Or tapping three times on the salt shaker with our index finger, rhythmically, the way the Zen monk taps on his gong. In so doing, we can reconstitute the salinity of the inland sea, that of the ancestor we once were. Could this bring back the sense that we were once a sponge? We could sense the ancestors still moving below the surface of our skin – they are our foundation, they have bequeathed to us our living powers. I was sponge, bacterium, an ember among the embers. From every life form all around, a lineage full of possibilities can be born.

Raising our glasses, finally: 'To the promises of the living world!'

3

Cohabiting with our wild beasts:
the diplomatic ethics of Spinoza

The unconscious part of our mind is conscious of us.

R. D. Laing

Swim calmly in the current of your own nature and act like one single man.

Sir Thomas Browne

My aim here is to track down the metamorphoses of interior animals. In Western history, we have often depicted the inner life of humans, their passionate, sentimental life, through animal metaphors: the instincts are represented as wild animals; docility as peaceful tame animals, courage as a lion, while greed assumes the face of a pig. This inner menagerie has played a fundamental role in the history of traditional Western morality, inspired by Greek philosophy and Judeo-Christianity. These traditions are very powerful, because they have shaped our way of understanding our most intimate, most shapeless, most evanescent passions. And the paradox I want to track down here is that, while we have inherited a morality that depicts our inner life in animal form, yet our tradition is *wrong* about what an animal actually is. How, then, can our ethics of the passions be correct?

For there to be an ethics, we must first realize that every person is split in two: there is the one who wants to give in and the one who wants to hold on, the one who acts and the one who judges. There are different forces pulling us in different directions, and ethics consists in choosing the right one. Without this original doubleness, no ethical project is possible. But these instances are very often depicted as animals, albeit deformed animals: not understood. The point here is to do justice to our internal animal natures, by better understanding the animals outside of us that we have taken as models of our intimate passions.

The object of this investigation therefore amounts to reinterpreting an aspect of Western philosophical ethics from the point of view in which they constitute split ego theories, in which animal metaphors play a special role. The ethics proposed by philosophers do indeed tell *stories*, in which the ego is composed of several characters, and *torn apart*. In the myth of Plato's *Phaedrus*, for example, reason is a charioteer who must drive a winged chariot drawn by the horse of concupiscent passion and the horse of noble passion. The ego is composed of a rational 'soul' which must dominate and control mismatched animals: the horses of the passions. This figure of the self split between reason and animal nature deserves to be analysed schematically, and then rethought in the broader context of the relationships that our tradition has with animals. Thus it becomes possible, more speculatively, to set out new boundaries in the field of philosophical ethics, to highlight those which maintain an original relationship with our inner animalities: this is a kind of diplomacy with a non-inferiorized aspect of the self, rather than the domination of what is coded as the 'lowest' within us. The ethics of Spinoza is a prime example.

Taming the horses of the passions

It is Plato who formulates the necessity for all ethics to be based on a dual *conception of the self* (that is to say a cartographic representation of the self divided into two regions fighting for power). But Socrates immediately isolates the logical paradox of this doubleness: 'He who is master of himself is also, I suppose, a slave of himself, and he who is slave, a master.'[1]

To resolve this Platonic paradox, we must postulate a *natural hierarchy* between the two poles. The Western ethics of this tradition then comes down to a game between forces in oneself, one being seen as what is *most* authentically myself within myself (my reason), and the other as what is *least* myself within myself (my bad passions). Thereafter, ethics is seen as a problem of *liberation*: when what is the least myself within myself dominates the other, 'I' am his slave ('he is a slave to his passions'). When what is most myself within myself dominates (reason), then 'I' am said to be free. The daily experience of this potential inner slavery is regret. Sometimes, in fact, the least myself within myself does something, and then the most myself within myself regrets it ('I wasn't myself'). So the one must be more myself than the other. While doubleness is necessary for ethical life, it is the division of roles, and the nature of their relationship, that I wish to criticize here.

The history of Western ethics thus resembles a drama in which the question is that of who plays the two roles. What is fascinating is that the first and supporting roles, the most myself and the less myself within myself, vary greatly in history, and sometimes even *swap sides*. In classical ethics, I am above all my reason, and that is why reason must dominate my passions so that I do not become their slave. In a certain romanticism, on the contrary, I am above all my most vibrant feelings (my passions), and cold reason is merely a secondary social device for normalizing coercion, from which I must free myself to *finally* be myself. The roles are reversed, but the play is the same.

The subject of much of the history of moral philosophy has been the poles involved in the split ego staged by Plato. Peter Sloterdijk, the latest philosopher to analyse the entire history of European ethical systems, shows that what is missing in this tradition is an attention to the *relations* between the poles.[2] Throughout history, these relationships use the same metaphors, whose origins remain unquestioned: training, control, domination, *enkrateia*. It is surely strange, however, that all the words used to describe the moral relationship to oneself are about taming, controlling, restraining, subduing a fierce rebel.

The philosopher Spinoza was among the first to see that, in this immemorial duo, if the roles change, the *relationship* remains the same. And it is *this relation* that is toxic, involving as it does checking, dominating, controlling. So what I understand by the 'ethics of the charioteer' is this map of the interior life, where Reason must control, *as their master*, the passions and desires, which are thus assimilated to irrational beasts, unable to behave by themselves. (This ethics, strictly speaking, is not the same as the ethics of Plato, Christianity or Descartes, which are far richer.)

We can read the *Ethics*, Spinoza's masterpiece, as an attempt to end this internalized relationship of self-domination, where to live is *to oppress yourself*. Spinoza invents another map of inner life, where passions are not irrational, dependent and rebellious beasts, but autonomous wild animals within us, which must be influenced, guided, coaxed, with the aim of promoting the joys that emancipate us, to the detriment of the sadnesses that make us helpless.

For Spinoza, this is not a return to the myth of some noble savage within us, to an ethical laissez-faire, to the egalitarianism of the inner life demanded by those who suffer from too much discipline imposed from outside: nothing is more dubious or misleading. Instead, he proposes another ethical demand, higher and more subtle, as far from the undivided domination of the passions as it is from an unchecked unleashing of the passions. For these two versions are based on a misunderstanding of the animal nature of the passions.

Spinoza thus opens the way to another relation to oneself, one which will be shown to inaugurate an exit from the immemorial error of traditional Western ethics, which consists of thinking of ethics as a *rational domestication* of oneself by oneself. We must freely reinterpret the *Ethics* (not according to the letter but according to the spirit) as a manual for living peacefully with the wild animals *within us* (these are our affects, sad and yet so joyful).

From one map to another: reason/passions vs joy/sadness

Spinoza's decisive ethical gesture is to replace the map of the self that opposes reason to passions with a different map which *connects* joy and sadness. In the first map of the self, the canons of reason are turned towards the passions: ethics is an attempt by reason to dominate the passions. In the classical ethics of Descartes, this domination is deduced from a strange law of human nature: the 'law of inverse proportion'. This law, structuring inner life, stipulates that between the two poles of ethical life (reason and passions, mind and body), one suffers *as much as* the other acts. This law is easily deduced from the first article of *The Passions of the Soul*, entitled 'That which is passion with regard to a subject is always action in some other respect'.[3] Reason acts only insofar as the passions are subject to its law. Ethics becomes a *psychomachia*: a struggle of the soul, in the soul, for the soul.

This law of inverse proportion between acting and suffering turns the individual into a battlefield, where an oppressed confronts an oppressor, a muzzled figure confronts a domineering protagonist. Any *psychomachia* thus involves a psyche in the grip of a bellicose schizophrenia. It necessarily oscillates between suffering and frustration (when desire is dominated by reason) and guilt and self-hatred (when reason is overwhelmed by the passions). In his ethics, Spinoza understands that this ethics of the domination of one side of oneself by another always creates an S/M game: when one triumphs, the other clinks glasses ('This time you play the slave and I play the master – tomorrow we swap').

This map that opposes passions and reason is, moreover, superimposed on the body/mind map. So the law of inverse proportion decrees that, in order to uplift my mind, I must mortify my body. This aspect too will undergo the Spinozist revolution.

Spinoza redraws this bellicose map of the self by changing the basic axiom of the mathematics of the soul: he replaces the law of inverse proportion with a law of *simple proportion*. This discreet but revolutionary transition is visible in the historical debate between Spinoza and Descartes on the relationship between the soul and the body. The law of simple proportion is formulated by Spinoza as follows: 'If something increases or decreases, fosters or prevents our body's power of acting, the idea of this thing increases or decreases, fosters or prevents our soul's power of thinking.'[4]

This is known as parallelism:[5] raising the mind *elevates* the body. The body's increased power of acting and being acted upon increases the power of thinking.

However, as we said above, there is no ethics if there is no *split* in the inner life. We require at least two possible paths for the self, for action, if the ethical issue is to emerge. But now – and this is Spinoza's brilliant theoretical move – this split is no longer between two *parts* of the soul, but between two *types* of affect or desire: joy and sadness.

Indeed, there can be no war within the self unless the split identifies reason and passions as 'parts of the soul' (Descartes), that is to say as fixed regions of the self. They exist face to face, and in direct struggle with one another. With Spinoza, joy and sadness are no longer *parts* of the self, but transitory affects of the self which each time involve the *whole* individual:[6] they are processes. These affects are defined as *passages* to a higher or lower perfection. That is, they do not oppose each other statically, but they replace each other: I am a trajectory of power that rises towards joy, or a sad trajectory which sinks towards powerlessness. So there are still two forces involved, but *this is no longer a dualism*, as these two forces are two possible but mutually exclusive trajectories that a now unified self can follow, under the name of Conatus, or Desire.

Relationship with our animal nature, relationship with ourselves

To make this revolution in ethics possible, we have to rethink our relationships with our passions; we must no longer see the self as a charioteer who needs to subdue his bestial passions or be overwhelmed.

It is the classical moralists, contemporaries of Descartes, who provide the clearest instructions for a charioteer's ethics when it comes to the relations we must entertain with our passions when they are seen metaphorically as wild beasts.

Yves de Paris, for example, declares that a passion is 'like a beast that we hold by a chain, and that we cannot quite tame'.[7] Pierre Le Moyne replies: 'When we cannot tame [passions], we chain them up.'[8] Ceriziers, more measured, qualifies this: we have to 'conquer our body, not kill it'.[9] If the charioteer is to overcome his passions and bind them together, one condition is necessary: it is a question of 'reducing them to mediocrity when virtue demands it'.[10] ('Mediocrity' must here be understood in the old sense, as weakness.)

However, if we pay attention to the relations between the *poles* of the self in this ethics of the charioteer, we may be surprised at the way the metaphors are systematically those of military-style control, of taming, of the domination of our inner animals.

This quirk becomes intelligible if we allow ourselves to take a detour through the history of the relations between civilizations and animals. This detour was made by the ethnozoologist André-Georges Haudricourt, in a brief article published in 1962, as revolutionary as it was discreet.[11] In this text, he argues that the original relationships that a society maintains with animals are often a model of the relationships that the same society establishes *between humans*. Our relationships with nature are consistent with our relationships with humans: for example, the exploitation of cattle is, according to Haudricourt, an origin of slavery. Extending this idea, we can advance the hypothesis that the relationships we establish with the living world *outside of us* constitute models for the relationships with the living world *within us* (our 'wild' emotional life). The domestication which controls and exploits the animal world, characteristic of the relationship to the living world found in Western civilization, is also the model of the relationship that reason must maintain with the inner life. The slavery of the living world outside of us lies behind the slavery of the passions within us.

This conception of the domestication of the animal world is, however, a local cultural phenomenon, and far from being universal. But it is such a long-standing relationship that it has become naturalized within us. Countless types of relationships with non-human animals have been invented by humans, but Haudricourt isolates the one that in his view characterizes our dominant Western history, insofar as we are the heirs of the Near-Eastern Neolithic period, eleven to eight thousand years before our time. He calls it 'positive direct action'.[12]

The old system of sheep farming seems to be a model of positive direct action. The animal must be guided by the shepherd's crook and dogs, and is considered not to be autonomous. It has to be carried through difficult terrain; you have to go looking for it when fear has immobilized it on narrow ledges and sometimes even roll it over when it has fallen on its back and is unable to get back on its feet. It is as if it had to be monitored constantly – and this is made possible by virtue of the fact that it has been made docile, fearful and somewhat helpless due to artificial selection. It has been 'reduced to mediocrity' as demanded by the needs of control, just as the passions will have to be reduced in the ethics of the charioteer. Domestication with positive direct action thus constitutes the model later internalized in the self by this same ethics. Its sacred duty is to heteronomize nature (to make it dependent), and then to govern nature outside oneself and within oneself.[13]

But Haudricourt shows that there is at least one other type of relationship with animals, a profoundly different one which he calls 'negative indirect action'. In this, we postulate that the other animals are autonomous and complete in themselves. Domesticating them does not consist in making them dependent, but in influencing their wild nature by means of negotiation. It is then through a detailed knowledge of the animal's behavioural logics that we can influence its action and weave a harmonious relationship with it. That relationship can be seen in the way the Tuvans of Siberia (a shamanistic and animist people) herd their reindeer, as described by anthropologist Charles Stépanoff. Reindeer are intentionally kept in their wild state, but are nonetheless involved in mutual cooperation with the humans who influence and guide their behaviour. He concludes that, 'paradoxically, humans can only domesticate reindeer if they keep them in the wild state'.[14] In this other conception of our relations with animals, we live better with them if we influence them in their intact vitality, rather than weakening them so as to control them.

I call 'Stépanoff's paradox', here applied to cohabitation with the living world *within us*, the strange idea that, in order to tame the fiercest desires, that is, to live well with them and through them, we must *keep* them in the wild state.

The ethics of the charioteer is based on the original mistake of believing that our inner desires are deficient beasts that demand positive direct action – demand, that is, to be devitalized and then controlled from start to finish. The intrinsic error of the ethics of the charioteer comes down to the postulate that we need to devitalize desiring life in order to be virtuous: 'reduce it to mediocrity when virtue demands it'.

This is where Spinoza's intuition about human nature reaches its full extent. We are intrinsically *made up* of desire. Desire is not a lack, but a power – the power by which we persevere in existence: 'Desire is the essence of man.'[15] Consequently, stifling our passions and desires means weakening the only vital force with which we are able to move forward in life.[16] What Spinoza saw is that we are *nothing but desire*: it is the intensification of the joyful and wise vitality of this desire, at the expense of morbid sadness, which comprises virtue, and becomes the name of wisdom. This vivification of joyful desires requires another relationship with the passions in oneself, a relationship that I will call 'diplomatic'.[17]

An ethology of the self

The passions in the ethics of the charioteer are like exotic animals on old maps: we fantasize them into monsters because we do not know them very well, we project things onto them that are actually in us.[18] We try to keep them at a distance without understanding what they need (this is repression) or how to let them converge on our desires; eventually, they return in such an intense form that they *seem* bestial and uncontrollable (chase away the repressed, mistreat it, and back it gallops).

However, treating the wild desires in ourselves is not the same as unleashing bestial passions. Here we need to understand 'wild animals' not as the ferocious beasts fantasized by Judeo-Christian pastoral writers, but in the light of what contemporary science teaches us about wild animals. The ethology that observes them closely shows that they do not have the unbridled ferocity that the charioteer's ethics attributes to animalized passions. 'Wild' here means 'fully alive', but with a logic of its own.

The whole problem of ethics is that the inner life is metastable: it has an infinite metamorphic richness, and no established forms. Consequently, we need metaphors to describe this inner life. These metaphors allow us to visualize it and manipulate it, but, like any metaphor, they are both solutions and obstacles – they solve problems, but in other situations they also create problems.

What happens if the founding metaphor of ethics is based on a misconception of animal life?

Traditional morality sees desire metaphorically as animal, and is mistaken about the nature of animals.[19] So it is also mistaken about the metaphor of our relationship to animals: it demands the domination of a dependent beast, rather than a cohabitation with the very lively animals that inhabit and constitute us.

Diplomacy then comes down to knowing in detail, by means of an ethology of the self, the delicate and ardent behaviour of its emotional life, thus appeasing and influencing desires that preserve their vitality intact, and enabling them to converge in an upward, and therefore generous direction – just as we constantly whisper adequate stories into our own ears, to temper our inner speech ('Patience, my heart', as Ulysses put it).

The originality of Spinoza is that he offers a self-to-self relationship much closer to what Haudricourt calls 'negative indirect action', and to what I here call 'diplomacy'. Diplomacy with the living world inside and outside the self is a type of relationship that becomes relevant when we live together, on the same territory, with beings who resist and insist – beings who, however, must not be destroyed or unduly weakened, because our vitality *depends* on theirs. So it is with our passions.

Plato vs. the Cherokees

Perhaps it is time to seek models for an ethical relationship to our inner animals inspired by cultures whose relationships with animals are less domineering and more diplomatic. Cultures that do not rest on the hierarchical separation between humans and animals that prevails in our naturalistic West.[20] We find examples in animistic ontologies.

In this respect, let us compare the ethics of the charioteer to that presented in a tale often attributed to the Amerindian Cherokee oral tradition. In it, the self is made up of two wolves: one is white, noble and happy; one is black, arrogant and base. Here, in essence, is what the tale says:

'In every human there are two wolves', says the old sachem.

'One black and one white.

The black one is sure of his due, afraid of everything, and therefore angry, resentful, selfish and greedy, because he has nothing more to give.

The white one is strong and calm, lucid and fair, open to others, and therefore generous, because he is strong enough not to feel attacked by events.'

A child listening to the story asks him:

'But which of the two am I, then?'

'The one you feed.'

One can be struck by the resemblance to the ethics of the charioteer, especially in its Platonic form (two animals, one white and one black, each embodying one of the opposite poles of the human psyche). We must however note the difference: the ethics of the charioteer thinks of the self as made up of animal slaves doomed to obey, which must be trained and dominated, and *to this end* devitalized; the Cherokee theory of the self thinks of it as made up of wild animals, autonomous and fully alive, animals that one must frequent and *foster*.

We can take inspiration from this Native American parable to interpret the Spinozist ethic which consists in favouring positive passions (the white wolf) to the detriment of negative passions (the black wolf). 'All right, my wild beast, you're fine, gently does it, it's okay, that's the way', the Spinozist Cherokee tells himself.

What does human life – that experimentation that comprises life – resemble when the self no longer thinks of itself as a master dominating devitalized impulses with an iron fist, but as a strange collective with wild animals full of life?

Probably something else, another way of existing, as an individual and as a civilization.

It is no longer a question of reducing and controlling, but of feeding *certain desires to the detriment of others*, to bend them in the direction of what is 'truly useful' to us according to Spinoza, towards what contributes to the power to act and think about oneself and others. It is Spinozist diplomatic reason, which consists in understanding rather than obeying, a nuance that in Deleuze's view distinguishes Spinoza's ethics from any morality – and distinguishes the attitude of the diplomat from that of the charioteer.[21] To influence the ecosystem of desires within ourselves, we need to associate intimately with our animals, to know their modes of behaviour in all their subtlety, to form 'adequate ideas': this is an ethology of oneself, of the animal life in ourselves.

In what concrete sense do we need a subtle ethology of the behaviour of desire to replace domination with diplomacy? The science of addiction provides us with one good example. Getting rid of an addiction, or obsessive thoughts, seems to require courage at every moment: an endless challenge for those who try to quit smoking, for example. The ethology of the black wolf, however, teaches us the discreet but decisive fact that the urge to smoke tobacco (like many other addictive cravings) lasts, at each physiological peak, between two and five minutes. Whether the person who is tempted gives in *or not* to temptation, the urge will disappear *no matter what happens* at the end of this period. If the diplomat knows the rhythm of his wild impulses, he simply needs to arouse a joyful and competing desire for this brief period of time, without any superhuman effort or having to bully himself, so as not to experience the helplessness of the will. All that is needed, in life, is often just five minutes of courage and cunning.

What 'spiritual exercises' of desire can be found, then, in a diplomatic ethics? Excellent examples can be found in *The Chimp Paradox* by psychiatrist Steve Peters, a specialist in the psychology of high-level athletes. It is based on the metaphor that living involves cohabiting with a chimpanzee inside oneself. When you say things in the heat of the moment that you later regret, Peters says, or eat compulsively, or do not take exercise when you really want to, look no further: it's your chimpanzee that's taken you hostage. The originality of Peters' practical metaphor is basically that it shares some fundamental intuitions of the Spinozism defended here: 'As the Chimp is far stronger than you are, it is wise to understand it and then nurture and manage it.'[22] He suggests that we move from our difficult and conflicting relation with our chimpanzee to relations of mutualist cooperation. A concrete example of this diplomacy involves a detailed ethological understanding of one's chimpanzee. For example, you should know that a message always reaches your chimpanzee first rather than you (this is one of the principles of how the brain works), but the chimpanzee reacts emotionally.[23] All stoicism is based on this asynchrony: the chimpanzee always receives events a few seconds before you do, and Stoic asceticism lies in not adding judgment to the impression you feel. One of the techniques of cohabitating with the chimpanzee consists in always feeding it *before* influencing it. If you take good care of your chimpanzee, if it is well fed, it is very likely that this little animal will be happy, that it will not be a problem, and will be easy to manage.[24] In order to influence it, then, you have to be an ethologist. For example, when the chimp is agitated or upset, Peters recommends systematically allowing it to express itself, letting it say exactly what it thinks, however irrational it is and for as long as necessary[25] (he wisely recommends that you only let it speak alone or with people you trust, who won't take what is said seriously . . .). He estimates that ten minutes will be the time it takes for the chimpanzee to express its most intense fears and emotions, until finally being able to shut up, listen and be influenced (sometimes it needs several training sessions).

Deleuze said of Spinoza's *Ethics* that it was an 'ethology', a science of the behaviour of things, a method for learning how to behave towards beings, showing consideration for the relationships of composition and decomposition that they maintain with us: an art of organizing the encounters of existence. Virginia Woolf is a Spinozist when she says: 'What one wants in the person one lives with is that they should keep one at one's best.'[26] Knowing the ethology of desire is knowing the way in which things affect us.

Diplomatic ethics consist in fostering and nurturing the *feeling* of strength or power in oneself: it is *this feeling* that is the white wolf, from which flows all generosity, if we are to believe the Nietzschean aphorism that 'all generosity is superabundance of strength'. Sad life is helpless, and has nothing to give to others: it pulls towards impotence. It feeds the black wolf. The latter is the feeling of helplessness, the ethological form of which is *fear*, which leads to any encounter with the outside world being experienced as an assault. It is like when we are ill and feel the most mundane encounters in everyday life (a bill to be paid, an object that resists, another person who seems distant from us) to be aggressions which make us tense up in an aggressive-defensive attitude. What this myth means is: 'Feed the strength in you and in the other, but do not bully your weakness and fear.' For the black wolf and the white wolf are not *parts* of oneself, but mutually exclusive ascending or descending trajectories that the self can follow.

From taming by force of will to diplomacy with your wild animals

The classic objection made by defenders of the ethics of the chariot-eer is that the diplomatic influencing of oneself (as found in Marcus Aurelius, writing down his 'thoughts for himself' and tirelessly murmuring into the ear of the wild horse that he himself is) is too *weak* in the face of the excessive power of the passions, their instability, their blind virulence. This objection is typical of terrified people, postulating that the only solution to what they are afraid of is violent coercion. To these, Spinoza replies that, in any case, the will as a charioteer *does not exist.*

The diplomatic relationship with oneself is evident in Spinoza's thought when he criticizes the Cartesian myth, inherited from a certain stoicism and formulated in article 50 of *The Passions of the Soul*, of a potential 'absolute control' over our passions. This despotic will is a fantasy, according to Spinoza. But if we cannot control something in every respect, we are fated to influence it. This is how Spinoza transforms the idea of reason, which is no longer conceived as an abstract will capable of imposing itself on desires, but as desire's way of influencing itself, moving from passion to action.

What is really Stoic about Spinoza is that there is no intrinsic

excessiveness in the passions: the reason they can become disproportionate, uncontrollable, toxic to oneself and others, is that they are
misled by a deficient reason (by mutilated and confused ideas). For
harmful passions do not exist in themselves, as the other of reason;
they are, as Epictetus said, the same as reason, that is, the guiding
principle of the individual – but they are badly governed, diverted
from their true course: they are simply an individuated form of the
flow of desire that constitutes a human being – but they are misrep-
resented as a destructive tsunami by external causes and mistaken
representations.[27]

But how do we continue to act if there is no sovereign will? By
incorporating good habits that can modify the deployment of even
the most ardent passions. Not by giving ourselves orders, whip in
hand, but by setting up, in the environment that surrounds us, small
devices that can encourage joyful desires to emerge spontaneously
and deprive sad desires of their vitality. It's a matter of organizing
encounters. The philosopher Ferhat Taylan uses the term 'mesopol-
itics' (literally 'politics by the middle') to refer to a way of leading
citizens without ordering them, simply by transforming the environment in which they live, so as to influence behaviour.[28] I use the
word 'mesoethics' for a diplomatic relationship to oneself which
consists in modifying one's inner life without commanding it, simply
by transforming the living environment, so as to influence desires by
adopting habits, by incorporating second natures that will inevitably
increase the power to act and think of oneself and therefore of others
(see Spinoza's lucid argument about the causal diffusion of joy as well
as of sadness).

Mesoethics is lucidity about the non-existence of any pure will
or pure reason, and always being able to live on good terms with

oneself, so as to piece together devices, externalize them in the daily living environment, so that they help us to incorporate habits, good habits. Until holiness itself becomes a good habit.

Organizing one's environment using technical artefacts is a great and original skill of the human species. These devices may be tangible or intangible (protocols, values, maxims of action, alarm clocks, schedules, new ways of organizing our activity, ways of posing problems). Once they have been put in place, they speed up life and problem solving, and make energy available for the plans made by other desires. The spiritual exercises that writing and reading comprised for Marcus Aurelius are powerful examples of mesoethics.[29] Reading a few pages of *The Interior Castle* is a discreet and powerful mechanism, in times of crisis, for feeding the white wolf at the expense of the black wolf. A book titled *The Daily Stoic* proposes that every day, when we get up, we read a fragment of Stoic thought, revamped so as to speak to our complicated circumstances.[30] It's a first-class mesoethical device.

The problem of mesoethics comes down to reappropriating the power to transform the territory of life that transforms us. 'Build the environment that builds you, modulate the environment that modulates you': this is the inscription over the gate to the mesoethical path.

Diplomatic ethics is a permaculture of the self – not an intensive and interventionist agriculture practised on oneself: it is based on an understanding of the ecology of passions, a channelling, an irrigation and a potentiation of desires. 'I' am a permacultural forest-garden, where classical ethics wanted me to be an impeccable formal French garden, where romanticism fantasized about an English garden, and neoliberal morality demands that I be a bit of high-yield monoculture.

The error of classical ethics, as I have suggested, is that it took the animal as a model of the passions, and that it was fundamentally wrong about animals. In its view, the passions are intrinsically in excess, and this excess is the foundation of their instability, their dependence: they must be led (they are blind) and they must be subdued (they are prone to hubris, excess). But my hypothesis is that it is partly this particular form of domestication with positive direct action, made of inadequate ideas and inappropriate treatments, that makes passions disproportionate and blind – that bestializes them, turns them into beasts. As long as we maintain diplomatic relations with them, relations that are not domineering and do not impel these passions to rise above their 'low' animality or crush the animality in ourselves, they have a certain quiet metastability, because we are broadly speaking an animal well designed by evolution; looking at other animals, we can easily see that excessive madness is not the norm of living beings. It is clear that the thesis of the ferocity of bestial passions does not describe any real animal observed by ethology. So something must have happened. This is not a return to the myth of the noble savage, to the goodness of nature. This is not an apology for laissez-faire. On the contrary: diplomatic ethics, like permaculture, implies a greater demand for 'design and information',[31] which replaces the demand for control and domination.

It's like the life of the soil in agriculture: already depleted and damaged by intensive farming, a soil needs more input to remain productive, it requires constant control by positive direct action: it has become dependent and unstable. But a soil that is still living, cared for, with a lively microfauna – a soil that we have influenced in its native powers and its evolutionary potential – does not need a huge amount of backup control: we can diplomatically influence its expression towards a cultivated biodiversity, sustainable and healthy for all.

From the coercive charioteer to the diplomat of the passions

In this respect, it is the question of control over our passions – in other words, the question of will – that marks a fundamental divergence between the ethics of the charioteer and the ethics of the diplomat. It is this absolute power that Spinoza challenges, first in its absoluteness, and then in its form of victory and coercion, which has not been highlighted enough.

Indeed, while Spinoza, as a man of his century, continues using the lexicon of the mastery of passions, we see that what is now at stake has nothing to do with control in the strict sense: a grip or a domination, as conceived by classical morality.

For Spinoza, we cannot acquire absolute control of our passions, because we are a part of nature, a finite part, and as such subject to bad encounters: 'Man is necessarily subject to passions, follows the common order of nature, obeys it and adapts himself as much as the nature of things demands it.'[32] Where classical morality advocated dominating nature in ourselves, Spinoza conceives the relationship to the passions as a relationship of obedience and creative adjustment to the common order of nature. But what does it mean here to obey, and to adjust ourselves? And what is meant here by 'nature'?

For Descartes, the will is like a pilot in his ship. Spinoza's critique of this model could be formulated as follows: the real problem of navigation is not the sailor's will, but the behaviour of the wind. According to the Cartesian model, man believes that, when the boat is heading in the right direction, it is the will at the helm that willed it so; while, of course, it is actually always the wind that drives it. The wind should here be understood as the flow of causes in the affects, the force of causes.

In the Spinozist ethic, there is no power of reason, but some desires that are more reasonable than others. The desire for truth is a desire. Thus, ethical liberation no longer consists in overcoming, through annihilation or domestication, a part of oneself. Rather, we need to ride another, equally wild horse within ourselves, another flow of desire, one which goes in the opposite direction – in the right direction. Spinoza's ethics is not based on a staging of the sailor's struggle against the elements, but on an attention to the winds, a transformation of oneself into a being that is 'half-ship, half-squall', ready to change direction, to play one wind against another, to round the cape.

We can see yet again how Stoic he is: as Epictetus says, the problem is not to overcome a part of oneself, but to harness one's inner discourse to a 'noble representation', to go elsewhere. The problem is still the use of representations. We then move from *psychomachia* to psycho-navigation, sailing along, needing to know the wind first, then deal with it and follow it, tacking. There is no longer anyone to impose a pure direction: there is no consciousness or pure will that would be the pilot – the pilot is also determined by causes.

But are we to deduce that man cannot really act if there is an absolute determinism of causes and effects? In the classic moral map, freedom was understood as free will, as the mind's ability to control the body. Once we have replaced this dualistic map with a map made up only of desires, that is to say of causes – when there is no longer a chief in a watchtower giving orders to the populace of desires, but just the complex mass, the crowd of intersecting desires confronting each other – what can freedom correspond to?

For Spinoza, humans *can* act – by becoming a cause themselves. Ethical life in Spinoza is not built on an opposition between an alienated submission to the course of things and an act that is free because released from this chain of causes, but on a difference between *two types* of causes: adequate causes and inadequate causes. Freedom then corresponds to allowing the appropriate causes to express themselves. You are a cause among causes. Your desires are causes among causes. Above all, your adequate ideas are free causes among causes. Hence ethics, that is to say the question of the value of actions, for all causes are not equal.

Freedom therefore consists in letting the adequate causes express themselves; in being a good cause of one's actions, and not a mutilated cause, captured and used by external things, that is, an inadequate cause. It is the model of the pawn, the model of the secret agent as assassin, used against his will by some dispensary: he is an inadequate cause of his actions, he is driven by external causes. Now, we have inadequate causes within us: anger, hatred, all the sad passions. They are not our true selves within us. These are our bad masters within us. They use us, and we then repent.

Nor is it a matter of turning our joyful desires against the sad ones, but of simply letting ourselves be overcome by the joyful ones: no more direct struggle, but a theory of voluntary possession, letting ourselves be possessed by a wild affect which expresses more power and joy. It's a well-organized voodoo that consists in leaving more room in oneself for one desire than for another, in bringing the one to life. We know that when we are tempted by something that hurts us, and let ourselves get carried away by an opposite joyful desire, the first desire is not bullied into submission and frustrated, it is just *forgotten*. No inverse proportion, no inner struggle, just joy instead of sadness, and not against sadness. It's hard enough to cobble all this together.

Wittgenstein, with his conception of the resolution of problems, concurs with Spinoza here: 'The solution of the problem you see in life is a way of living that makes the problem go away.'[33] The problem is not to be solved intellectually or by force of will; rather, you need to find a way of living such that the problem becomes meaningless.

Fortifying the white wolf without subduing the black wolf

Generations of teachers and priests have repeated the ethics of the charioteer: that reason should dominate the passions ('Control yourself!', derived from 'Control your horse, your slave, your wife!').

To this refrain, Spinoza responds with a limpid intuition that everyone has probably realized: we cannot silence a desire except by an even *stronger* desire. He formulates it thus: 'An affect cannot be thwarted nor suppressed except by a contrary affect stronger than the affect to be overcome.'[34] We must not subdue the black wolf, but strengthen the white wolf. Reason must therefore actually *be* a desire, and its practice must be a great joy, otherwise it will be powerless to influence action. If being reasonable devitalizes all passions, then it makes us sad. So it makes us weak, since sadness is a weakening of power: weak in the face of undesirable desires.[35] Or: it feeds the black wolf.

On the map of the Spinozist self, there are only desires, but some are more rational than others (i.e. oriented towards increasing the power we ourselves and others have of acting and thinking, and the political harmony that contributes to this). And some are likely to be subverted, diverted and influenced by this reason, thus becoming happy. Reason is the hand that feeds and fosters the white wolf – starting off by forming the adequate idea of the behaviour of the passions (the ethology of the wild animals in ourselves).

Thus, in Spinoza and in a diplomatic ethic, there is no confrontation between will and desires, but a map of an inner life composed only of desires and affects. The force that can resist a temptation that will cost us dearly is still a desire, but a wise desire. The noble desire to respond to hatred with love is also a desire (based on an adequate idea). As Nietzsche wrote much later: 'The will to overcome an emotion, is ultimately only the will of another, or of several other, emotions.'[36] There is no more disembodied reason hanging over us, but a life on the surface of things, where the point is to orient ourselves with the right maps – those of adequate ideas, or those of the 'Great Reason of the body', wiser than the 'small reason of the spirit', in Nietzsche's parable from *Zarathustra*.

If I am made up entirely of desires, we could then ask why some should be preferred over others. Why am I not just as much my sad affects, anger and hatred – the black wolf in me? Why is it reasonable and good to feed and foster the white wolf?

I am not my sad passion because I am a *fully living conatus*, that is to say a force that prefers health to disease, food to poison, quiet and noble power to frustrated, resentful helplessness. Every living thing strives to persevere in its being, in its trajectory of increasing its power to act and to think, so that sadness diminishes. It is the *living conatus* that is my basis: we can represent it as a vigorous beast that tracks and sniffs down great health (the white wolf in me). Thanks to this conatus, I cannot wish to be unhealthy. But sadness is a disease of the soul, because it decreases my powers. I am a wild conatus that spontaneously flourishes in active joy and spontaneously withers in raging helplessness. So my reason is not a separate force, but just the intelligent and vital tendency of my power to move towards joy, towards the relations of composition that strengthen me and give me an overabundance of strength to share with others. Diplomatic reason is not a cold calculating faculty – it is the name of the intelligence proper to the vital desire within me, which seeks joy, and knows how to recognize and flee intoxication and sadness.

It is the sense of vitality in oneself that has not forgotten Musil's idea that we need to judge whether another person's presence lowers us or elevates us.[37] This idea is rigorously Spinozist in its understanding of the relational character of ethics (some beings, in fact, demean us, while they elevate others. Some beings are truly toxic: they lower everyone).

The confusion in this history of ethics stems from the fact that, before Spinoza, moralists did not sufficiently distinguish between dominating our passions and exercising them, between passions as beasts to be subdued and as powers to be ridden the way one rides a spirited horse.

According to Sloterdijk, 'The worse part can only take over after "bad education" – whose criterion lies in leaving untethered (*akólaston*) something that requires tethering, and, if all were as it should be, could be tethered with ease.'[38]

Of course, the destructive attacks launched by virulent passions need to be contained but, as soon as habits are formed, it is the passions themselves that in their spontaneous behaviour embody the measure and the vitality of an individual. Here there is a confusion between asceticism in the sense of mortification and asceticism in the sense of the composition of a higher self through the incorporation of vital habits.

Good habits make it possible to consider the passions as merely powers to be ridden – but in an 'ethological' display of horse riding where rider and mount form a hybrid, become extensions of one another, attentive partners engaged in joyful negotiation.

So those who continue to wallow in toxic passions are not struck by an intrinsic *weakness* of will or reason. Their drama, rather, is that they cannot arouse within themselves higher and more intense desires than their harmful passions. It is because they have not sufficiently strengthened the white wolf with good habits. The ethics of the charioteer, obsessed with his fear of the passions, has confused discipline with bullying. The demanding discipline of diplomatic ethics comes down to finding, forming and strengthening in ourselves emancipatory desires so ardent, so irresistible, that they can effortlessly replace the toxic passions that make us unhappy and unhealthy. We need to use living reason to cobble together the experience of a wild joy so vibrant that alienating, morbid pleasures, the lousy desire to demean others and to do evil, lose their interest, and even their shine. We need to weave with these passions a robust joy, a power of *being acted upon without being subjected* – without suffering unduly from the inevitable harmful encounters. Diplomatic ethics is the art of incorporating and influencing the *habits of desire*, of influencing the ecosystem of the affects itself. Freedom exists: it is the art of arranging the irrigation systems in ourselves so as to bring out emancipatory desires and feed our noblest wild animals. Ethics no longer means proudly rising above the animal in ourselves, but being in a certain *way* the animal that we are.

It is the status of reason that is transformed in Spinoza, and even into a diplomatic ethics. It is no longer a pure mind controlling the passions, but a certain figure of lucid desire, the desire to live well, according to our nature. To cohabit among the fully living wild desires which are its true essence. It becomes an art of diplomacy: an art of living *on good terms* with what, inside and outside of us, does not want to be tamed.

The secret of the will is that it exists, but not *within* us. No one *has* a will.

'Will' is the word people invoke when they see from the outside, *in another person*, the energy streams of an inner life converging and flowing superbly in the same upward direction, however steep the slope ('what strength of will she has!'). The will in fact is only the a posteriori name given to the irrigation system of desires, in the blessed moments when they are so composed that they converge in the same direction, one that has been chosen. The fact that we don't have a 'will' doesn't mean it doesn't exist, but that we don't possess it: it is not a quantity, and it is not in us a priori.

Will is not an abstract quantity that we possess in ourselves, but a skill in cobbling together devices to enable our desires to converge. We piece them together outside ourselves and inside ourselves, we incorporate them. In this reading of Spinozist ethics, the diplomat becomes a developer of interior channels for the flows of desire.

It is the art of smoothly aligning flows in a certain direction, piecing it all together outside ourselves, in diaries, in the rooms where we live, the meetings we organize with things and people, the little devices that direct the flows of desire. They are spiritual exercises that help us cohabit with the wild animals in ourselves, so that their native powers can converge on what is good for us. The good diplomat delicately enables the free play of the flows of desire to converge and gather in a powerful, vectorized bundle that, from the outside, we call the 'will', believing that it expresses a sovereign 'I will!', whilst it is in fact just a sailor's acquired habit of reading the winds, using them, and navigating with them.

Ascensional ethics

However, I am not here defending a strictly horizontal ethic with no ascent possible. I think on the contrary that the whole ethical problem is powerfully built on vertical metaphors which, freed from their theological folklore, are merely the practical metaphors of improvement. There is only ethics if there is a will and an opportunity for improvement. But this ascent does not necessarily go from animal to angel, from beast to man. And it does not ascend merely by domination, rising above the smouldering ruins of the animal nature within ourselves. The common metaphor of ascending (raising ourselves) in the figurative language of ethics traditionally captures the poles described in the historical philosophies of a culture, even if these poles are arbitrary, even if they are wrong. These poles, the high and the low, the desirable and the detestable, often differ in their mythological content: the animal, the archetype of what is low, can on the contrary, in other cultures, be seen as up on high. For example, there is an ascent towards non-willing in Zen – and this is an ascent towards the animal. This animal is a good metaphor for the need to reduce associative thinking, fantasy, the alienating imagination. We need to become one of those animals that mainly think by solving problems related to encounters in experience, rather than thinking in phantasmal associative ways, parasitical and judgmental – for this latter, according to Zen, makes human animals unhappy, unhealthy and wicked. The Western saint wants to rise as far as possible above the beast within, whereas the Zen sage wants as much as possible to resemble her cat. The animal wisdom of your cat: an original model for a type of thinking not blinded by false desires.

We are the heirs of a culture that overall has thought of wisdom as elevation above the animals inside us and outside us. This involved a misconception of what an animal is really like, setting it up as a straw man onto which are projected all the vices of the human being. Other heritages are more lucid: certain ancient forms of wisdom (the Cynics and the Sceptics) endeavour to regain an animal-like tranquillity that comes before language. The Native American shaman Davi Kopenawa also has this strange wisdom: he cherishes his macaw parrot feathers, because they give him the wisdom of the bird and its animal power of eloquence, when he goes to talk to the white chiefs in three-piece suits who are destroying the forest.[39]

We can even hypothesize that perfectibility, therefore ascension, therefore the possibility of ethics, is immanent in the living. It is present in living matter: muscle, unlike stone, is matter that improves when exercised; the nervous system too. The ontological problem comes down to determining what it means to 'ascend' when there is no divine plan above, no angel to act as a role model. There is no one upstairs (a perfect male ideal already constituted by a form of transcendence, a god-template). There is no upstairs: each step we take upwards invents one more step on the stairs. Any act of self-improvement is not a reaching up to some divine sphere that is already there as a given, but invents one more dimension to reality, a dimension that is each time new. And this problem has already been posed by the Asian ethics of the Way. The Way, in some traditions, is the concept of an ascension without any pre-existing ideal, an improvement without any a priori model of perfection. A somewhat more perfect storey of the human being needs to be invented; it will be plural and it will resemble a chimera – a face made up of animalities.

4

To the other side of the night: towards a politics of interdependences

✦

Nights on the watch

Positioned in silence on an outcrop in the middle of the plateau, we point a thermal imager at the darkness: it captures the heat differential between bodies in the landscape and restores it in contrast in the viewfinder. Wolves' silhouettes made of harsh light appear in dark glades, playing, repeating the rituals that comprise their existence, heading off to hunt or patrolling their territory. The camera in question is a military object prohibited for sale: so-called 'sensitive' war material. It was designed for army border posts, and it is used to identify, among other things, immigrants seeking to illegally enter the territory. Even if our goal is not the same, using cameras made to monitor immigrants to observe wolves leaves a sour taste in the mouth. The technical device materializes the common basis to our relations with the foreign beings who live right up close to us. Any technical object incorporates an embedded theory, which directs its uses. What is intriguing about our activity is that it involves hijacking and subverting the theory embedded in a surveillance camera, turning it into an instrument of diplomatic metamorphosis.

In recent years I have spent many nights like this, on the watch in the South of France – part of an interventionist research project to observe the nightlife of a pack of wolves and its relationship with the herds of sheep and guard dogs. We're observing these animals from a military camp: at dawn, as the helicopters fly over us, we catch sight of four wolf cubs playing in disused tanks. One night, the howls of the wolves are heard against a background of bursts from a sub-machine gun. As we walk we can hear the detonations of the shells, in a nature emptied of humans. In the distance lurk ghost villages. From this desert, wildlife is reborn with explosive vigour. Amid the tanks and the flocks of sheep, all this human and technical wildlife, the wolves settle down and take control: they learn to inhabit and transform those environments that are heirs to a complex human past. In these ruins, the living re-weave new assemblages for themselves.

This research project is called CanOvis; it was dreamt up by ethologist Jean-Marc Landry and his team. I worked with them for three years in a row, for several week-long sessions, in summer, as a volunteer, fellow traveller and researcher,[1] mainly on the Canjuers plateau, in the Var. This experiment mainly brings us into contact with shepherds and sheep farmers, sheep and dogs, flock routes, meadows and groves, night skies, and finally wolves. In constant dialogue with the protagonists of this pastoral scene, we follow the herds across the territory of a pack. Shepherds can graze their sheep in the camp: the herds exert a constant grazing pressure on the landscapes, which allows them not to become forested; they keep the meadows clear and thereby limit the risk of fires. It's a strange alliance between the military and the shepherds which explains the presence of the latter when all the villages have been evacuated. The shepherds are alerted to the military exercises and move their sheep according to the schedule of the gunners and the infantry simulations.

CanOvis is a research programme focused on understanding the nocturnal ethology of wolves in contact with herds, through the use of thermal imagers, to anticipate and better protect against the risk of predation on sheep. The aim is to restore the power to act in the face of that natural hazard, the wolf, through the reinvention of forms of knowledge and know-how. The diagnosis starts from the idea that we have underestimated one of the problems posed by the pressure of wolves on shepherding systems: beyond the economic or technical dimensions, the problem is mainly linked to the *effective, lived helplessness* of shepherds when wolves attack their herds. These are unpredictable events and difficult to control. The challenge is to concoct an approach that gives the shepherds some leeway and capacity for action, in the form of a new ethology, and various decision-making tools.

Vita incognita

Contemporary scientific ecology and ethology teach us that, in order to understand and influence living beings, we need to be sensitive to the invisible relationships between them, relationships that go far back into the past and that govern ecosystems. To observe these discreet relationships, the thermal imager is a crucial device. As part of the CanOvis project, we use this technology to film at night. Because we can access the 'world of the night',[2] we learn from this research that the relations between wolves, herd, sheep dogs and humans are infinitely more varied than had been thought, the act of predation itself being only 'the tip of the iceberg'. The thermal imaging camera allows us to observe a multitude of other interactions that were initially incredible, and usually invisible: wolves who play with sheep dogs, and share with them the remains of sheep, or even court them. This, according to Landry and his team, is where a real understanding of the system can be gained: 'It is in this "invisible" part of the relationship between the predator and the shepherding system that scenarios are constructed which will, or will not, lead to predation, with more or less regularity and intensity.'[3]

These new data are likely to revolutionize what we thought we knew: for example, some spectacular images captured by CanOvis thanks to the thermal imager show a quiet wolf in the middle of a flock of serene sheep, who examine him from up close. It's almost unimaginable, given our traditional conceptions of wolf and sheep. This opens up new spaces for ethological reflection. How are we to understand the absence of panic in the sheep and the placidity of the wolf? Should we assume that the sheep do not have such a homogeneous category of 'wolf' as we do? That for them, there is no *essential* wolf, just differentiated wolves? That, here too, they are not as 'essentialist' as humans, not as inclined to project onto a whole group (or race) characteristics that can be seen in only a few examples? That they have a more subtle and vigilant relationship to the difference between *individual* wolves (some are dangerous, others not)? Or that they are more sensitive to the context: one day a particular wolf can be a predator that they need to flee, and another day the same wolf can be an interesting bypasser they just have to keep an eye on? Riddles emerge from this night world revealed by the camera's images. They undermine what we thought we knew about both sheep and wolves. A wolf is no longer just typecast as a hungry predator, whom we imagine as instinctively prone to devour its prey the minute it comes across a 'sheep-as-stimulus'. A sheep no longer bears the stigma of being 'just a sheep'. Might solving these enigmas allow us to imagine more effective arrangements of protection and cohabitation, to be better adjusted to the complexity of reality?

When we investigate the ways of existing, any life form appears as a *vita incognita*. An unexplored outcrop on the atlas of our practical and scientific knowledge. To find our way into its depth, we 'should never doubt the invisible', as the forester and philosopher Aldo Leopold says. But never doubting it doesn't mean that we fall back on merely fantasizing it: rather, we learn to investigate this invisible realm, to make it intelligible, and to make our modes of action more intelligent.

Becoming-diplomat

Briefing in the open

The CanOvis experiment consists of entering into a strange device that discreetly alters the trajectory of individuation of anyone who penetrates it. We enter it in a state of knowledge and ignorance, with aversions and affinities, a mythification of the shepherd or a love for the wolf, esteem for the countryside heritage or contempt for the predator, a marked empathy for one or other of the belligerents. We return home almost as diplomats, albeit of a singular kind: diplomats of interdependence.

For the sake of narrative clarity, we can relate this initiation by merging it into the story of one night, since it's always at night that we work. One evening, one night, one dawn, but woven with reminiscences, so as to enrich the story of the whole experience compacted here into one cycle. (In every dawn there are so many dawns, and in every night so many nights.)

It all starts in the cool of the evening, around 6 pm, with the briefing. Jean-Luc Borelli, the operational leader of the Canjuers project, outlines the plan of operations. We ask him about the behaviour of the wolves, about the meaning of the interactions between wolves and herds recorded the night before, which we watch together on a computer screen, in the military dormitory allocated to us by the camp.

He has spent a considerable amount of time behind the camera, thousands of hours, including hundreds specifically observing wolves, synthesizing, isolating invariants. Yet when we ask him about the observations that have been made, he often replies, 'Honestly, we don't know.' This attitude sets the tone. Interpretative probity is one of the keystones of the project. Its scientific position, mapped out by ethologist Jean-Marc Landry, gives the experiment a very particular tone: circumscribed ignorance is the most honest kind of knowledge, and the art of not concluding *just yet* becomes a virtue. It's all about gradually drawing a clear map of the known and the unknown, and the latter predominates. Still, the knowledge accumulated is already eloquent: in summer 2018, we documented, on the basis of our images, the largest litter in France (ten cubs, probably born from the same mother) and the most populous pack (to my knowledge) in the history of the wolf in France since its return (sixteen wolves for certain, maybe seventeen).

There remains a span of sunlight

In the evening, in the abandoned bastide of Bourjac, the sun falls with generous slowness behind the line of the plateau, flooding the plain with new shadows. The hoopoes are jubilant as dusk falls. We are passing some time with the shepherds. Around this bastide, the sheep come back in the evening to drink from large troughs, and the dogs are fed there. We chat with the shepherd as she extracts big bags of dry food from her huge white pick-up van. She's reluctant to ask us to help too much, despite her condition. We joke, we ask her about her rounded belly, then we examine the sheep together, and tell her what we saw the night before in the thermal imager. Last night the wolves tried to attack the herd, the dogs repelled them, but the commotion lasted quite a while, the sheep ran everywhere. It's the end of August and the females are pregnant, though not yet close to giving birth. The shepherdess looks at the sheep with an expert eye, she looks for those that are wounded, or limping, or shedding blood from the hindquarters, which would indicate that the ewe has lost its lamb; and then she looks at them from a different perspective. She says something like this: 'When I think about what you saw last night, I imagine the sheep; in my head, she's a pregnant woman running all night long trying to escape from the wolf.' She puts her hands on her stomach. Our minds begin to open up to this world. Step by step, through encounters, we are woven together with those who live on this isolated plateau by threads of affect.

But ambiguity quickly emerges as the dominant tonality. The region has its rumours. It's said that, among the sheep farmers, there are some who inflate the number of sheep killed, for various strategic reasons. It's said that other sheep farmers don't always take the trouble to protect the sheep as effectively as possible, because they will be systematically compensated by the state, once the experts have examined the sheep and concluded that they have been killed by wolves. It's said that, with the compensation money, a sheep farmer had a new house built from scratch; the locals call it the 'Villa du Loup' ('Wolf's Villa'). When one looks at the sociological surveys, the government data, the expert knowledge, it appears that it's difficult to determine the real extent of these practices: there is no doubt that they exist, but they are unlikely to be dominant or even representative. Some radical advocates of the wolves are reducing the problem posed by their return to the dishonesty or laziness of the sheep farmers. This formulation of the problem does not seem to be a fair or exhaustive way of capturing the complexity of the situation.

Another anecdote worries us. Some people from the shepherding world or elsewhere maintain that, among the 'sampling shots' carried out on the wolves, some specifically target wolf cubs near their den or meeting site. If this could be proved, it would be contrary to the spirit of the law: the killings would be being used to regulate the population (which is illegal in the case of a protected species) and not to provide effective protection for the herds. For, as we observe on several occasions, this year's young wolves do not really leave their meeting place before early September, and never attack the herds. Empathy then shifts towards the other belligerent, towards the wolf cubs who are the targets of snipers as they frolic in disused tanks. Another thread is woven.

In the evening, as night falls, we encounter one of the shepherds. He comes to 'swap jokes' with us every day. We tell him where his herd is, we help him as much as we can, we'll locate the injured or killed sheep for him, we sometimes help him to take care of them. He's one shepherd among others, each shepherd has his own personality and charm but, as the days go by, we bond with this one, so much so that, one morning, he tells us about an attack that had taken place one night. At dawn, he came out of his caravan – the sheep had been parked all around. There's something wrong: the silence . . . and one by one he finds their remains, dead, wounded, sometimes half eaten, bleating in distress. About twenty sheep. He turns his gaze from us, towards the ridge. 'It's hard', he says, 'it's hard'. Looking at the same point as him, we mumble: 'It's hard, yes, it's hard.' One more thread. Empathy comes and goes, sometimes, like the tide. The generalized figure of the arrant shepherd taking advantage of the situation becomes a facile caricature, an escape from the irreducible moral ambiguity, the tumult created by the wolves' return to France.

The threshold of twilight

We have swung between empathy for the sheep to empathy for the wolf cub, then for this shepherd, and at nightfall there's a scene where we see the dogs at work.

The shepherd has just left, he's heading off home to sleep. We are left alone with the herd, the dogs and the plateau. After they've been tended to, the sheep drift away slowly, following their leader, towards the place of rest for the night, where they lie down. We are at our posts with the thermal imager. An extraordinary pack of twenty-five Anatolian shepherd dogs and *patous* is protecting the large herd on the Plan de Canjuers. They're now lying down, under the Collet des Mouches, in an area of short grass and thickets of boxwood. Suddenly, five wolves who have stealthily crept up manage to isolate a sheep far from the herd. Only one dog has smelled their scent; he joins the isolated sheep. She is motionless, injured or else petrified with fear. The dog sniffs her, then positions himself in front of her. On camera, we can make out the dog standing in front of the five beasts. He raises his head, he swells his chest. He barks to rouse his comrades, and the wolves advance towards him in a fan. He some-times turns to look at the sheep. He does not move. The wolves are all around him. He could run away, he could outrun them. He sizes them up, barks at them, challenges them. He won't budge. Three white tornadoes then charge to the rescue, three galloping Anatolian sheepdogs, and the wolves scatter among the bushes. The solitary dog bounds after them, now re-woven into his pack, on the heels of the fleeing wolves.

The dogs have done a wonderful job as guardians, triggering an ethological gratitude in us for all heroes, in the living, immemorial sense of the term: the strongest who protect the weakest by a simple superabundance of unused force. So the dogs join in the dance. In the evening, at the watering hole, we stroke them; there are puppies among them, who will be colossi next year, but they're still adorable here, although it's best not to surprise them at night among the herd. And a thread of affect is woven between us and them; they are caught up one by one in the web of affiliations and bonds.

'Do not go gentle into that good night'

Night time on the watch, the moon is high in the sky, there's a dead calm; here, it's the eye which is the sense for tracking, the gaze rendered incandescent for hours on end, scanning the plain with the eyes of an owl, tirelessly, looking for a white spectre with a singular gait, a movement, an event. There is an asceticism of immobility: our hands should no longer touch the thermal imager once it has been focused. We strum in the air like musicians, a few centimetres from the camera levers, to ensure the most delicate touch and so that we can move the camera without blurring the image, just in case we need to start video recording to capture an interesting scene. The hundreds of hours of video, archived, will then be analysed during the long winter evenings. And the category of the 'interesting' is not closely defined a priori; anything can enter its vibrant field: an interaction between wolf and dog, between wolves and herd, but also between a fox and a sheep, a dog and a deer, a human and any other form of life, and other shards of strangeness that we haven't even imagined yet. We go into apnoea, unconsciously, so as to disappear, to the point where not even our breath can disturb the experience.

Then the wolves come.

We start by hearing a few howls scattered across the landscape. It's often around 10:15 pm – the so-called 'golden hour'. Guided by their howls, they come together. Parents trot home daintily, their silhouettes made of harsh light, like ghosts against a background of darkness, sliding over the steppe of the Var (the wolf's trot and gallop are so fluid that in the thermal image it sometimes seems as if they aren't really touching the ground). They run crazy races, lick their chops, indulge in mysterious rituals, adopt different postures. And then another type of howling emerges: this time, it's collective, and the wolves that are howling are all together, side by side. This is called a 'chorus howl'. It is often a ceremony preparatory to a collective activity, for example hunting: when it's over, one of the leaders starts off in one direction and the pack follows him; the tone changes. They go into action, they're coordinated, silent, determined. Chorus singing is a ritual whose function is obscure, but its liminal status is explicit, since it changes the tenor of the group relationship.

There is one threshold that tips everything over into another age of the night.

This is what we note in our notebooks:

'10:15 pm, patrol departure, 10 individuals with 6 adults, 4 cubs, towards den site'.

'3 am, 3 adults, the hunting squad disappears from the Grand Plan, towards wildlife, direction of Aiguines'.

Or: '6 am. Near Loubière. There are 4 (maybe subadults?), they fidget, run, regroup, separate: enigmatic behaviour'. This attitude reduces the ethologist and the specialist to silence. But if we put a child behind the camera, he would turn towards us after a few seconds, saying: 'Duh, they're playing.' It's obvious.

The notebooks are dotted with scientifically dubious words. We write that a wolf is 'draggling along', that three individuals are 'funning around'. These words are in fact ethological instruments: their vague outline formulates as best it can our inability to isolate the intention that governs their behaviour.

One night, I note:
'10:30 pm: departure from the meeting place, all of them, with cubs. Just one line. Looks like the adults are keeping tabs on the youngsters for efficient, fluid travel, thwarting their habit of strolling around, exploring, stopping at every bush. 10:40 pm: return of the little ones to the meeting place in scattered order. Hypothesis: is this a lesson about how to head off on patrol, in an operational line, without playing, frolicking, dispersing?' The next day we observe a similar phenomenon, but the radius is more extended: the cubs have gone further from the site before turning around, a little scared, their tails between their legs. Every day we see an increase in the radius of the circle of familiarity: the cubs are gradually being taken further and further away.

First to the ridge, then to the valley behind it, then to the plain behind the valley. None are going to hunt yet, but they are clearly expanding their domain. They are learning to travel in groups.

One night a muffled noise approaches us from the sky. It's huge and stealthy. Our hearts race (is it an alien spaceship?). A few metres above us, it halts, as black as night. It's a stealth helicopter: it pins us with its own thermal imager, it distinguishes our slightest movements, we are powerless, unable to hide – and suddenly we make the connection with the wolves that the moment before we were looking at in the viewfinder, while we ourselves remained invisible. The roles are reversed.

The camp colonel will explain to us the next day that you have to stay still if you hope not to be detected. It is the speed differential between you and the unfolding landscape that makes you visible from a patrol helicopter.

One night, I note: 'It's fascinating the ease with which we start talking to them: come on, big guys, come out of the woods, all in line, gently does it, we can count you.'

'Sing us a song . . .' This is an experience that we also often have while tracking. Certain practices encourage us spontaneously, without the need for any metaphysics, to switch to more animist relationships with the world. The shepherd who speaks to the lost sheep who are several kilometres away from him seems quite understandable.

One night, a terrible mistral sweeps the whole plateau. The best point to place the camera is in the full wind. The task gives us little choice. We will need to keep watch standing in the windstream and the whirling of the gusts, for a full half of the night. We curl up in our down jackets, we cover ourselves with a random selection of layers, we come back the next night with everything we need to keep warm and to waterproof a body whose every atom of heat is getting stolen and swept away by the icy wind. We have to hold on, there are things to see and document. Out of doors, there's no such thing as bad weather. Just bad equipment.

Tonight we howl to entice the wolf cubs to answer us. This will allow us to confirm the year's new brood and precisely locate the meeting site. They reply and, some moments later, the pack goes out into the night, in battle formation; we can see it advancing, in line, magnificent. The wolves in France do not need to feed on sheep: there is enough wildlife, and they are perfectly capable of hunting it. Moreover, despite its proximity to the herds, and the fact that the latter are not always well protected, the pack that we are following frequently neglects the sheep to go deep into the forest, hunting for deer or wild boar. We can sometimes see the line of wolves, casually skirting the flock of sheep, interested in another, more difficult type of prey. And when the herd is well protected by sheep dogs, and the wolves have had their noses bloodied by them, they feel that the game isn't worth the effort. But sometimes, for mysterious reasons, they decide to go after the sheep. On this particular night, we follow them, continuously, for almost three hours; at five o'clock, they confront a pack of dogs five times the size of theirs, and twice as heavy; we observe their courage and cohesion in the face of adversity, returning to the charge against the dogs to get the pittance with which they will feed the hungry litter that awaits them at the meeting place.

That evening, we see wild animals living their lives, building them, shaping the world – all collectively. We see them making decisions involving how they live together. We see them in full possession of their existence, and we feel a whiff of sadness for what we have done to the animals that have been domesticated – domesticated to the point of making them affectively and concretely dependent on us, like those toxic lovers who produce fragility and dependence in their partners, binding them more tightly, and in so doing losing any consideration for them. The recurring words of the shepherds and sheep farmers, who keep saying 'Those sheep are idiots', take on a different meaning. As do their shining eyes when they talk about the wolf and repeat at leisure this enigmatic phrase: 'his intelligence'.

We can sense here what that somewhat hackneyed phrase the 'beauty of the wild' means: we experience the specificity of this form of life, which over-domesticated dogs or sheep have lost, that way of being complete, in one sense perfect, by themselves, without us, far from us, among us. This is a spontaneous form of life which has in fact been that of the majority for four billion years. But this state is stigmatized as wildness by our metaphysical tradition which sees it as the 'other' of civilization. It is disfigured by the strange myth that we sometimes hear being repeated by shepherds, according to which 'nature needs us, otherwise it's a mess'.

And here, it is loyalty to the whole pack that is being woven, the pack as a pack, in the face of adversity, in this military camp, surrounded by exploding shells, rumbling tanks, wolfcatchers, sniper brigades, sheep farmers going round in their pick-ups with their rifles propped up in the seat where they'd put the dead wolf ('I killed two', says one sheep farmer, with a wave of his hand).

'Before nightfall you must light your torch'[14]

One night, we witness an amazing scene. The pack has left the meeting site, there are six individuals on a sovereign patrol down a forest track. They arrive at a pass, it's the crossroads: six tracks radiate in all directions. Which will they choose? It will take them just a few seconds to make their minds up. We are witnessing a magnificent scene of collective decision-making, where each individual character will shine through for a moment, enacting the power of the social bond. All six halt in line for a few long seconds, like Hercules at the crossroads. The leading adult, probably the breeding male, takes the northern trail. Behind him, the breeding female, more puny than her male (usually she leads the whole pack), procrastinates for a few moments, then follows him, but half-heartedly. A subadult swerves west, maybe to go and sniff at a scent, or instigate a collective change of direction, but no one follows him or seems to notice him, and his trajectory makes an arabesque that soon brings him back to his mother. A small cub, with a less confident demeanour, immediately follows the leading adult. Further down the line, another youngster plays the waiting game, he hesitates, halts as if in the middle of a ford, drawn by something to the east. For someone has moved away from the line.

There's always one rebel.

He's just a small cub too. But he's trying out a different path: he heads directly east, sure of himself, his head held high, without looking at the pack. Maybe he anticipates the future direction of the pack, or is he following the memory of a previous decision? Everyone has slowed down. The timid one, motionless, procrastinates, he's torn, he's seen his brother or his sister heading off following some desire or other, but dad is there in front, and mum has stopped to make a territorial marking. The leader has slowed down and seems for a moment to turn back towards the doubter then, following his gaze, towards the impetuous rebel (but when we look at the video recording several times, this movement isn't clear, it's difficult to identify, we're far away: perhaps it's an a posteriori projection meant to restore narrative continuity to this silent ballet?). So the leader does something strange: he changes course. From due north, he veers north-east, he bends his course in a direction which *combines* the two vectors (his and that of the rebel). And the rebel, without further ado, heads off at a slight angle, without turning towards the others, tail still held high, as if he had chosen for himself this oblique path; but he then innocently rejoins the pack a few hundred metres further along. He follows the new combined direction, at a calculated pace, so as to enter the line of wolves in third position, behind the alpha female. We are too far away to hear the vocalizations, distinguish the changing bodily postures or the interactions of facial masks. We play the video ten times. It seems that the decision-making was mainly driven by the adult leader, but it was modulated by the stubbornness of the rebel, negotiated, silently debated. What mysteries are at play in fifteen seconds of nocturnal life?

The rebel, female or male, has the disposition of a future leader, of a future 'disperser' in any case, one of those wolves who leave the pack to go and found another dynasty on another territory. This is someone who knows where he wants to go. Another young wolf seems to love being guided; the third is immobilized between multiple loyalties.

And for a few moments, we catch ourselves being the young wolf torn apart here, the doubter: he's there on the screen, in the camera, torn between conflicting affiliations, and it's us that we see, torn between our loyalties to the shepherd, to the sheep, to the wolf, to the dog, to the pack, to the environment, to the grass itself. But we have to choose a route and act, and the idea is to navigate in a way that will serve the relationships among all of us: if there is a way to cohabit here, despite interests that conflict on certain points, that is our course, even if it looks like from the outside like endless compromise, endless negotiation. But this is the tragedy of true diplomacy, as Nelson Mandela showed when he tried to reconcile an entire country that had been bequeathed the most violent rapine and domination, through the founding idea of his Truth and Reconciliation Commission: not to work for one side against another, but in the service of the relationship, the good of the relationship – since we all need to live together. Mandela among the wolves – this is the secret ideal I have for the CanOvis project, or the interpretation that means the most to me.

The next night, in a hidden valley, there is something we can barely see: we think it's a sheep, it's limping on its hind leg, that's for sure, the gait is what we can most clearly isolate on camera, we suffer with it, we breathe between our teeth, feeling the pain in the bitten thighs and buttocks, and suddenly we realize that it's a wolf, a wolf that has been bitten and wounded by these huge dogs, heavier and more powerful, that prevent wolves from accessing the easy prey with which they could feed the litter of cubs waiting impatiently in the den.

The camera as a night eye, an owl's eye, requires that the observers are at ease with uncertainty. No moving being, when it is far enough away, can be identified with any certainty at a glance: we need to interpret its look, its gait, its style, clumsy or light-footed; and even after that, we have to accept that it can be read simultaneously as two different possible beings.

At 2 am, eyes struggling to stay open, fingers clenched, after an hour of dead calm, enervated by the desert of the landscape, I detect the silhouette of a canine that seems to be heading towards the herd. Who is it? A dog on the prowl coming back? A young wolf investigating? Our eyes burn, we mustn't blink, spurred on with adrenaline, but the mind must hold on to the idea that it might be both dog *and* wolf, an in between. As they approach the herd, the dog and the wolf have very similar motor patterns; the first is greyer, but in the heat of the moment this nuance is too weak to cast any light. The two enemy brothers look alike, and yet we need to distinguish between them. On camera, all distant animals are Schrödinger's cats: simultaneously in two different states of existence, two different species at the same time. They are chimeras that the mind must domesticate so as not to make errors of interpretation. When the canine-chimera rushes at the herd, we can try to read his identity from the way the sheep react. But even that is not obvious: sometimes it even seems that the sheep *confuse dogs and wolves*. Here the sheep do not flinch when the canine arrives, and its tail straightens in an arc, he bounds joyfully around a *patou*: our attention relaxes, it's a dog back from patrol.

The spiritual exercise required by the situation amounts to living on several different maps: simultaneously holding two or three contradictory interpretations of the situation together, consistently, with different bundles of concordant and discordant clues concerning the nature of what is being played out here, concerning the identity of *one and the same* being.

But other living beings also live on several maps, with multiple loyalties; they can sometimes play together, dogs and wolves, with she-wolves and *patous* courting each other, and they can equally well fight to the death. They can behave according to the most reductionist of naturalistic predictions, and at other times be as full of spirit, as impossible to pin down, as animism serenely assumes.

The dark side of the night

And then of course, finally, the night arrives, the last night, the night when everything comes together as if it were really a story, as if sometimes life were as coherent as a fable, but without any moral, an undecidable fable – rather more like a work of art, quite literally: something that creates in you waves of paradoxical, powerful and inexhaustible affects and senses, that cannot be summarized or reconciled.

We are positioned in the middle of the plateau, the night seems calm. A movement in the herd to the north attracts our attention, things start to stir, hundreds of sheep, like flocks of starlings, are running in all directions, they merge and separate, we hear their panicked bleating, the barking dogs, just over there, near the Grand Margès. It's an attack. We point the camera at these myriads of fire-flies, we clumsily follow the herd, now transformed into an infernal school of fish. And in the uncertainty, where all merge, we confuse the sheep with the wolves, the wolves with the dogs; a dog is being chased by a wolf who is being chased by a dog (or is it the other way around?), the attackers become defenders, the fugitives turn around and charge, roles change in this time of metamorphosing creatures, on this exposed hillside near Bourjac. Glued to the thermal imager in the middle of the Grand Plan, we are little panoptic and one-armed gods, tightly focused on the stage, bathing in the whirr of old cinemas, produced by the hyper-technological thermal imager, the whirr of spools of celluloid running on an old projector, and the images in black and white pass in front of us, like an Eisenstein film, with its thousands of extras at war, in dark, chaotic battles, where no one can tell their friends from their enemies.

Dogs, wolves, sheep, the shapes merge into one metamorphic dialogue: you are my ancestor against whom I fight; you are my old prey that I defend at the risk of my own life; I am your descendant who sometimes plays with you, and whom I kill when you get close to my protégés who were still my booty *only yesterday*; I am your ancestor, who desires you and deceives you.

That is, if you look at things from an instrument as strange as the thermal imager – a philosophical camera that would see all of this on an evolutionary timescale: I am you that I kill, you are me that I protect, I is another.

These images evoke that old truth that those who are only themselves, and are sure of what is their due, refuse to hear: the contingency of singular forms. Schopenhauer explains in a famous passage that what we would now call empathy, in the sense of a moral emotion based on ethology (which he himself calls, using the nineteenth-century lexicon, 'pity', *Mitleid* in German, literally 'to suffer with'), needs a certain condition if it is to emerge in the emotional flow. He calls this condition the 'consciousness of the contingency of singular forms'. For a migrant to move me, for his fate to distress me, I must realize that the fact that he is *him* and that I am *me* is a contingent fact: I could very well be him and he could be me – our differences are happy or unhappy coincidences, and not necessities linked to fate, election, merit or value. It is this experience that, paradoxically, the camera technique reproduces here: the very difficulty of identifying animals at a glance, the labour the eye-mind performs in discriminating who is running after whom, gives access to this philosophical truth of the contingency of singular forms; it opens a breach to restore to these living beings their long history. It reminds us of the fact that they are originally indistinguishable in the evolutionary flow, and that they are intertwined in their ecological relationship to the present. Evolution over millions of years is made visible in these images by their sheer uncertainty: originally, wolves, dogs and sheep – these three different animals – had a common ancestor. And this ancestor, over successive generations, each indistinguishable from the previous one, produced sibling lines, one of which ended up living by devouring another, while that one derived its grace, its vitality, and the health of its populations, in part from being devoured by its brother.

What moralizer can wield universal principles for sorting out the wheat from the chaff here?

On this particular night, we sense that the worst for the sheep, perhaps, is the night of panic, being chased, panting helter-skelter, with all the pain of the bites, the feeling of helplessness and incomprehension. To our surprise, we catch ourselves insulting the wolves on the camera, encouraging the dogs. The paradox, however, is that it is humans who are largely responsible for this panic: the sheep descends from a wild mouflon – and the mouflon knew how to defend themselves, to flee, to organize themselves. They foiled wolf attacks almost nine times out of ten. But artificial selection has, for several thousand years, juvenilized the wild mouflon into a docile sheep: in other words, the *adult* sheep, when faced by a threat, is kept in the emotional state and helplessness of a juvenile. It is a classic phenomenon of domestication, which allows domesticators to use the developmental possibility invented by evolution which we call neotenization (it consists of delaying the maturation of individuals), so as to keep in the herd only the most impressionable, manoeuvrable, malleable, manipulable specimens.

Hence our feeling of responsibility to protect the sheep by killing the wolf. But the historian Michael D. Wise puts us right: this story of the shepherd protecting against the predator is also a fiction told to hide the predatory dimension of breeding. The *topos* of the shepherd who defends the herd against bloodthirsty predators has served to forge the image of a pastoralism that protects the weak (made weak *by* this very pastoralism itself) against a fierce nature, and to hide the predatory nature of pastoralism behind the image of the protector. In *Producing Predators*, his environmental history of the ranchers of Montana, Wise has a powerful intuition: he analyses the construction of the representation of breeding as a 'production' of meat.[5] He shows that, in this American context, the 'producer' of beef is a predator who must represent himself as besieged by other 'predators' (wolves, bears, Native Americans) and as protecting his innocent beasts (that is to say his prey), so as to redeem the predatory ambivalence of his own activity, and present it as productive and not destructive. Here, of course, those involved are not capitalist ranchers, but the conclusion is the same: it is hardly defensible to want to eradicate wolves to protect vulnerable sheep, when it is our heritage that has made them so. One can no longer say with innocence: 'the poor sheep . . .'

It's impossible to decide. It's night in the steppe, among the lives – no, slipped into the lives of each other. Moral certainties are for the broad daylight of churches and ministerial offices.

The next morning, the project leaders, much more expert than we are at deciphering images, will examine the videos taken at night, a few slices of time that are admittedly less complete than what we have seen, and not always properly filmed by us; but according to them, there was only one wolf involved in the whole business, who came upon the herd late. The unrest remains a mystery. These videos cannot be used for the scientific project: they are the threshold experiments of a diplomatic process.

The philosophical emotion propagated here is disturbing, and this disturbance is converted into a riddle. It's this formulation of the enigma that leads to the concept of diplomacy that we will now explore. This emotion lies in the ambiguity of our being shapeshifters too: we recognize the shepherd in the pregnant ewe paying attention to her round belly; we recognize ourselves for a moment in the pack that makes its way up the track before our eyes, disciplined, cohesive, in commando formation; we see the wolf cubs playing all night long, far away, in the thermal imager, we find their cheerfulness endearing, then we come up to the herd at dawn the next day and watch the puppies playing, in the same postures, with the same little faces and invitations to love, so we stroke them and roll around with them as if by *transference*. It's a contingency of singular forms, an indistinct crossbreeding.

We are woven into all the living beings present on the plateau, one by one grafted onto them, so as to grow with all of them and suffer with each of them, pinned to them with a nail gun. We are woven by the great diplomatic spider, she binds us all together, one by one, by affiliations and links, in such a way that at the end, entwined in these threads of attachments, no one, no wolf, no sheep, no meadow, can move in the distance without your heart ringing.

Going over to the other side

But we are also chimeras because we are partly wolf scientists, partly helpers of shepherds. Should we have reacted that night, should we have gone to make contact with the herd to stop the wolf attack? Sometimes, in cases where the herd was accessible and where the pressure was unbearable, some of us intervened to push back the wolves. That night, the darkness was too deep, the herd was too far away, inaccessible in fact, so we didn't go. We felt remorse afterwards. Remorse always towards everyone, the feeling of not having made the right decision, because, quite simply, there is no right decision: on the contrary, it's the sign that we're at work.

How to choose a course in this chaos? At sea, there is the practice of *negative navigation*, it's often useful when we need to orientate ourselves in existence. It's practised when we don't know where we are and cannot know it. The main thing then is to know where we absolutely must *not* be on the map, and carefully determine on paper what should be observed around these places of death. What landmarks (lighthouse, coast, Genoese tower, cliff, archipelago) would be in sight if we *were* where we should not be, at the risk of being driven onto reefs, cannonaded, carried by the tide, stranded on the shoals. Then the main thing is to keep away from these landmarks: navigating consists of not seeing them – reacting so as to remove them from the field of attention every time they enter it. Navigating well means systematically trying to lose sight of any mark. It's an intriguing art. Navigating away from the only identifiable known point each time: taking the unknown as a compass, the absence of any visible reference point as a sign that we're in the right place, because every known landmark is a sign that we're in the wrong place. We can be reassured, sure of our way, certain of our own course, only when we reach the unknown. It's the art of staying on the empty spaces of the map, on the areas not surveyed: uncertainty becomes security, a heading to follow as we move forward.

Well, in real diplomacy, the diplomacy of interdependences, the diplomacy that's in the service of relationships, and not of one member of the relationship against the other, negative navigation is an important art, an everyday art. The compass is clear: the landmark to avoid, the one from which we always need to move away to be brought back to the high seas of uncertainty, that is to say, to the shelter, is peace of mind, it is the feeling of moral purity. It is the feeling of being at the service of the exclusive Just Cause (for the innocent wolves against the dishonest exploiters); at the service of Holy Wrath (against the thieving wild beast, the sadist), of Revealed Truth. The conviction of being among the Good against the Bad, the Righteous against the Beasts, the innocent against the criminals, the Noble Savages against the vile humans, or Civilization against Savagery.

Any feeling of being *sure in one's heart*, of being within one's rights, needs to be banned, otherwise we do not do justice to the relationship itself, to all those who are caught up in it, entangled in a thousand weaves of relationships that extend from conflict to care, from exploitation to love, with this slight exception: we share the same territory, in which the habitat of one is the interweaving of all the others.

You have to accept being a shape-shifter to the end, a chimera until the bitter end – even in ethics, heart of a sheep and maw of a wolf, and no crocodile tears.

Dawn on the other side

Back to Canjuers, after this long night, this night of intense attack, where we shuddered for the sheep, cursed the wolves, encouraged the dogs in battle, suffered for the bitten animals (none were found killed), shivered for the young wolf manhandled by five dogs. After this episode, one of us, a woman, slept and dreamed.

When she wakes, she says she slept 'as if on morphine', as if overwhelmed by the chemical cocktail of all the emotions of the world experienced in one evening. She says that she dreamed she was sleeping there, out in the open, in the middle of the Grand Plan, under the immense sky, surrounded by steppe, on this grassy flat, exactly where we did indeed actually sleep.

But something woke her up in her dream: she sat up in her sleeping bag, with that view all around of ourselves that we have at this precise point of the plateau which allows the camera to observe everything that happens in a circle surrounded by the horizon.

And she saw them. All the animals in the world (she was certain). They were running there in this steppe-savannah-scrubland of Provence: there were elephants, moose, giraffes, bears, baboons and impalas, reindeer, elk, deer and sheep. And they were chased by the wolves, which flew just above the ground as they seem to do on the night camera, at full speed, like winds or rivers without obstacles, with that calm ferocity that characterizes them when they are onto their prey. But it was not a nightmare, she adds, nor an oppressive scene. For simultaneously these dream wolves were dogs, guiding the animals to a secret place where they would be safe, secure.

The dream is sometimes a nocturnal art that can smooth the emotional journey of the day's events, and metabolize them. Here it is as if the dream had worked on this ambiguity of the canine, indistinguishable, simultaneously *canis* and *lupus*, running with the same power, charging with the same courage, returning to the attack with the same fighting spirit.

In the Neolithic, we invented a new form of life: two million years ago, we lived like wolves, seeking and hunting. With domestication, living was no longer a matter of seeking, but of keeping, like the guard dogs who are fed to keep the sheep – to keep what we had appropriated.

This night's fight between dogs and wolves has philosophical power because it stages two faces of the human, the essential conflict of life forms, the conflict between hunter gatherers and domesticators, as played out throughout the history of human peoples: in the Neolithic period against the last nomadic peoples, on the Western Frontier between Blackfeet Indians and capitalist ranchers, and between Maasai and Hadzas in sub-Saharan Africa. Dogs keep and wolves seek to take: two forms of life that we have gone through, that we reactivate daily, passing from one to another. Two forms of life that already exist in living beings, with birds who hide seeds and birds that hunt in flight, ants who explore and ants who protect the fungus that they have domesticated. This ambiguity is a shared heritage – shared between dog and wolf. And the sheep is also there, somewhere, in our inner menagerie: we too have had predators. Nothing that is living is a stranger to me.

Each of us carries within ourself the entire living condition.

The political philosophy of night

'If the night turns dark, make yourself even darker'[6]

We can now dwell on how these field experiences impact on the practice of philosophy. This is a field in a very particular sense: not a field in the sense of the methodological standards and epistemological aspects of the social sciences, but a philosophical ground. In the social sciences, the field is precisely what calls for empirical description and elucidation by theoretical instruments (it is simultaneously the material to be described and the practice that collects empirical evidence). This descriptive ambition is not the primary meaning of philosophical activity, even if it can contribute to it. The relation to the field of traditional social sciences is thus loosened in philosophy. The question then becomes: what is it for? What does the field do *to* philosophy? That is, what does it do to philosophical activity in its originality? Here I am adopting the Deleuzian approach where the philosophical activity par excellence amounts to *creating concepts*. The question becomes: what does 'being on the field', and not necessarily 'having a field', do to conceptual creation? So far I have showed how the immersion in practices on the field has contributed to a series of experiments that could be called 'philosophical' (neither more nor less than life, when it is not stripped of its enigmas and ambiguities, accessible to everyone). These experiences are decisive insofar as they contribute to the creation of the concept of an *interspecies diplomacy of interdependences*.[7] This is what I now want to explore.

I am for the moment taking from the field simply the affect induced by empathetic circulation between all the sides, from which the formulation of the concept can be woven. This affect is the symptom of an original position in the space of relationships.

What emerges from this experience is that the best compass for finding the diplomatic position is within yourself. It's a morally blurred attitude towards each belligerent on the territory, because we are working for the relationship – for the benefit of the lasting relationship between these belligerents, in the interests of the relationship – while each of them, as is only normal, often works for his or her own interest, and to the detriment of the interests of the others, when the relationship is first and foremost conflictual.

It is a threshold experience which takes place at low noise levels, with CanOvis. We ride through the night in the big trucks, with men of the locality, hardened by the needs of keeping watch, endowed with a quasi-military organization, using espionage tactics on the wolves; we travel down tracks strewn with splintered shells to capture images of the pack and its interactions with the herd. And yet, the emotional tone of this experience is not that of action, of adventure, conflict, or hardship. It's a moral blur of many different and contradictory empathies. I distinctly remember the predominant emotional tone in the words of the operational leader, a weather-beaten man, when he felt compelled to go for another drink with his shepherd friends, then check the dogs again: it meant his having to feel bad successively for all the 'misfortunes of the world', for all those involved in the conflict. 'On the ground', he said, 'from one minute to the next, I feel bad for the sheep who has to spend a lonely night there; I feel bad for the wolf that the brigade will come to shoot; I feel bad for the lamb attacked by that bastard wolf; I feel bad for the injured guard dog; I feel bad for the shepherd who won't sleep that night; for the cubs of the litter that will no longer have anyone to give them milk. I feel bad for this little meadow that will be eaten bare by over-grazing, without any possibility of renewal.'

'Feeling bad' is a rather vague formula for conveying the ambivalence of this feeling. But there is an untranslatable formula in Spanish which expresses the affective nuance more adequately: this is the formula '*Lo siento*', literally 'I feel it', 'I feel it inside' – a formula used to tell someone who has suffered a drama in which one is powerless: 'I'm sorry'.

We are in a truly diplomatic position when we feel internally, morally, slightly treacherous towards everyone. The clearest path is the sense of disquiet.[8] We don't have the comfort of purism, of having chosen our side against one system or another, one ideology or another. We must, strangely enough, be prepared to persist in the vague underlying feeling of being a traitor to all, by dint of not choosing one side *over* the other. We have to make a firm decision *for* ambivalence, to remain in uncertainty, in the plurality of contradictory points of view, to seek healthier and more viable solutions in the service of interdependent relationships.

This feeling of moral blurring is in my opinion the symptom of a particular philosophical and political position: diplomacy in the real sense of the term, as the *diplomacy of interdependences*. And here, specifically, an interspecies diplomacy. 'Feeling bad' is the strange inner compass indicating that you are a diplomat, here and now.[9] One fascinating feature of ethical skills has not been remarked upon often enough: these are the only skills where, if you sincerely suffer from a lack of them, it means you *already* have them to some degree. This is a discreet but profound point. It is enough to sincerely suffer over not having been generous or empathetic enough towards someone who needed help – this already makes you something of an empathetic, generous person. But suffering because you can't play the violin doesn't actually mean you can play a Bach suite.[10]

Being a guardian of interdependences

We can now specify what the diplomatic position covers, that strange position at the crossroads of interdependences. In the historical figure of the diplomat, we already find a similar attitude; the diplomat reminds his constituents that they cannot go it alone, that they do not exist without the external world. But the historical diplomat between nations in the *traditional* form is not the right model, because such a diplomat's activity is often limited to continuing the war by other means, in the service of his or her own side. The diplomat 'of relationship' here portrayed is of a different nature, placed at the service of interdependences.

This character of the diplomat is at once an intercessor, an interspecies translator and a go-between. The latter is not a superior sage who knows better than others where their interests are; not a new Patriarch, able to hand down the judgment of Solomon. On the contrary, the diplomat recognizes the collective intelligence, the intelligence of the protagonists, the fact that they are the ones who know what they are doing, and the main lines of practice and life. The diplomat is on the same level as other living beings. But the strangeness of the diplomat's position is linked to its 'between-ness': it is 'positional-relational'.[11] In other words, it is linked to its contextual *position* in a field of *relationships*. The diplomat knows that there is no lack of intelligence in those involved – wolves, sheep, shepherds and ecologists – but also recognizes the positional dimension of the conception they have of their own interests: each side spontaneously has a tendency to neglect its less obvious interdependences with other sides, to believe itself to be self-extracted from interdependences. If the shepherd keeps guard of the sheep, the diplomat keeps guard of interdependences, that's what monopolizes his or her ontological attention.

And that's why the diplomat can intercede to remind the different sides of the times when they forget their inseparability from others, and can piece together solutions, deal with the situation so that these interdependences can emerge in all their clarity for all to see, or can be respected, even if they seem to oppose the short-term interests of each side.

There are several initiatives, for example PastoraLoup in France,[12] which allow those who harbour friendly feelings for wolves to act as volunteers to help the shepherds protect the flocks. What fascinated me about these experiences was that I had heard of several people going along feeling quite certain of the wolf's innocence and the guilt of the pastoral mode, and coming back changed: still passionate about wolves, but a lot more perplexed, confused, less assertive about where the fault lay and less keen to defend the 'wild' side against the idea of pastoral 'exploitation'. Now feeling more affiliated to sheep,

sheep farmers, *patous*, certain landscapes and certain practices, to the extraordinary relationship between the shepherd and his sheep-driving dog, they wanted to defend the whole spider's web, in all its intimate contradiction.

An organization such as PastoraLoup impels them, as defenders of the wolf, to help the shepherds, and on their return they are more diplomatic, in the sense of accepting the complexity of what is being played out in these territories, and seeking the benefit of the two belligerents. And yet they are still defenders of wolves, and critical of the absurd policy of indiscriminate shooting; but their commitment is more mature, deeper, more nuanced. Their criticism has become more lucid as a result: enemies are drawn more vividly, more precisely defined, militant action is fluidized, since the adversaries are no longer anonymous, they have been extricated from an abstract system (the 'exploiters' in general, 'harmful humans' in general). Their transformative energy can then be about specific public policies. This energy can target, for example, the shift from a paradigm of protection of herds based on a shoot-to-scare policy to the surreptitious and illegal regulation of populations of wolves, based on sample shooting, in the development of national plans between 2007 and 2018. It can criticize the killing of wolves en masse as a last resort given the refusal to implement a serious policy of support for the protection of herds, and aid for those who protect them. It can concentrate on the wording of laws that can be fought, on localized cultural attitudes that can be targeted.

The fight can then be cross-linked to larger issues, as when, for example, it is understood that the crisis of this relationship between wolves and pastoralism in Europe is largely due to the economically devastated situation of French sheep farming, linked to economic logic (the devaluation of meat from the French sector brought about by the Common Agricultural Policy and the globalization of the mutton market).

If this idea of the diplomacy of interdependences is so difficult to theorize, it is because we have inherited a tradition that thinks of ethics and politics as a hierarchy of relations between well-separated *primary terms*, caught up in conflict, with a victim and a culprit (myself and my neighbour, Abel and Cain). But in a world where relationships are primary, more real than separate terms, and where to live is to be caught up in and made by relationships, this approach is tragically pointless.

It is also partly because of this habit of thought that we are tempted to believe that this empathetic circulation among all points of view depoliticizes, because it becomes impossible to choose a side. But this is a very impoverished conception of politics (bordering on chauvinism). What takes place here, in my opinion, is the opposite: moral blurring does not depoliticize those who encounter it, but politicizes them more effectively. Once you have examined all the viewpoints, you feel that some do *not* have the legitimacy they claim. We see the emergence of specific axes of mobilization and relevant devices for action, and the pointlessness of the great moral condemnations that are the daily lot of computer screen activists. Diplomatic devices politicize in the sense that they drive those who encounter them towards the concrete analysis of a concrete situation, where they are captivated, as we will see later, by the point of view of interdependences.[13]

When we emerge from an examination of these devices, we can no longer lecture anyone about ethics – but we *can* activate our disagreement in a focused struggle; we can no longer decree where the pure and the impure are to be found, but paradoxically we can better identify enemies in a new sense, enemies of the relationship; and that's what I call a 'becoming-diplomat'.

Thinking like an alpine meadow: profiling alliances

Because we are so little used to thinking this way, it may seem difficult at first to imagine what the point of view of interdependences might involve exactly, in a given situation. What exactly does it cover? And how does it emerge? Let us return to the case that occupied us: the cohabitation between wolves and pastoralism. What would the point of view of interdependences look like here?

Take Thierry, for example, a shepherd who works with CanOvis. He spends his summer days 'on the tail of the sheep', as they say in the trade. That is to say, he follows them and gently leads them throughout their daily journey. As we push the herd in front of us, he explains his attachment to the meadow: the sheep must be moved delicately so that they stay for *just* the right amount of time on a patch of pasture. If they graze for too long, they even destroy the roots and deplete the soil, they lay everything bare. If they stay the right amount of time, they will 'smoke' the meadow with their droppings, which will enrich it with nitrogen and allow it to grow back even stronger next year. But if it is smoked too much, the grass will be too thick and the sheep will not want it the next year. They have to be able to deposit their natural fertilizer, to smoke the grass so as to invigorate the flora, but not too much, so as not to burn it or suffocate it. This is how a shepherd pays careful attention to the overlapping interests of the different living beings woven there. It's really not about biodiversity in general, since each living thing by its presence favours certain partners to the detriment of others: the presence of sheep favours a certain floral diversity on the dry lawns of the South, but it weakens other species. One social question here is the extent we want to give, in the future, to pastoral landscapes. But the question that interests *me* lies elsewhere: independently of this debate on what floral biodiversity should populate the mountains, there is a huge gap between the pastoralisms that *take care* of the meadows that keep the pastoralists alive, and other pastoral techniques in which huge herds, unguarded or badly guarded, wring the meadows dry and kill them by putting unbearable pressure on them. Ecologist Aldo Leopold notes this and states that the mountain lives in deadly fear of herbivores,[14] whose grazing can lay its slopes bare for decades. The shepherd concerned by interdependences, then, is as attentive to the fear that his sheep have for wolves as he is to the 'fear' that the meadow has of his sheep: he is obliged to take care of the meadows that welcome and feed his flock, and this is the great problem of the forms of pastoralism that need to be fostered for tomorrow.

We can see here how the usual alternative – stigmatizing pastoralism as a whole as if it were the dishonest enemy of biodiversity, or hailing it as a whole as if it were the crucial link in the preservation of landscapes – does not work: it all depends on the practices adopted, and we must imagine a transformation in the pastoral use of territories which will move towards an increased protection of meadows, wolves and of the profession itself; it is the axes of these communities of concern that need to emerge.

The challenge is therefore to defend a certain pastoralism that treats the meadow, and the environment, with consideration. Now what is important here is that this consideration for the meadow requires smaller flocks and a more intense pastoral presence; and a pastoralism that follows these precepts will be more considerate of the profession of the shepherd, in the sense of the ancestral art of leading sheep. Finally, and it's here that the community of concern emerges, it's a pastoralism more compatible with the presence of *wolves* (as the presence of the shepherd and small flocks are an effective way of *massively reducing* predation on herds).

The technical paths that best protect the different environments are therefore also those that best protect sheep from wolves, and protected sheep imply policies that are less reactive, less destructive of wolves: this is the last resort when active herd protection is not successful. Such paths are also the best protection for the profession of shepherding as an ancestral art, a practical skill, one which has long consisted of staying with the sheep, moving them from neighbourhood to neighbourhood, taking detours, getting them to move around and make invigorating use of the meadow that they have helped create as a landscape, but that they often destroy when there are too many of them, without a guide, in farms designed to churn out cheap meat and compete with the cheap meat that comes from the rest of the world, especially the British Isles and New Zealand (islands which very quickly eradicated their predators, which is one of the reasons why their meat is so inexpensive). They are bound to lose in such a competition. Here we have a measure that works with and on interdependences: when they are possible, the pastoral practices that best protect the sheep also protect the wolf, along with the meadow and the profession of the shepherd. This is one specific case of a community of concern, but there are others to be explored, defined and defended.

This certainly involves reducing the number of sheep raised for their meat, but in the current situation, when it is necessary to reduce our meat consumption so as not to contribute to the climate crisis, is this seriously a problem? At a time when animal suffering is an issue, at a time when whole species of flora and fauna are becoming extinct, at a time of global warming when ruminants are a major cause of deforestation, we need to rethink sheep farming so as to transform its uses towards greater sustainability.

This is not to say that all sheep farming should be done in one and the same way: a variety of techniques is necessary depending on the type of farming and the landscapes involved, but we must give priority to those that defend the richest communities of concern, as is done elsewhere, often without their being formulated or presented as such, in Italy and Spain. And, at the same time, we must not give in politically to the demands of those who seek to cut down the wolves' numbers, a huge pastoralist lobby that refuses to shift its practices towards more sustainability and interweaving. In this regard, any compensation for attacked sheep from a herd that was not protected adequately or at all is not acceptable. This happens regularly: sheep farmers who refuse any measure of protection, even subsidized, are in fact compensated as much as those who are doing their level best to adjust their practices to the return of the wolf. And this despite it being part of the national Wolf Plan that compensation should be in accordance with protective practices (a common sense measure, never applied). This public policy must be criticized and withdrawn: it weakens any attempt by sheep farmers who want to transform their practices in the right direction. After all, what is the use of wearing yourself out inventing a pastoralism compatible with the presence of predators, if those who do not protect their herds receive more economic rewards than those who force themselves to do so? This is a political mistake: we are wasting the state handouts to pastoralism by promoting practices that refuse to protect the herds, and then we exploit the media pathos over the death of unprotected sheep to ensure that wolves are killed. It's an avoidable suffering, exploited to produce another avoidable suffering. A twofold death, one serving to justify the other – rarely good policy.

This is indeed a diplomatic situation, since there are several sides, which live as if they were at war. And the stake is diplomatic, since it is a question of defending a modus vivendi, creating alliances between those involved. This is not an irenic injunction to love everyone, since there are excluded parties: forms of pastoralism that definitively refuse to put in place protective measures and that demand the killing of wolves at the slightest loss of sheep will not be part of the covenant. Wolves who persist in attacking herds despite the most effective non-lethal protective measures (which are in fact messages to alert predators of the limits of their use of a shared environment) will also be excluded, and can be shot. The unsustainable pastoralism which destroys meadows, and the hunters and herders who poison and poach, will be the enemies of this alliance. They will be fought step by step.

The line that separates interest groups no longer passes between wolves and pastoralism, between humans and wild nature, but between different forms of pastoralism allied to the living beings that they foster or destroy, different ways of interweaving a human use of the territory with its non-human uses. What we have here is a multi-use approach to environments, extended to other forms of life: a multi-purpose approach to the environment that negotiates animal, plant and human life.

Consequently, the pastoralism which deserves to be defended implies a transformation of uses: it must be making progress from the point of view of animal suffering (i.e. slaughter and husbandry practices) and, from the point of view of nurturing the ecosystem, it must become more resilient and sustainable, able to coexist with the wild dynamics that shelter it and endure it, conspiring with the pollinators of summer grazing, able to make room for wild ungulates and less convivial forms of biodiversity, such as the wolf. It can also rethink its economic values, moving towards short circuits capable of adding value to meat produced on the basis of these commitments and practices. Many sheep farmers, from the younger generation in particular, are already raising the problem in these terms. This reinvented pastoralism can make a watchword of such alliances with the environment and its wild protagonists, and from this watchword it can reap the social and economic benefits. It can defend other relationships with the territory besides that of a practice based on the idea of heritage, in 'arts and crafts' mode, preserved as a memory of the past. Future sheep pastoralism deserves to become a spearhead of the sustainable relationships with the environment that we need for the future, constantly seeking the form of consideration best adjusted to the forms of life it involves, with which it cohabits, which shape the environment on which it is based. And this may well mean pioneering sustainable relationships by intelligently managing its inheritance from the pastoral arts and from the love of living beings that these arts imply, extending that love to the sheltering environment in all its richness and complexity. The wolf then appears, in a gentle paradox, as the accelerator of a transformation of land uses towards greater sustainability and greater ecological awareness.

The creative dimension of the intercessor

It all starts, then, with increased attention to relations and a refusal to accept the monopoly of terms. The idea that reality is mainly constituted by relationships has been defended in the twenty-first century, and ecological thought has learned this lesson. But what does this imply about reality if we neglect to ask the question of who *is responsible for* this relational dimension of experience? There are no angels of relationship, there are no Wise Men arriving as if by magic. All discourses that speak of relation in the abstract sense must remember to ask this question: from *whose* point of view is this relation envisaged, defended, represented? Who works for the relation? It will never be the relation itself. A relation has no hands and no voice. It has no rightful place. We must never forget, at the risk of simplification, that in our metaphysical tradition we always start by coming from a side that is seen as separate, *against* something else (which is probably less the case in those cultural habituses, documented by ethnography, where the awareness of interdependences with the giving environment comes first).

To activate a way of thinking about relation in the field of transformative forces, we must find intercessors between the logic of terms (namely, our whole heritage) and the logic of relations. We must give hands to the concept of relation, to the concept of interdependence, and these concepts also need voices.

And this is where the character of the diplomat takes on its full force: in the gallery of characters invented by human culture, there are few who have this logical dual feature of coming from *one* side, while being able to structurally place themselves at the service of the relation. To my knowledge, only the shaman and the diplomat have this strange and fascinating status (the former is more difficult to activate on the basis of our Western heritage).

This serious consideration of a need for the relation of interdependence to be embodied by an avatar[15] may be inspired by a little-known text in the philosophical tradition: *The Philosophy of Loyalty*, published in 1908 by Josiah Royce, the idealist philosopher.[16] Royce underlines the necessity of an intercessor, to enable a logic of relations to become established in the field of transformative forces.[17]

The clearest example is that of the interpreter in the field of international relations. The two sides that come into contact may not speak the same language, or share the same codes, habits and customs: the intercessor makes the interaction possible, because he is not a transparent mediator, but a real protagonist who bears the relation and transforms it, giving the relation itself a rightful place. In a 1914 text, *War and Insurance*, Royce mentions the intuition that sets him up as the political theorist of interdependences that I am trying to conceptualize here.[18] The very existence of the intercessor implies a particular logical status: a logic of the 'between' – between already constituted communities. As Scott Pratt comments, the agent cannot simply be the spokesperson for one side or the other, but needs to be distinguished from each side, even if he shares a language or common interests with both of them.[19]

Sometimes the intercessor, named B, will slightly modify his translation of the message from A to C, so as not to trigger a conflict or in order to guide the interaction. He will to a small extent betray the translation. Why? Because he thinks that the relation between A and C is more important to A than what A believes to be crucial for him, namely his side's interests. As the intercessor has no decision-making power, he is not likely to control everything from the point of view of relation; on the contrary, he allows us to keep in mind the point of view of the relation, between two sides that can at any time retreat into themselves and no longer see anything other than their exclusive and short-sighted interests.

This intercessor named B, writes Royce, 'desires, just as any reasonable agent desires, not to do A's will alone, nor C's will alone, *but at once to create and to make conscious, and to carry out*, their united will, insofar as they both are to become and remain members of that community in which he does the work of the interpreter'.[20] I prefer not to endorse Royce's over-ecumenical idea of a 'united will', as I favour another formulation that will emerge later (that of the 'community of concern'), but the main thrust of this quotation lies elsewhere: it consists in the creative dimension of the intercessor. He must remain distinct from the two sides, even if he comes from one of them. This situation structurally puts him in a position of contradiction: contradiction is the hallmark of his art, when it is well practised.[21] But this contradiction is a fertile one: 'In order to serve as a mediator, the agent is forced to go *beyond* what is given in the situation to *create new options* and to make choices not guided exclusively by the principles of either side.'[22] To this extent, these intercessors become real agents, dedicated to *allowing something new to emerge*, precisely, in my reading, because they have an original point of view on the collective situation, that of interdependences. In one fell swoop they create and carry on their shoulders the community of concern that emerges when we are made to perceive things from the point of view of interdependences.

Placing Royce's logic in a double context – that of ecological interdependences as a condition and that of interspecies relationships as a framework requiring specific forms of translation – allows us to see the conceptual character of the interspecies diplomat of interdependences emerge.

The diplomat thought of as the activator of a viewpoint focused on interdependences is, however, different from the 'spokesperson' who, like some elected official, represents an ocean, the Amazon rainforest, the living waters.[23] In reality, the 'spokesperson' character is sometimes problematic. Because if we represent every non-human on the model of the liberal protagonist, the bearer of a predefined interest to be defended, then this produces a very clear effect in a specific situation: it adds to the split, plays out again and perpetuates the exclusive and contradictory character of interests (theirs against ours).[24] Thus, non-humans always lose in the end, because anthropocentrism grows with the intensity of the crisis.[25] The diplomat portrayed here does not represent wolves, oceans or nuclear power, but activates the point of view of interdependences. It is the force field of interests which is jostled: from the liberal topos of separated individuals engaged in a struggle for exclusive and rigid interests, we move on to other arrangements of identity and desire which form fluent communities of concern, weaving several species into one place, one time, one fight. And this diplomat is actually a *Janus bifrons*. One of his two faces is turned towards other living beings to envisage a diplomatic relation with them (he practises his diplomacy *directly with* living beings, it is not a diplomacy carried out among ourselves *about* them). His second face is turned towards networks of institutions, towards humans, so that he can be a spokesperson not for wolves or sheep, but for interdependences.

He therefore speaks in the name of interdependences: he is their point of view in action. 'Interdependence', in fact, like 'relation', is a concept without hands. In the environmental nebula, everyone talks about it, but who defends it? It's difficult, as we have seen, because we are dealing with a relation, and our political and metaphysical tradition focuses on separate sides, that is, on terms. The point is to *arm* the point of view of interdependences: to give it hands so that it can get them dirty, to give it a voice so it will not be silent, and to give it a political pugnacity.

Communities of concern

This diplomatic agent, then, insists as much as possible on the point of view of the relation. In so doing, he does not defend compromises between *wills* that remain intact, but activates the creation of a new arrangement of desire that displaces the original dividing lines. This is what I provisionally call a 'community of concern', in an attempt to escape from the liberal lexicon which haunts us with its 'interests' (which are given in advance and linked to a separate individual with fixed limits who is inclined to draw up contracts in order to maximize those interests).

Far from this idea of interests *defining* individuals, the community of concern is a way of envisaging the fragile connection between interdependent collectives of human and non-human living beings, who have this much in common: the habitability of their shared living environment is *important* to them. Even if they don't say it, living soils, wolves, sheep, meadows, the taciturn shepherds have this in common: it matters to them. We saw a community of concern at work above, in the example of a pastoralism capable of seeing itself as more populous than it had imagined, as it felt concern for the meadow, the sheep, the profession of being a shepherd, and its untamed cohabitants.

The shift from exclusive interests to the community of concern involves a creative transformation of the identity of the humans involved. As with the sheep farmer whose sheep had been attacked several times by wolves, and who was among their first opponents, but who now defends the point of view of interdependences and reveals how his identity has shifted in his encounter with the wolf:

What's rather odd is the way this wolf who, as it were, stirs you out of your complacency also triggers a sensitive relationship you can have with your environment. It's pretty awesome. [. . .] It means that you're with your sheep, you *are* sheep, they pay attention to you, you're recognized by the intelligence of other beings who inhabit the same space as you. So somewhere you give in to a form of consideration for this intelligence, saying: Maybe you get irritated, maybe you get het up, he's a spoilsport, but all the same, he repopulates the land, he recolonizes, he's just defending his rights a bit, despite all the means we have to eliminate him. And so it's a real initiation into nature and the environment.[26]

If we are caught up in the point of view of interdependences, wherever we come from, we can shift the identity of what we believed ourselves to be, propelling collectives into an interweaving where they become others: where a desire that wasn't there before is surreptitiously invented, with another weaving of the self. Ultimately, it's all a matter of inventing tools for a modus vivendi whose embedded theory is diplomatic – tools that will enable communities of concern to take shape, tools that invent them by displacing the lines. And these communities of concern are in fact always already there, it is not a question of inventing them ex nihilo, but rather of invigorating, strengthening, shaping them. Indeed, once practitioners of the land or of the forest become sensitive to the mode of existence of the living world which includes them (a world entirely made up of interdependences), they have already diffracted their identity in the environment which makes them live, and they experience it as a community of concern. It is often external forces, either economic (the priority of output), political (exogenous regulations) or ideological (the cult of self-extraction vis-à-vis a nature viewed as inferior), which sometimes force the practitioners of the living world to forget what they know very well.

From the point of view of interdependences, it is thus creativity which is important, the possibility of bringing out new arrangements, new mediators, invisible alliances, communities of concern.[27] Then the diplomat of relation becomes something else: the creative voice of interdependences. Without this creativity, all we do is reach a basic, weary compromise between the two sides, we do not invent the right relationship, fair and relevant, and constantly renegotiated: adjusted consideration.

However, 'interdependences' are not to be understood in the strict sense of functional ecology, as what is biologically necessary for a species to survive materially. The interdependences here are to be understood as the weavings that make possible more prosperous forms of life, more fulfilled, better connected, more varied, richer in the consideration they can show to the living world. The wolf is not interdependent on us in the sense that its disappearance condemns us to death, but in the sense that its presence encourages a more sustainable land use, one more invigorating for the different environments involved and for human practices themselves. For it can rightly be claimed that a practice is more emancipatory and richer in meaning for a practitioner when it enriches the environment that supports his life rather than impoverishing it, when it weaves itself into the other inhabitants of its giving environment rather than eradicating them.[28]

Consequently, it must be understood that interdependences are not givens, facts of 'nature', formulated by ecological experts and dictating to democratic collectives the right way of using the land. Of course, interdependences reveal the multispecies *requirements* of the living environment which hosts the human collective, but they are also partly constructed, they imply decisions. It is the *course* of these democratic decisions that has changed: the aim is no longer for us to extract and free ourselves from a 'nature' thought of as a constraint on the sovereignty of the collective which gives itself its own law. It aims to weave us more effectively into our giving circles: in these interdependences that make individual, collective and other-than-human life more viable.

You are not born a diplomat, you have the role thrust upon you

The logic of the 'points of view' that I am exploring here explains the positional and relational dimension of the diplomat: he is not an official, but a position in the field, a moment of individuation, a place where you can find your bearings after being pushed out of your place. This idea makes it possible to resist the idea of professionalizing the diplomacy of interdependences, institutionalizing it too rigidly, in a Ministry of Ecological Affairs, personalizing it in an individual or an expert.[29] This would produce problematic confiscations, because this diplomacy is not a profession, a contractual mission – and moreover, it has no official mandate. It is a mobile, fluid position in a dynamic multispecies force field. It's a position that falls on you, or falls to you, whether you are a group, an individual, a profession, or a corporation. This can happen to anyone. The only reliable indicator is the inner compass (the moral blur of feeling that you're a bit of a traitor to everyone because you're in the service of the relation). Of course, we are traitors only to those who do not see their interdependences.

It's a relational position: we find ourselves in it, in this interspecific weaving, the minute we take the interests of interdependences *more to heart* than the interest of sides that believe in their independence. It's not a mission that's given to someone by any authority, but a free position in a field of relationships: we find ourselves *pushed* into the diplomatic position when we can no longer neglect the point of view of interdependences, when we are *captured* by the point of view of interdependences. We are diplomatic agents almost in spite of ourselves.

In this regard, the CanOvis team is an eloquent example: its original mandate is not obvious, its members initially join in order to produce knowledge on interactions between wolves and the pastoral system, with the ultimate goal of improving the protection of the herds. In my opinion, it's by letting themselves get affected by the terrain that they can become something else, because they are captured by the point of view of interdependences, due to the weaving of contradictory empathies.

The diplomat of interdependences thus differs hugely from the classic character of the diplomat between nations, because he has no official mandate.[30] Fundamentally, the diplomat of interdependences is not called upon by any external authority; he is called upon by himself. This diplomat is called upon by himself when he is called – summoned – by the point of view of interdependences; his mandate is moral blurring itself. This is his fragility (his power has no institutional guarantees) and his strength (absolutely anyone, even the most obtuse, can be captured by this role, the minute he is prompted to feel from the point of view of interdependences). This makes him a very original type of diplomat, almost unrecognizable. If this subversion of the original character shocks you too much, call him by another name, it's not all that important: he's the voice and the hand of interdependences, their agent, their attaché.

The concept of a diplomat of interdependences thus gives a name to the person who finds himself fighting for interdependences (no matter where he comes from). He is a diplomatic 'attaché', literally – he is attached to the relationship, as we say about a landscape that we inhabit: 'I am very attached to it.' It's like the way some people choose to attach themselves, by metal chains, to an Oregon redwood tree. But he's not attached to a tree; he's attached to interdependences. He doesn't work for nature alone, for wolves alone, for bees alone (we need all these, however, and the associations for the protection of nature often fulfil this task admirably). Nor does he work for humans alone, shepherds or farmers (there will always be enough of these). He is not against them either. These two sides are too monolithic, they exist less than relations. Their monopoly in the formulation of problems weakens the real interweavings, which are always localized interdependences of human and non-human living beings. He is for living weavings, against everything that devitalizes them.

The diplomat is here a radical, working *for* the relation, he is the guardian of the point of view of the relation.[31] The interests of interdependence will come first, at the risk of making enemies among members of both sides who think only in terms of the interests of their side. This diplomat must serve to bring interdependences into our struggles for the fabric of life. He is an avatar of the thousand metamorphoses of the living world as it defends itself.

Being captured together from the point of view of interdependences

This makes it possible to imagine diplomatic forms in which multispecies communities play the diplomatic role.

This phenomenon is as intriguing as it is interesting: the possibility that this active view of interdependences is not occupied by humans *on their own*. In this regard, some very odd collectives find themselves in this position of alternative diplomacy, forging alliances between human and non-human living beings. For example, we can consider beekeeper groups as figures of this kind; they are the *allies* of bees, and they demand a massive reduction in chemical inputs for agribusiness (phytosanitary products contributing significantly to the 'empty hive syndrome' and the weakening of domestic and wild pollinators).[32] It can be claimed that the chimerical collective 'beekeepers-bees' constitutes a de facto diplomatic alliance, between agricultural practices, on the one hand, and the soil microfauna woven into the wild biodiversity of rural areas, on the other. For input agriculture not only weakens bees, but also soils, environments and the sustainability of agriculture itself. The alliance finds itself defending the transformation of land uses towards practices more sustainable for the interdependences themselves. It shows us that it is not only beekeeping or market gardening that are weakened: it is the interdependence between pollinators and environments that suffer from chemical inputs. If the inputs seem beneficial to one side (agroindustry), they are not *really* so, since in the long term they destroy the pollinators which allow the return each spring of all the fruits and flowering vegetables, fertilized in their cross-marriages with insects and birds. This diplomatic alliance, however, does not call for the halting of all exploitation of ecosystems for the benefit of pollinators alone; nor does it call for the ending of inputs solely for the benefit of *sustainable* industrial food production (an anthropocentric approach).

You might think at first that these beekeepers are only out for their own interests: they would like bees to flourish so they can sell their honey, regardless of agriculture and the environment; but that would be to misunderstand the vital geopolitics in which we are all caught up in the new age that is dawning. It is rather that the attack on their interests (the bee crisis) has surreptitiously pushed beekeepers into this very strange relational position, where they have started to see their food landscape with the eyes of interdependence itself, the inter-dependence between pollinators, market gardening and agriculture. They have started to see the feedback loops and the interweaving, all of which imply that the best form of consideration for each side is in fact a consideration for the relation between them. And this is at the risk of engaging in a massive critique of one of the sides and a struggle to transform it (i.e. to transform the agricultural practices, which are then instructed to move from intensive and monocultural agribusiness to an agroecology of interdependence).

There is nothing pure, then, in the diplomatic position: it's not a moment of overcoming the ego in which, since nobody would any longer have any self-interest, we would finally have become wise, able to take seriously the interests of an abstract relationship and act as an intercessor between the egoists. Not at all: it is not thanks to the disappearance of our own interests that we find ourselves migrating into a multispecies diplomatic middle ground; it is thanks to the sat-uration of interests, their cross-linking and interweaving, their mine-theirs-yours, in a skein so subtle that we can't see things any other way than through the eyes of the weaving itself.

Bees are whistleblowers here: their *unique sensitivity* to the doses of environmental inputs allows them, as sentries, to make visible the invisible attacks on the *entire* living tissue. They become political deictics in the sense of the philosopher Carl Schmitt: they point the finger (the antenna), in silence, to the enemies *and* the friends of sustainable use of the tissue of living beings. They are political allies for those who want to change practices, in this sense: their interest (their vital requirements), combined with others, weighs heavily in the balance of alignments and power relations (would beekeepers who militated for their income *alone*, that is to say without any sense of kinship with the fate of bees, have the same political significance?).

The alliance between bees and beekeepers in struggle constitutes a diplomatic focus almost in spite of itself, going beyond the health of the former alone. It's not just that beekeepers fight against chemical inputs to save bees, it's that the alliance between bees and beekeepers constitutes a form of diplomacy between, on the one hand, agribusiness and its 'demands' for performance, and, on the other hand, the wild biodiversity of the environment (soil microfauna and pollinators in general), which suffers from extractivism.

It's the biotic community of these environments as a whole which benefits from the capacity of this alliance to adopt the point of view of the interdependences between agriculture and soil life.[33]

The possibility of diplomatic alliances involving bees, or soil springtails, which seem a priori poorly suited to diplomatic negotiations, nonetheless shows that the possibility of engaging in explicit dialogue with these life forms is only a prerequisite for a certain degree of diplomacy: on the first level, there are interdependences and the possibility of taking their points of view together and working for the relation. There is no need for 'higher' cognitive skills in other living beings to engage in diplomacy, even if such skills sometimes facilitate exchange. It is at the second level that translation skills can enable communication with other forms of life, modulating collective behaviour in the diplomatic sense (this is already what the beekeeper does when he paints coloured pictograms on the hives to indicate to each bee its home).

Finally, it is not necessary for humans and non-humans to have any *intention* to forge an alliance for there to *be* an alliance (this is already the meaning of the descriptive concept of 'objective alliance'). Three conditions are enough for a plural force field to manifest something like the crystallization of an interspecies alliance: it is enough that a common front can be woven *between* two or several protagonists in a community of concern, that this front can act *for* a transformation in the use of the territories important to them, and that, in so doing, it can fight *against* other uses. The mental intentions, signed pacts and verbal negotiations are of little importance: three prepositions make an alliance, you just need a *for*, a *between* and an *against*.

Composition and struggle

The moral blur of contradictory empathies has an emotional and ethical tone very different from that of militant struggle, and one might get the impression that they are opposed. How are we to conceive of the ways they are connected?

My approach is situational: both are necessary depending on the context, and every person spontaneously switches from one to the other when prompted by the nature of the situation, when we need to do justice to the latter.

I am trying here to distinguish two moments of diplomacy, often present in the same conjuncture: the diplomacy of struggle through interspecific alliances, and the diplomacy of composition, which relies on creativity from the point of view of interdependences. In both cases, it is a question of arming the point of view of interdependences; but in the first case, the political struggle against an adversary of interdependences is a major issue, in the second it is secondary.

Faced with undue domination or injustice, the conflict is necessary, creative: the balance of power is the only decent attitude and, in these cases, diplomats have a specific function, they busy themselves shaping alliances to be set up *against* the enemies of constitutive interdependences (for example, the aforementioned struggle against pesticides).

In cases that call for militant action, cases that are ubiquitous these days, interspecies diplomats endeavour to forge unexpected alliances *between* living beings and certain human uses of the land, *against* other uses.[34] Against extractivist uses, usually, and all those that weaken the maintenance of weavings, all those that participate in the process of cheapening the fabric of the living world.[35] This process cheapens in every sense of the word – it makes things less expensive and of less value; it simultaneously devalues them ontologically, depoliticizes them, and converts them into raw material for productivism. But it would be wrong to innocently call this fabric of the living world 'Nature' as the moderns have done, with nature as something that should be protected, loved or exploited. (Not that we can do without the word 'nature': rather, a thousand reflective words are necessary, to release, to invent, to hijack.) Because, as Patel and Moore put it, Nature is not a thing, but a way of organizing, and cheapening, life.[36] Under these conditions, it is ambiguous to assert that 'we are the *nature* which defends itself'. We are the living world that defends itself – including against its conversion into 'Nature'.

And, of course, we don't ally ourselves with *all* living beings against *all* humans demonized in a misanthropic way: it is *certain* human collectives that, in the name of interdependence, ally themselves with certain living beings, against other alliances, sometimes also between humans and living beings (for example the link between the company Bayer-Monsanto and its GMO Bt soybeans also constitutes a multispecies alliance, between humans and non-humans).

How are we to know where to draw the lines between allies and enemies? By collective intelligence, by the concrete analysis of concrete situations. For not every relation is an interdependence: the latter, first of all, always has its place somewhere. It starts from an environment, a biotic community, with its history. Monsanto's relationship with its GMO soybeans is not an interdependence, first because it is off-ground, and also because this relation weakens the weaving of the living wherever it imposes itself. An interdependence between human and living uses of a territory always implies, as a necessary condition, that we live in the environment we exploit. This is where the interests of exploitation alone can be undermined: by living in a specific place, we are forced to live among the effects of its exploitation and, consequently, to feel its effects on interdependences. There are no interdependences that are off-ground.

But the dimension of struggle must not obscure the fact that there is another problem to be dealt with: we must not confuse the enemies of a certain side with the enemies of interdependences, at the risk of considering all divergent points of view as enemies and believing that the struggle will solve all problems of usage. In situations without obvious culprits hostile to interdependences, in those cases where it is necessary to share the land, diplomacy is about working – however odd or indeed impossible this might at first seem – for the relation. Those are times when diplomacy is a matter of 'composition', where it is about reinventing uses of the land to do justice to communities of concern, beyond short-term contradictions.

We can try to generalize about this difficult point. Carl Schmitt's view of the essence of the political as the act of distinguishing between friends and enemies is enjoying a comeback today because it helps revive the idea that politics is not confined to consensual forms of deliberation and negotiation – that it is not confiscated by the limited institutional room for manoeuvre of the citizen who votes, but that it is made up of struggles, power relations and conflicts. Today, in the field of political ecology, there is a split between the supporters of negotiation and those of conflict. I believe that the monolithic positions on this question – with, on the one side, the pro-struggle side which sees any negotiation as a compromise with the 'system', and, on the other side, the reformers who think of any radical struggle as romantic immaturity – hide from us the real intellectual and political stake: how to find an *organized* way, with appropriate targets, of connecting negotiation and struggle. The main difficulty here is therefore to think simultaneously about the need for a diplomatic approach towards other forms of life and their several uses of the same territory, an approach involving the invention of ways of living together and negotiating uses, while maintaining the need to fight some of the protagonists.

The politics of interdependences responds to this challenge as follows: by negotiating with all those members of the weaving who keep their woven structure together and are kept together by it; and by fighting all those who destroy it and exploit it by weakening it structurally.

In the field of forestry practices, for example, 'non-violent forestry'[37] exploits forests, but it is part of the weaving, because its practices do justice to the specific dynamics of the forest, and they are rich in the consideration with which they treat the woods. For these foresters have brought about an empathic circulation between the points of view of the forest, of its wild denizens: they take account of the point of view of their former 'resource'. Conversely, monocultural forestry, whose investors live thousands of kilometres from the exploited areas, and whose function is to transform the forest's plots into wood factories to feed global markets, is an opponent of interdependences which hold together the living denizens of the environment.

I am not saying that it is an obvious matter to distinguish between allies and opponents: I am proposing a compass to navigate a little more easily, in the light of concrete analyses, through inextricable situations. Our relation with the allies we can negotiate with, and with the enemies we can fight, is no longer carried out in the light of the different sides (that of humans, that of nature, that of wolves, that of shepherds, that of trees, that of 'degrowthers', that of capitalists) but in the light of the interdependences on which the life of an environment is based. It's a fragile compass, as I am aware, but it is the best I have found so far to shed some light on our bleak situation; and perhaps it will serve to clarify certain situations.

The attempt to feel from the point of view of interdependences then allows for a new political mapping in which empathetic decentring and the need to struggle no longer appear incompatible. For arming the point of view of interdependences does not mean relapsing into a consensual and pacifying empathy towards everyone *indiscriminately*, but is rather a *different* way of showing who are friends and enemies. The enemies are not the enemies of my human side outside the context of our interweavings with the living world, but the enemies of the process of weaving itself. And there are many necessary and possible struggles from the point of view of interdependence: specifically, against all the uses of the land that destroy or despise interdependences. This struggle is waged in the name of a community of concern of many species, of a weaving of sustainable interdependences, against human uses that endanger it.

Seeing from the point of view of interdependences enables the enemies of this fabric to stand out clearly. This politicizes us 'better' because we no longer defend off-ground ideas, but communities of concern, collective transformations in the use of living territories, which do justice to their evolutionary, ecological and human history.

It's an uncomfortable process, however, because centuries of liberal political philosophy have taught us otherwise: one's own side was the stable political unit (here we say: interdependence is a metastable political unity). One's own side was what required closed empathic identification (flag, anthem, homeland) and the prohibition of all empathetic movement towards the opposite side (the enemies from the nation next to ours are cockroaches, we are swamped by migrants, foreigners are barbarians). This model is in all its shapes derived from forms of struggle between sides: those who are pro-wolves do not have the right to feel empathy for sheep farmers, under penalty of being charged with treason; sheep farmers do not have the right to mention, in a shift from their own point of view, the right of wolves to life, under penalty of reprisals, sometimes violent, from the radicalized anti-wolf fringe of pastoralism.

In the approach outlined here, however, empathy must circulate even *among* the 'enemies', among all the different sides, so that we can clearly see *who*, despite the underlying interweavings, opposes them: who destroys them, and fails to play the game of what sustains life.

This circulation can be fostered by anyone, from either side; it may impel people even against their will to sense where the midpoint of all these interdependences lies. So the problem takes a different shape: how to create, to raise new, creative arrangements that will make the community of concern visible and make it *real*.[38] This agent, at the service of constitutive relations, becomes the living memory of interdependences, he stands up for them, he reminds those who forget them that they exist, while being a creative force to open avenues of action, and to shift lines. And this is something made possible by the new point of view itself (in the mountains, everyone knows how much the landscape changes when we see it from another pass, another point of view: new paths, which remained invisible from everywhere else, start to emerge).

Concern for interdependences as care for the self

What the field does to philosophy appears here: it activates the work of the concept, it brings out its potentialities, its plurality of meanings, other interconnections. It helps to clarify some of its aspects in order to guide its development, such as the positional-relational dimension of diplomacy, and the inner symptom of moral blurring that shows us when we find ourselves in this position.

This moral blurring is however only a symptom, and not the affect itself which binds us to other living beings. The affect that binds us is above all a feeling of their importance, a requirement that we give them the attention they deserve; in a nutshell, it's a form of solicitude. A concern for the living world outside of us and within us. This point is interesting because it restores the importance of philosophy on this journey. Pierre Hadot, the great theorist of the originality of philosophical practice, thinks of philosophy as a *conversion of care*.

Thus he writes: 'In principle, we give value to what we care about. To change the object of our concern means to switch values and to change the direction of our attention.'[39] This is why philosophy is for

Hadot 'a transformation of the perception of the world', 'an effort to relearn how to see the world'.[40]

Hadot here reveals the order of the phenomena: it is not because we rationally demonstrate or logically deduce that living beings are of value that we care about them, it is because we care that we grant them value. The concern comes first, it is the force that shifts the architectonic lines of political attention, between what is important and what is not. Concern is founded on this ambiguity: it is at the same time preoccupation and care. It's a signal that tells us that something matters. How can we bring living beings into this concern when we have rendered them invisible? How can we bring into the field of political attention our contradictory empathies for those forms of life that are so divergent but woven into *one* environment?

More than appealing to the love of Nature, or brandishing the fear of the Apocalypse, it seems to me that one way, better adjusted to the challenges of the time, amounts to trying out many approaches, practices, types of language, processes, devices, and experiences that can make us *feel and live* from the point of view of interdependences. Make us feel and live as a living creature in the living world, also caught in the weft, sharing ascents and ways of being alive, a common destiny, and a mutual vulnerability.

Paradoxically, it is the current crisis that is the most effective device of this kind: the crisis of the bees, the crisis of soil life, the crisis of the Amazonian forests as carbon sinks, because the weakening of one form of life caught in the weave makes the web vibrate *all the way to us*, and reminds us that we have never been alone, that we are living only when we slip into the lives of others, in a situation of mutual vulnerability.

It is the experience of *mutual* vulnerability with pollinators, earthworms, ocean life, that impels us to feel from the point of view of interdependences, and to broaden the spectrum of our concern. For we are now dealing as living beings with other living beings, not as 'Mankind' dealing with 'Nature'. If we are vulnerable to their weakening, it is because they are important. And if they are important, why shouldn't the others be so too? And from then onwards, the breach is opened in our political attention, and the rest of the living world can flood in. This is one way of understanding the sudden upsurge of a movement like Extinction Rebellion, and the deep meaning of its paradoxical slogan: 'With love and rage'. The love is concern for interdependences, the rage goes against all that destroys them.

What I have in mind is neither more nor less than a transformation of our self-understanding: the political concern for ecological interdependences is not just a strategy for responding to the systemic ecological crisis, it's also the experience of another answer to the question of who we are, that is, from whom we are made.

For this concern for the living is indeed a 'concern for the self' in Foucault's sense, but for an expanded self, made up of its weavings. A self that is no longer the isolated and egotistical term, alone in the universe facing the absurd cosmos, but one that has risen to the point of view of its real being: as a node of connections with other living beings, its concern for self is a concern for interdependences.

There is an important word in the Bantu languages, a completely untranslatable word: *ubuntu*. It means in essence: 'I am what I am because we are what we are.' Or: 'I am what I am thanks to what we all are.' The idea, as a political compass, reached its apotheosis with the end of apartheid in South Africa, as part of the Truth and Reconciliation Commission led by Desmond Tutu. This formula is the key to a political philosophy for the south of the African continent, which centres the identity of each individual on their relationships

with other humans from the community. But, without anyone noticing, this fine formula is also a rigorous and almost perfect definition of
eco-evolution: of the living world. It's a question of bringing to light
the immemorial fact that this slogan, usually confined to relations
between humans, in fact deserves to be extended to our relations with
the living world. It's as a living being that 'I am what I am because
we, the living, are what we are.' This concern for oneself as a concern
for interdependences is an *ubuntu* extended beyond the human realm.
A multispecies *ubuntu*.

Shifting the lines of concern is thus a reconfiguration of the metamorphic body of attachments and detachments that constitutes a
human being. We detach ourselves from a monolithic fixation tightly
focused on the exclusive interests of our own side, a fixation that
obscured our links with the giving environment (there is no agriculture without the soil life being weakened by input agriculture); and,
in the same move, we become attached to a community of concern
that weaves together different participants who are seemingly in
conflict over how to use their environment, but where the conflicts
in fact constitute the giving environment itself, the one that makes
our activities and our lives possible. We focus on our 'real' interests,
which are no longer thinkable in terms of the 'exclusive interests' of
the liberal, off-ground individual, freed of any bonds, but in terms of
bonds that liberate, bonds that vivify. Shifting the individual and collective lines of detachment and attachment is crucial to a diplomatic
experience, where one is brutally pushed to feel and fight from the
point of view of interdependences. We need to detach ourselves from
what yesterday mattered so much that it defined our identity ('anyone
who interferes with my interests is attacking *me*!'), but which no
longer really counts, if everything that was invisibly supporting it is

corroded by my interests; and we need to become attached to what yesterday was invisible, but in fact constitutes what makes my life alive: the fact that it is woven into so many other lives. To detach, to attach ourselves – that is the point.

As a result, the problem is no longer one of being autonomous in the sense of being *unbound* from the whole biotic community, as in the modern understanding of autonomy. To be interdependent here does indeed mean to be autonomous, but in the sense of being *well connected* to multiple elements of the biotic community, that is to say in a plural, resilient, viable way, so as not to absolutely depend on the instability of the environment. Since autonomy as detachment from the living environment does not exist, the only real independence is *balanced interdependence*. An interdependence that frees us from a dependency focused on a single pole (for example, fossil fuels, or chemical inputs as preconditions for crops).

The modern contrast between independence and dependence, which has given shape to our political imagination, vectorized the time of social progress as a move from youth to adulthood, through an emancipation interpreted as the conquest of two parallel independences – from Nature thought of as a constraint on our freedom, on the one hand, and from social affiliations interpreted as alienating for the individual, on the other. In an ecopolitical thought of interdependences, the problem is no longer one of playing independence against dependence, but rather one of learning the art of differentiating between *bonds that free us* and bonds that alienate us. In this world, the problem becomes cartographic; it consists in distinguishing the bonds which enslave from those which give us the power to act, and the detachments that weaken from those that give life. We need to discover how to intensify the living affiliations that drive us, as societies and as individuals, in the right direction: how to transform our uses of the Earth towards more sustainable forms, forms more habitable for interdependences.

This politics of the living world, a politics associated with another conception of the self, may seem, to a modern ear, to go against the founding political project of modernity, which rests on the idea of a human collective that extracts itself from the natural environment (thought of as a constraint), so as to give itself its law without suffering the injunctions of 'Nature', after having triumphed over it. However, we must not see interdependences as the spectre of a normativity external to politics, by which ecosystems impose their laws on democratic collectives.[41] What forces us to think our way through the ecological crisis is not the return of a Nature which dictates laws to humans, as in the modern myth from which modern democracy claims to have emancipated itself. It is quite another matter: it is the call of the interdependences which indicate the limits to the range of possibilities that the human democratic collective can explore. Ecological limits are not constraints *external* to human politics, but the inner life lines that shape our human condition as *woven*: woven into other forms of life that make up the environment, in an *ubuntu* of living beings. If the human collective is only a knot of relations with the environment in which it lives, the limits in the use of this environment are no longer *external* constraints imposed by a Nature from which we need to emancipate ourselves, but the very lines of our face. Of our real, non-fantasized face: the face of a living being into whom the biotic community that carries it at arm's length breathes life.

Epilogue

Adjusted consideration

Our era of systemic ecological crisis is a time in which our relations with animals, plants and environments are at stake. These relationships must be reinvented. To this end, we can allow ourselves to be affected by animist traditions, given that their relationship to living alterities is richer than ours. But I doubt that blindly embracing the full cosmology of Amerindian peoples, in a kind of mass conversion, would constitute an adequate solution to our situation.

By what specific aspects of animism, then, could we permit ourselves to be affected, when we are the heirs of a naturalist modernity (that cosmology which contrasts 'Nature' on one side with humans on the other)? It seems to me that the relationships between animists and animals, plants and rivers are of a kind to allow humans to *make contact with non-humans*, to allow a sustainable 'commerce' with them, in the old meaning of this word, which designates negotiated interaction, as peaceful and mutually beneficial as possible, in a cosmopolitan, contingent context, always at the risk of discord and conflict. A common point of these animistic relationships with other living beings – if we look for example at the animism described by Descola when he talks about the 'political' relations of the Achuars with the woolly monkeys they hunt and the maize they plant – is that they must make it possible to establish an interaction, the negotiation of a modus vivendi involving forms of reciprocity and not equality, as the latter is impossible both de jure and de facto (what equality can there be between you and each of the millions of bacteria that populate your digestive system?). In animist cultures, the invariant of these relationships, what characterizes them all, is not abstract egalitarianism, but rather the fact that they always require *consideration*, even when hunting to kill and eat a monkey, even with a so-called 'pest' animal, or with a raspberry bush or a grove of wild trees that we do *not* use. This is what we have lost and negated in late modern dualism.

The other living beings, and their environments, were entities to which we owed consideration, forms of reciprocity, because first of all they make the world that makes us. The essence of the animist, i.e. non-modern, relationship with other forms of life is consideration, while the essence of the modern relationship invented by those who invented the recent idea of 'Nature' is the *uselessness* of consideration for living beings and non-humans: such consideration is irrational. This is the essence of 'Nature' for the moderns: nature is a matter devoid of sensitivity and of any autonomous meaning, a reserve of resources from which to draw; so nature is that towards which it is irrational and childish to be considerate. This can clearly be seen in the language of the allegedly 'serious adults', the men in suits who rule the world. It would be 'sentimental, absurd, backward, superstitious' to show consideration or compassion for animals or plants, rivers or environments. Worse: we must dominate this 'Nature', organize it, put it to work, subject it so that it doesn't overwhelm us. Here is the basis for the quiet but real contempt of the average modern person with regard to all ecological thinking: he condescendingly regards as irrational the 'Greens' who demand consideration for what is for him mere 'matter'. That naturalism, that late Western conception of the world, created by inventing 'Nature', has had a profound impact: these are the first relationships to the world that lack consideration. In my opinion, mankind had never invented such a crazy idea before.

And this contrast could be extended to other human collectives, other cultures, other cosmologies; this would highlight the oddity of the dualist metaphysics of the moderns. If we re-examine from this angle what anthropology calls 'pagan religions', involving the worship of the little deities of gods and groves in ancient Greece, Roman penates and nymphs, Gallic deities of the fertility of the fields, or the kami of Japanese Shintoism who dwell in forests and springs, we can understand them differently, outside of Judeo-Christian ethnocentrism. They are not gods in the spiritualistic sense, but *bearers of consideration*: they are the immanent entities themselves (*this* spring, *this* forest) and not a Spirit who is added on top. They are this river as it calls for consideration. It is the responsibility of each culture, then, to invent nature and the ritual form of this consideration.

This is what we discover when we shift our attention not to 'nature' or 'culture' as separate blocs, but to our *relations* with the beings of nature, and with human beings. It is this methodological shift in focus that permits this strange discovery and brings out the hidden essence of modern naturalism: the great invention of modern cosmology is not dualism. The specificity of naturalism, rather, is that it invented the first cosmology which postulates that we are not bound to treat the world that made us with consideration, or the living world with which we share the Earth, or the ecosystems that nourish us, the environments that generate the water we drink and the oxygen we breathe. What a strange story ours is.

Why should we treat the living world with consideration? Well, because it is this world that made our bodies and our minds, capable of emotions, joy, meaning. It is the living world that sculpted all our faculties, including the most emancipatory, in a constitutive interweaving with other life forms. It is the living world that keeps us upright in the face of death, by its continuous and joyful infusion of life (this is called, among other things, 'breathing'). Unplug this connection to the living world, and it's all over. This is called eco-evolution. Thus, the question is reversed: how could we have become crazy enough to believe that it is irrational to treat what made us with consideration, since at all times it ensures the conditions of our life and our potential happiness? The burden of proof must be reversed. It is up to the ideologues of modernity to show us that this consideration is irrational (good luck with *that* . . .).

How did they carry off this sleight of hand over the last four centuries? They simply needed to mechanize the living world, to de-animate it, to disenchant it – to imagine a creator God, then to project him outside the world of the senses, which thus became profane, that is to say a reserve of resources made for our good pleasure, and intended to produce economic 'value'. But it was our giving environment, in the sense that it has given us everything, up until today and even tomorrow.

What is at stake today is that our relations with the living world, with pollinating bees, ancient forests, farm animals, soil microfauna, and all the rest need to be reinvented: it is this consideration that we need to rethink.

This is not, however, some anti-modern nostalgia dreaming of ancient times when 'Nature' was worshipped as sacred: the concept of 'consideration', indeed, is aimed precisely at shifting the whole field of the problem *outside* the opposition between sacred and profane, between worshipping and exploiting. For this is still the same dualism. And besides, sanctifying is not a good ethnographic description of what non-modern peoples do towards their surroundings (which do not comprise some version of 'Nature'). Sacralizing is the dualistic concept that *our* tradition has developed in binary contrast with 'exploiting': there is the profane world, matter to be extracted without consideration, and the sacred, an immaterial realm not to be touched *at all* (the non-moderns do in fact kill, eat, trick, exploit, and gather, but also sow and reap their 'sacred'). The modern ethnographers of the early twentieth century were often simply projecting their provincial dualistic concept of the sacred onto the ritual and practical forms of other peoples – which were not a matter of absolute veneration and sacralization, but relations that were *never devoid of consideration*.

And consideration is deployed on another cosmic map than that of the dualism in question. Consideration does not *oppose* use or exploitation, on the contrary: the more you exploit an environment, the more you owe it; the more you take from the earth, the more you need to restore to it, but it is to the land that restoration is made, not to a transcendent God outside the world, nor to the intact sacred grove or the nature park. Western conservationist logic makes our dualistic heritage perfectly visible: let's completely sanctuarize a small percentage of our national territory, scatter some confetti, and then we can exploit all the rest with a clear conscience, treating it as matter to be pressured and managed (in a singular twist of history, the moderns following Locke called this 'improving' the land, making 'good use' of it, in other words putting it to work through agricultural practices organized so as to maximize biomass yields, mainly grain and cash cattle, to feed growing urban populations and, more insidiously, generate surplus value for capital accumulation).

While it is absolutely relevant to leave extensive spaces free of exploitation and able to evolve,[1] it is the corollary with regard to all the *rest*, the inhabited space, which is false (it can be pressured without consideration). So there are not two spaces, profane and sacred, there are not two logics of action (exploiting or sanctuarizing), there is only one world, and one style of sustainable practices with regard to it: to live off the territory while showing it consideration. And we need to imagine a whole gradation of consideration, which sometimes goes as far as the prohibition of all forms of exploitation of the environments that are left to evolve freely; this consideration takes the form of sustainable, diplomatic agroecologies at the other end of the spectrum.

The idea here is that modern dualism has drawn the whole sphere of the sacred towards the human person, and left the rest of the world bloodless, drained of all higher value, of all ontological consistency, of any ethical requirement. It is far from innocent, this idea that naturalism invented the first range of relationships to the world that *can dispense with consideration*. The choice of words is important here: 'consideration' doesn't sound like much, but it's actually an elaborate concept, a virtuoso at ducking and diving; it's a concept that slips in and out of the modern dualist division between our *moral* relation towards people (ends in themselves) and our *instrumental* relation towards everything else (means for ends in themselves). This dualism was limpidly formulated by Immanuel Kant, who is in many ways the most important thinker of the ecological crisis, in that he theorized this opposition which became the basis of our daily ways of living.[2]

Thinking of modernity as a prisoner of this specific dualism sheds a different light on the most contemporary movements, and the mistakes they entail. For example, antispeciesist attitudes are fundamentally stuck in modern dualism, because they replay the dualistic drama between sacred and profane, exploiting and sanctifying, basing their view of the sacred dedicated to sanctifying animals not on the model of the premodern form (sacred Nature), since that has been rejected by modernity, but on the hypermodern form of sacredness, the only survivor of the de-divinization of ancient Nature: the human person, considered as an end in himself, because endowed with dignity (unlike the rest of the cosmos, which is only a means to an end, and thus profane). By shifting sentient animals into the category of persons, antispeciesism re-enacts and perpetuates this dualism, which condemns all the rest (plants, non-sentient animals, environments) to remaining a 'nature-resource', a means for persons (human and now animal). By claiming to revolutionize modern morality, it perpetuates its most toxic structure.

In fact, this dualism, so obvious to us, is very provincial, very late and local, despite its universal guise. The true field of our relations with the world and its beings, which has unfolded in all its diversity in the Earth's cultures for more than three hundred thousand years, is a halfway house from the point of view of concrete practices: it neither sanctifies absolutely nor exploits blindly (because it's on another metaphysical map); it's the field of consideration. In non-dualistic cultures, when it comes to our relation with the world, there is always even a requirement to show consideration for what we kill and what we eat (so they are not persons or ends in themselves); even towards the giving environments that we exploit, and above all *because* we exploit them, consideration is demanded. Consideration is discreetly located between the moral and the instrumental dimensions, it is a position of reciprocity which is not an egalitarianism nor a sanctuarization of the other. It is here that everything is played out.

It is in this sense that I want to redefine, finally, the interspecies diplomacy of interdependences as a 'theory and practice of adjusted consideration'. The consideration that needs to be invented is 'adjusted' and not 'fair', precisely because the beings involved are beings whose powers, in truth, are unknown: their definitive moral status (in terms of person, dignity, end in itself, means, pure matter) is not available to us; we must constantly adjust and readjust our consideration for them depending on the answers they give us, on their ways of reacting, of altering our actions and sending them back to us in a different form. As the pollinators of the French countryside unexpectedly send us back our massive use of pesticides and phytosanitary inputs, 'telling' us: 'If you carry on like this, we'll go on a pollination strike (a strike that means death), and you'll have no more fruit, vegetables or flowers, no more spring, no more anything.' Adjustment requires work, a journey, a permanent co-adjustment, a negotiation; it's not just about discovering the right thing and moving on, because that right thing doesn't exist; we need to constantly restart the effort to ensure that the relationship stays balanced, to strike the right note as in a piece of music where everyone is playing in harmony. It's not morality, but practical craftsmanship, sensitivity, empathetic taste; the fitter is a craftsman, like a tailor, sensitive to singularity, always ready to resize his garments. That is why this reinvention is not the direct and exclusive object of the law, which must by its very essence over-stabilize legal statutes, for reasons of sustainability: this reinvention is also and first of all the major stake of all practitioners in contact with other forms of life (peasants, permaculturalists, foresters, developers, conservationists, town planners, architects, etc.), towards a transformation of our land uses.

But how do you know what consideration to show to whom? From this point of view, the current situation has huge potential: the revolutions in access to information and knowledge allow us to reconnect knowingly with living beings.

This is what these contemporary practitioners and naturalists show us when they spend their nights on the Internet, reading blogs by 'expert amateurs', learning how to decipher the forms of behaviour, the relationships between their leeks and slugs in a permaculture vegetable garden, the behaviour of wild riverine forests that distil all the nitrates and phosphates out of water, the actions of intestinal microbiota and forest mycorrhizae. These expert amateurs spend the day out in the field, or getting their hands into the soil, asking new questions, shifting the knowledge they have acquired. It's this circulation between field practices and the extraordinary access to information permitted by the web, in particular in its amateur form, which is the basis of a philosophically enriched tracking capable of giving us incredible exploratory powers, teaching us to have an adjusted consideration for each form of life, each interweaving of living beings. The repeated opposition between the authentic reality of contact with nature, on the one hand, and the 'virtual' world, on the other, does not allow us to understand the contemporary situation: the Internet is a prodigious machine for enriching relationships to the living world, as long as it raises our consciousness in ways that immediately have an impact on our embodied practices. Hence the importance of defending a culture of the free Internet, rich in shared experiences and wide-ranging, accessible, freely available, non-copyrighted knowledge. What is reactivated in this shared information that enriches our connections to living beings is a 'culture of giving', an anthropological phenomenon reactivated by hacker communities: imagine a social world in which you would be valued not by what you monopolize and own, but by what you freely give.

It is by capturing these powers of circulation of intelligent knowledge, through the culture of the gift characteristic of the Net, that we can *democratize* the exploration of adjusted consideration for the living world. Here, sensitivity is nourished by knowledge, it becomes more intense, more vibrant, more intelligent. It connects spontaneously with struggles: citizens thereby become experts in ecological alliances with living beings in the territories where they live and for which they fight, against the expertise of the technocrats appointed by firms, in the service of the big useless projects which destroy those living beings. The Internet, with its horizontal circulation where everyone can track multiple forms of knowledge, is an amplifier of sensitivity towards living enigmas, and of the struggle for vital alliances of a kind never before available in the history of mankind.

What must be reinvented by this is a cosmo-politeness: it's a matter of rediscovering and inventing adjusted consideration for the other forms of life that make the world, so that we can at last be just a little bit cosmopolite.

Afterword

Why is it important? Why is it so important?

What, exactly? Well – this book. And, more broadly, all of Baptiste Morizot's books.

They're important not just for me as a squaddie, suddenly sent to the front to write this afterword; not just for my own creations, that have been fertilized by his works; and not just for any pathway that takes, as its luminous line of flight, the beauty of being alive.

They're important for this society of ours that turns all flesh into a number, for this Western world that's as devitalized as a molar tooth without a nerve, and that's had to be filled with metal. They're important for this Earth that never needed to be saved, but wanted simply to be left to its own resources, restored to its freedom to revitalize its sap and to bud and blossom. 'Naturally'.

So let's try to describe what's at issue, in simple terms.

Our modernity, for three short centuries, has been a torn rag – the rent fabric out of which our bodies are woven, insofar as they are alive. We are the dividends of this digital century, scattered in our techno-cocoons, bits of tissue, balls of fabric – the rags of a general attack on interconnections. Our connections to the world (as well as our connections to others and to ourselves, perhaps) have all been expertly frayed. And above all, sheathing them all, our connections to the living world – to this living world pulsating within us, and outside us, and through us, for the living world is a field and a rhythm, and thus, etymologically speaking, a way of flowing. In this hydrodynamics we are the pumps and the pipes, the geyser and the spring, lake, rain or river, just as are the smallest cell, the most sober bacterium or the most majestic of fig trees.

Baptiste Morizot puts his finger on it brilliantly: the current ecological crisis is first and foremost a crisis in our *relations* with the living world. A crisis of sensibility, in other words. A tragic impoverishment of the modes of attention and openness that we maintain with the forms of life. A discreet extinction of experiences and practices which play their part in the ordinary process of forming a body, of feeling that we are shared flesh with the world rather than bipedal meat, vacuum-packed by culture.

> The specificity of naturalism [. . .] is that it invented the first cosmology which postulates that we are not bound to treat the world that made us with consideration, or the living world with which we share the Earth, or the ecosystems that nourish us, the environments that generate the water we drink and the oxygen we breathe. What a strange story ours is.

Faced with the mirages of the Technocene, which believes it can terraform the globe as we would knead a ball of pie crust; faced with quiet ecocides, and shifty gazes; faced with the accelerated warming of this thin layer of air that protects us from the cosmos and is now immersing us at seven billion degrees in the pressure cooker, with the valve closed, we need, more than ever, to be philosophers. Nietzschean philosophers, that is, to 'strike out at the current stupidity', to put an end to *moraline*, the messianism of apocalypses, the antispeciesism of the supermarket and the mirages of law, those prosperous empires of reactivity. And to reinforce, as much as possible, a philosophy of the living world which is both a politics of the living and a praxis which this philosophy nourishes. This is exactly what this book does – and what makes it so valuable.

In this now intense and 'controversial' field, in the best sense of the word, of contemporary ecological thought, Baptiste Morizot is a door. He opens up to what will come. Not because he can predict better than anyone else, or project his visions further. Precisely the reverse: because he is *here* when too many others are looking elsewhere (behind us, beyond us, from too far or too high, in the manner of short-sighted eagles). Because he inhabits the present of our relationships, places himself there as if at the knot of the skein and thus makes us touch what we can be and *how we can live together* once we have moved beyond the abyssal absurdity of a world cut off from the world.

For the little *sapiens* that I am, one who, like so many others, is a rag torn between social struggles and ecological activism, and would like to escape from the capitalism that pollutes, plunders and torpedoes, but is floundering up to his waist through the avalanche of bad news from collapsology, while he desperately looks for a compass, an ice axe, a constellation that is not too hazy to guide him across the mountain pass of the Anthropocene and emerge on the sunny slopes, and who yet feels, in his grumbling body, in his heart dancing the batucada, that everything is already there, that we lack nothing, that the desire that moulds us is powerful and splendid – for me, Morizot writes books which are like lips: able to both articulate and embrace the world. And more trivially: to nourish us.

This politics of the living world which rises from his texts, irrepressibly, reaches the melting point of three burning issues. Sacrificing all elegance, I can formulate them as follows:

1. How to move beyond physical and cognitive technocapitalism, and finally ward off its addictive economy of desires (individualism, the postulates of independence, the drive to consume, the frenzy of accumulation, self-imposed digital slavery) by responding with a reactivation of our anaesthetized life forces, a renewed confrontation with our exterior and a re-empowerment of our weaving bodies?

2. How to reconnect with the living through an ecosophy that is sober, resilient and cheerful, that deconstructs our apocalyptic anxieties and fascinations, and gives us a glimpse, in our imaginations as in our experiences, of our post-hubris future, one which we can already start to build?

3. How, collectively, to construct a political approach that sees care and concern for relationships, in their breadth and complexity, as the core of its practices? In other words, how to foil, in our relationship to both humans and living beings, the drive for control and domestication that has been part of us since the Neolithic, and enter into this ethos of meeting and welcoming? Into this hospitality towards the not-like-me, into those circulating and crossed empathies which 'evastate' us, turn us inside out, when we believed that they were going to devastate us? In short, how to enter into that *adjusted consideration*, both agile and precise, for all that lives and yet differs from us, to recombine in it *their* powers with *our* own faculties (which we more often than not share with them)?

Let's here risk the 'protest slogan' mode: it's not a matter of making the *end of the month* and the *end of the world* converge. Rather, it's a matter of accelerating the *end of the self* to activate the end of selfish worldliness. And thus open up to a hunger for the world, a thirst to sign up as an accomplice, as a weaver, as a guest. It is therefore time to change the banners, comrades, and to graffiti them with: *End of self – hunger for the world: same combo!*

As I see it, Morizot's work seems to define itself by its striking originality and its three major contributions to ecosophical thought.

Originality? He starts out from fieldwork. He's an embedded, situated philosopher. Highly concrete. The reverse of a speaker on stilts. Hence his precision and the integrity of his pedagogy. No gratuitous virtuosity. No vague concepts. No idea whose potential for activation is not felt. He presents us with motivating thoughts, born of a lived, daily relationship with the living world.

The three major contributions? In my view:

1. *He gives the living world back its freedom.*
2. *He politicizes it in the best sense of the word.*
3. *He sews us to it, thread by thread, very finely, lifting the curse of the moderns by re-inscribing the human world in its rightful 'panimal' place.*[1]

Let's unfold all this.

Free living

1. He gives the living world back its creative freedom. He moves far away from the devices and determinisms that have long impoverished and disfigured it. He draws a distinction between function and use, and takes up the concept of *exaptation*, which shows that a function 'intended' for an organ can be superseded and reassigned to other practices, completely renewing the way we view evolution.

The conceptual nuance that I am proposing here between function and use aims to pave the way for a philosophy of the living world which accepts biological heritages without transforming them into determinism: on the contrary, they are the condition for inventiveness, novelty and freedom.

He grants importance to variations, to 'flows of variants', to the subtle combination of inherited faculties, based on notions of origin and model, and thus enhances difference and divergence against the background of common sources and evolutionary convergence. He uses Gilbert Simondon[2] to give back to species a pre-individual dynamic, prior to their taking of structured form; the same is true for territoriality, whose singularity, lying in a geopolitical experience of space, is shared by many species.

Of the animals we study, he reminds us: 'We should never read them but always translate them.' Again and again. 'To do justice to what takes place, to what they are, to the relation.' In other words: no living being can be reduced to an automaton or to a program. Everything is always a free and situated creature, operating under constraint and inventing its own emancipations. This freedom that we assumed to be inherent only in humans finds its specific form in reality everywhere – and therefore requires consideration. And interpretation. Cautious, intelligent, well-informed interpretation. Hence also the importance given to the perspective of Viveiros de Castro, which Baptiste metabolizes, for example in his geopolitics of wolf droppings:

Handling the analogies of perspectivist ethology simultaneously frees us from simplistic anthropomorphism ('droppings *are* coats of arms'), from the crass naturalization of the human ('human coats of arms *are nothing but* droppings') and ethological reductionism ('droppings are nothing but stimuli that are triggered by operant conditioning').

In a free, living world, you have to think and feel the other by *similarity of relation*, without flattening it out in our folds. If the other is free, 'like us', he is also a body *different from us* given the potentialities on the basis of which we must try to understand his behavioural choices. 'Each animal does not see or configure the world from its mind, but from its body: its perspective on the world is based on its body with its own powers of feeling and doing. This is the great idea of perspectivism.'

Think like a wolf, feel like a sheep, perceive like a *patou* sheepdog – yes: provided you are aware that it is the structures of relation to the world which are analogous, not the direct relationship, which is always singular.

Repolytization

2. *Baptiste Morizot politicizes the living world in the noblest and deepest way*. For me, this is absolutely decisive. In particular as a way of escaping from the current aporias between extractivism on the one hand, and putting nature on a sacred pedestal on the other. Or as a way of considering 'the planet' as something other than a crystal globe that we should condescend to 'save'.

He politicizes the living world first because, as we have just seen, he sees each living creature as based on its freedom, a freedom often denied. Less to make these creatures suitable 'subjects of law' for a puppet democracy in which humans are the puppeteers, than to place them at the heart of a 'commerce', in the old sense, in which all living beings are involved.

Politicizing, above all, means putting relation at the heart of every-thing. Starting from relation, whether it is symbiotic or predatory, mutualist or parasitic; restoring its knots and tensions, repotentializ-ing ecosystems, showing that it alone can really produce worlds. And deploying around and for it a constellation of concepts that comprise the shaping strength of Morizot's thought: encounter, cohabitation, interdependence, the art of diplomacy. Conceiving of ethology as an *ethopolitics* and, with even more delicacy, as a relational art, which raises with a new finesse the question of living together on this small bit of green and blue cosmos revolving around a sun.

At the end of the book, Baptiste Morizot goes even further. Onto the shop counter of available concepts he places a tool (or is it a weapon?) that in my view will lead to some extremely fruitful devel-opments. He calls it 'adjusted consideration'. The articulation of the two words in itself embodies the relation being indicated. It functions like multigrip pliers that express both the habitus, the fold, and the ethics that we need to bring to living beings and the ethical conduct we need to activate: *to adjust this consideration*, these forms of attention, to guard the vitality of the relationship, to treat interdependences with consideration and, even better, to (re)adjust them to help them regain their fluidity, to get them to cohabit and cooperate if ever they try to become autonomous in some morbid conflict. Morizot writes:

I want to redefine [. . .] the interspecies diplomacy of interdependences as a 'theory and practice of adjusted consideration'. The consideration that needs to be invented is 'adjusted' and not 'fair', precisely because the beings involved are beings whose powers, in truth, are unknown: [. . .] we need to constantly restart the effort to ensure that the relationship stays right, to strike the right note as in a piece of music where everyone is playing in harmony. It's not morality, but practical craftsmanship, sensitivity, empathetic taste; the fitter is a craftsman, like a tailor, sensitive to singularity, always ready to resize his garments. That is why this reinvention is not the direct and exclusive object of the law, which must by its very essence over-stabilize legal statutes, for reasons of sustainability: this reinvention is also and first of all the major stake of all practitioners in contact with other forms of life (peasants, permaculturalists, foresters, planners, conservationists, town planners, architects, etc.), towards a transformation of our land uses.

For this consideration, Morizot therefore offers many possible adjustments and readjustments, forms of immanent rightness and justice, stemming from the context. He also restores flexibility to a whole interplay of relationships that were believed to be rigid and determined and 'a whole gradation of consideration, which sometimes goes as far as the prohibition of all forms of exploitation of the environments that are left to evolve freely; this consideration takes the form of sustainable, diplomatic agroecologies at the other end of the spectrum'.

In our discussions, my own obsessions as an author have sometimes led me to criticize Morizot for the words 'diplomat' and 'diplomacy' that I sometimes found a little bland, sometimes restrictive (*diplo*- means two, while relations are always multiple), sometimes too reminiscent of its semantic frame where an individual is mandated to defend a particular side. I found that the word did not do justice to the very profound polyphonic, if not polyphrenic approach that he develops. But, arguably, a single term could not describe the complexity of a relationship. And by coupling a noun (consideration) and a verb (adjusted) in the past participle, he ultimately gives himself 'the means of its politics'. Or rather, of his *polytics* – a politics that goes beyond binary oppositions to organize inevitably multiple relationships. After all, is not the diplomat he invokes, fundamentally speaking, a polytic man or woman? That is to say, a human who accepts that s/he comes from a particular side and yet continues to put him/herself at the service of relationships, to be the considerate guardian of interdependences rather than the fierce guardian of identities, of one species and one side.

In animals, by the grace of the super-face, 'the highest degree of individual existence, the possibility of displaying inner states, is at the service of the encounter', as Portmann puts it.[3] Thus the *polytic man* is the one who goes to make contact with familiar aliens, who intercedes for them and produces tameness out of strangeness. He faces up to the labour of translation, he interprets the tracks, expressions and signs and he finds himself holed/split, crossed by this multiple life which he deciphers without certainty and articulates without transcendence. As best as he can.

For a generation like mine, educated under Sartre and Camus, bottle-fed with the Absurd and the ontico-ontological difference, stuffed with the mouldy and 'modern' but ageing myth of the silence of the universe, weighed down by the postulated loneliness of a melancholy slug facing the silence of the moors and the sea, we will never thank Morizot and his peers enough for having given us this vibrant perception of a world whose changing taffeta fabric rustles through us – and whose every movement stirs the intimate web of these bonds that we had thought to be lost. Thanks to them, we are already the children of a new polytization.

Always inside, never in front

3. And now I come to the third major contribution of this book. It re-inscribes us in the living world. It sews together our common

belonging. It gives us back our place and our chance. By breaking down the fourth wall of this theatre of humanism-as-the-centre-of-everything, it reintroduces us (almost like a new species) into the heart of the bonds that set us free. From an independence sanctified by liberalism, it makes interdependence not only a fact but a strength. Rather than a constraint experienced as a heap of chains, it reminds us that this interdependence is the main skein of our emancipation. This magnificent passage must be quoted in full:

> The fabric of the living world is a tapestry of time, but we are in it, immersed in it, never standing in front of it. We are doomed to see and understand it from within, we will never escape it.

> This is what makes it possible for us to envisage an *unseparated approach to the living world*: a philosophy that is simultaneously eco-evo-ethophilosophy, that is, sensitive to our horizontal interweaving with the biotic community all around (denaturalized ecology), sensitive to our vertical weaving with the manna of ancestralities plunging into the immemorial realm (demechanized evolution), and attentive to the power of the living world to open up whole dimensions of being: a space for inventive forms of existence (a philosophically enriched ethology).

> Denaturalized ecology is open to the political dimensions of interspecies relationships; demechanized evolution works on the sedimentations of available ascents and the exaptive reserve which makes new relationships possible; enriched ethology is a ethology of 'seeing as' built on the *perspectivist analogy* as a method. It embraces the biosemiotic dimension of communications and conventions, the agreements, mores and customs of living beings.

> [. . .] Animal ascents are like spectres that haunt you, rising to the surface of the present. Benevolent spectres, who come to help you – which makes you a *panimal*, a total animal, a shapeshifter like the god Pan

– when the need arises, to invent a brand new solution to the problem of living.

Of course, many contemporary thinkers and activists also express and encourage this reconnection with the living world. But Baptiste doesn't just go about it conceptually. He imports it into his practices and activates it through his modes of perception. He embodies it in his experience of tracking and reverberates its emotion through his narrative qualities and his style.

Enriched tracking is the sensitive and practical aspect of an unseparated philosophical approach to living beings – a style of attention. A way of always being on the alert, open to the lavish signs of life thick with time and woven from alien kin, an alertness immersed in the world, always inside and never in front of.

Style in philosophy

'Great philosophers are great stylists too. Style in philosophy is the movement of concepts.' Who has put this better than Deleuze?[4]

When we write, like Morizot, in the heart of the living world, a formidable question of writing arises. Or rather a host of formidable questions of writing! These ones, to begin with: how to insinuate animal effects into your sentences? How to write, not on the relation, but on the growling belly of the relation, as if starting from the sun to tell the story of its rays? How, above all, can we reach that pole of empathy with a life form, for example the wolf, where suddenly we will no longer be describing what the wolf does, but writing 'in wolf', wolving one's words as one stutters, ferociously poking our syntax in a teasing attempt to trap becoming-wolf inside a cage of words and digging, as a possible tunnel beneath it, the language that is foreign to all language from which amazing affects will be able to arise?

Baptiste does not dodge the challenge; on the contrary, he wallows in it, sometimes superbly, as at the end of Episode 3 of 'A season among the living' in which he illumines the senses with a single howl:

'I'm here, come, don't come, find me, run away, answer me, I'm your brother, your female lover, a stranger, I am death, I'm afraid, I'm lost, where are you? Which direction should I run in, towards which ridge, on what summit? It's night. Pierce the fog with a sounding star, so that I can follow it! And which of you is within earshot? Friend? (*Sotto voce.*) Enemy? Let's make a pack! We are a pack. Go! Let those who love me follow me! Are you there? I am incomplete, I am yours, I am the ill-fated. (*Allegro.*) There's a party to be had, we're about to set off, the ceremony is well under way and I'm a fragment. Anyone there? I look forward. Joy! O joy!' (*Someone has replied.*)

A single howl.

For writing from the point of view of another body, which embodies and activates other ways of being alive, demands that we seek within ourselves our buried bodies, layered with animal ascents, and awaken their powers. It is far from impossible. It just takes talent, an aptitude for diving, the wet porosity with states of being close to ours that can be transposed, in accordance with Mallarmé's inescapable suggestion: we just need to stick to the rhythmic correspondences of nature and transpose them into language by kindred correspondences, finding in the play of sounds and the twists of syntax something to mirror the play of relations and the twists of reality.

In other words, we need to experience in ourselves this affect of the pack or the gang, with the melting feeling of being both protected and strong, finding a way to express the tumble of biting mouths, this 'pure river of fangs, running along'. If the sudden perception of the neophile and joyful wandering of the dispersing wolf should arise, then give him this rhythmic movement of syntax, first hopping and nimble, with light commas, then anchor it with a deep-diving syntagm, so as to stretch it then, with small fanning movements, towards a throbbing, strange desire:

> tasting everything, trying everything, doing nothing, wandering around, getting bored, and then the sun sets over there, and you can feel a little bit of loneliness rising up inside you, the desire for a wolf mask to lick, the longing for the excitement of being together, the warm smell of others like a smoke that bathes us, the longing for others.

Or this predation on the indistinct beast of the landscape, as if coming out of the very body of the mountains . . . and the image then gives rise to 'smouldering wild boar-hills' which concatenate in two nouns the fusion of an inseparable lived world.

These are just, from Morizot's prose, humble examples, as if the demands of philosophy ruled out a poetry which alone would have the proper sensual ways to tip us over to the other side of the night, where the animal would finally melt into our blood, rehabilitated in our rhythms and recalled, in many cocoons of words, to our common ontological bases.

If, as Deleuze suggests, the concept can never be complete without the emotional and perceptual wing which will give it balance and finally ensure its full aviation, how can we claim to speak of the living world in all its scope without having to forge a style that is this life articulated into syntagms, hoarse with wild sounds, twittering with little alliterations to finally trumpet with assonances as pachydermal as elephants tramping noisily across a dry savannah? Baptiste is obviously aware of it:

> Adjusted consideration begins with an understanding of the form of life of others, one which attempts to do justice to their otherness: thus it involves honing an *adjusted style* to speak about them, to transcribe their vital allure into words – something they themselves can never do. And in a way it's always a failure, we never do them justice, but that's why that we must endlessly waffle on, translate and re-translate the untranslatable, try again. You have to be able to talk about them with the language we use to talk about ourselves, to show that they are not physical matter, not 'Nature'; but by bending this language so as to let their strangeness appear.

There would thus open – and may this dream fuel Baptiste's future books – a philosophy that would reconnect with all the necessary poetry, since the living world, more than any other concept, better than any other concept, calls for a writing full of a variety of timbres, thrusts, bursts and sensations, breaths and buds, in short an extreme stylistic vitality without which it will remain a mere demure alignment of woodcarvings. The living world does not describe itself or represent itself, it choreographs itself. It appeals for fluency. It demands its syntax, tempestuously.

The incandescent alloy

Ways of Being Alive, the book that you hold in your hands, is far from being a classical philosophy textbook, as you will have guessed, conceived at his desk, in the top-down rigour of concepts. It involves as many ways of writing as there are of bringing his thought to life: by the intense and scientific observation of the terrain ('To the other side of the night') or the adventure story, close to the ethological thriller, provided by the chronicle of wolf tracking ('A season among the living'); by the alert reading of great thinkers ('Cohabiting with our wild beasts') or the testing out of a brilliant hypothesis and the fiction of a ritual ('The promises of a sponge').

So much so that this collection raises a welcome, opens up to the outside imported into our skulls; it does not close the lid of a coffin on thoughts already cold. And I would even go so far as to say that it is a real hustle and bustle: this movement of the ice under the action of the wind, tide or current, as if a whole spring of melting disarray were necessary to finally thaw out the hierarchical dualisms that block us.

In my eyes, Baptiste Morizot is a mongrel. That's his strength. He's the failed novelist who writes wonderfully well, the sealskin trapper who makes circles in the snow and suddenly becomes the barbarian of a wild beast. He's the tracker who dissects droppings, explores caves and stalks scratchings, the shaman without mystique, the monomaniac and music lover who howls with the wolves. He's the psychologist at the bedside of the moderns and the ethnologist by proxy who refracts the Amerindians to us and, passing under a branch, is suddenly reliving the days of myth. Some nights he becomes alternately shepherd, *patou*, sheep and wolf, star and meadow, military spy and dispersing pack – but always a philosopher and de facto an ethologist, the interpreter, both careful and rigorous, of an animal world that fascinates him.

So it would be wrong to read in this, the album of an *ethosopher*, the nonchalance of a thought wandering along and seeking to make us witness to its happy wanderings. Because if we do walk that way, yes, from epiphanies in the midst of nature to lightning intuitions, we never lose the fundamental consistency. It's a thought that moves and unfolds, less like an archipelago than a growing forest, densifying its plantation and extending its hold on the fallow lands.

Baptiste Morizot is a great philosopher, for a very good reason (and in a very beautiful way): he puts life inside thought – *his* as much as *ours*, if these proprietary trivialities have the slightest meaning in a field that traverses everything and everyone.

Not so much life as an idea; rather, life as virulence, a sensitive imprint, a prodigality of tracks, a burgeoning of the assumptions which sense they will flower, then turn into theses which will become fruit.

And since the living is in us, at the heart of our lymphs and our microbiota bellies, within us as animal ascents that roar and emerge in a myriad of cognitive acts and running perceptions, in us as the living world is our common miracle and our common experience, what is strange about the way it crackles there as an *intercept* of thought? This is the way it electrifies itself, traces its openings, intersects our roads – and punches holes in our routines.

Baptiste's thought moves through the limestone blocks of naturalism, and breaks them up. It climbs up its crunching scree which makes it such a slippery task to even begin the ascents that a true philosophy of living beings should undertake. He's a troll who, as he passes by, pierces with a teasing arrow concepts that are as big and empty as advertising balloons: nature, culture, collapse . . .

He thinks as he tracks, dancing among the rockroses, his mental backpack full of readings, his shoulder in contact with the boxwood, ears pricked. And if his concepts are equally rich, he owes this, in my opinion, to the sites where they have been hatched, to his ability to ruminate while standing on ridges, leaning over a pawprint, his neck broken by following a path which fades and is then traced again in soft snow. A field philosopher, you say? Yes, earthy and earthly, even down to earth when needed, and the next minute lifting his gaze to the sky while savouring the jizz of a vulture, then going upstream, with the river for syntax, his muzzle sniffing and the wolf as his vanishing point. But a philosopher, above all, because he knows and feels how the pure concept is nothing without the affects and percepts that haunt it, without this incessant zigzag crossing, upstream-downstream, near and far, which goes from sensations (and even the most childish emotions) to the clarity of an idea. By seeking, with each coming and going, a whole host of modes of attention that will silhouette the real and frame it, sorting out its slag to release the nuggets from it.

Baptiste has given a name to this practice and this ability to set in vibration, joint and fusional, this triple relationship to the world – affect-percept-concept: he calls it, magnificently, the incandescent alloy. What in my novel *Les Furtifs* (*The Furtive*) I called, more blandly, the 'glow of red'. And tried to translate in the music album with this idiom, inspired by Van Gogh discovering the violence of the lights of Provence and approaching them with a form of terror: *entering into colour*. One 'way of being alive', fully and multiplyingly alive: in your mind, on your skin, your hand in the embers and through the palms of your eyes, to reach that very profane point of incandescence where the present is a sword from a forge, one that you grab without burning yourself.

As an enigma among other enigmas, the human way of being alive only makes sense if it is woven into the countless other ways of being alive that the animals, plants, bacteria and ecosystems demand all around us.

May this book give you, as it gave me, the intense joy – for the volume of his body as in the small box of bones of his skull – which feels like being enlarged, elevated and deepened all at the same time.

Like being just a little bit taller when you leave these pages: no more, no less.

What else can you ask for?

Alain Damasio,
October 2019

Notes

Notes to Introduction

1 Thanks to Estelle Zhong Mengual for this idea, and for the wealth of our discussions and her remarks on my manuscript: they have made this book better, like everything she touches.

2 That is, the extinction of the experience of nature. See Robert Pyle, *The Thunder Tree: Lessons from an Urban Wildland* (Portland: Oregon State University Press, 2011), especially chapter 9.

3 The survey was conducted in 2014 by Discover the Forest, the US Forest Service and the Ad Council.

4 Richard K. Nelson, *Make Prayers to the Raven: A Koyukon View of the Northern Forest* (Chicago: University of Chicago Press, 1986).

5 See Baptiste Morizot and Estelle Zhong Mengual, 'L'illisibilité du paysage. La crise écologique comme crise de la sensibilité', *Nouvelle Revue d'esthétique*, no. 22, 2018.

6 Charles Stépanoff, 'Human-Animal "Joint Commitment" in a Reindeer Herding System', *HAU: Journal of Ethnographic Theory*, vol. 2, no. 2, 2012, pp. 287–312; Eduardo Kohn, *How Forests Think: Towards an Anthropology Beyond the Human* (Berkeley: University of California Press, 2013).

7 Morizot uses the term '*les égards ajustés*' to suggest the specific, varied

kinds of consideration proper to other living beings. I have translated it as 'adjusted consideration'. (Translator's note.)

8 A character in Richard Powers's novel *The Overstory* puts it like this: 'You study what makes some people take the living world seriously, while for the majority the only important thing is other people. It's all those who think that only humans are important that you ought to study. [. . .] it's pathological' (translated from the French).

9 Jean-Paul Sartre's play *Huis Clos*, set in a room which the characters constantly fail to leave, is known in English as *In Camera* or *No Exit*. (Translator's note.)

10 Of course, people will object that Camus's *Noces* suggests other relations to the living world. But my argument here is on a more general level. (*Noces*, translated as *Nuptials*, is a lyrical work by Albert Camus celebrating the natural world and the pleasures of the senses. – Translator's note.)

11 Claude Lévi-Strauss and Didier Éribon, *Conversations with Claude Lévi-Strauss*, translated by Paula Wissing (Chicago: University of Chicago Press, 1991), p. 139.

Notes to Chapter One

1 Martyn Evans, 'Wonder and the Clinical Encounter', *Theoretical Medicine and Bioethics*, vol. 33, no. 2, 2012, p. 123.

2 E. O. Wilson, *Biophilia: The Human Bond with Other Species* (Cambridge, MA: Harvard University Press, 1984), pp. 139–40.

3 Marie-Françoise Guédon, *Le Rêve et la forêt. Histoires de chamanes nabesna* (Laval: Presses universitaires de Laval, 2005), p. 131.

4 Ibid., p. 132.

5 Barbara Cassin, *Éloge de la traduction* (Paris: Fayard, 2016), p. 10.

6 By 'biological trait' I mean broadly an organ, a behavioural pattern, an

inherited organized trait, of whatever kind. Here I accept as a premise the founding thesis of classical ethology, that behavioural patterns (like the sequence of acts that make up a howl, for example) are to some extent heritable and subject to evolution, like organs.

7 Karen Neander, 'Functions as Selected Effects: The Conceptual Analyst's Defense', *Philosophy of Science*, vol. 58, no. 2, 1991, pp. 168–84.

8 Vinciane Despret isolates this phenomenon powerfully, showing the existence of many types of 'territories' in birds, which are more than different conceptions of territory developed by ethologists, but in fact something like different uses of territorial behaviours to make different connections to a shared space and environment. She thus brings to light a continent of uses that escape the economism of behavioural ecology, while drawing her basic material from the behavioural patterns sedimented by evolution. See Vinciane Despret, *Habiter en oiseau* (Arles: Actes Sud, 2019).

9 Like the work of art according to Kant, the wolf's howl when heard seems to manifest a 'purposiveness without purpose'. According to this reading, Kant's purposiveness without purpose is not a reality, it's an experience: it is the name of one's experience of a work of art as opposed to a technical object. Faced with a sailboat, you feel that it is shaped to perfection, and you know for what purpose, so you understand why every part, from the mast to the rudder, from the cleats to the bow, took this shape. But when faced with howling, one experiences purposiveness without purpose: one feels that it has in a certain sense been shaped quite matchlessly for millions of years, but it's impossible to know for *what* (because its functions and uses have accumulated and been diverted from time immemorial, and this whole story is *in* the form of the song).

10 John R. Krebs, 'The Significance of Song Repertoires: the Beau Geste hypothesis', *Animal Behaviour*, vol. 25, part 2, 1977, pp. 475–8.

11 Roland Barthes, quoted in Barbara Cassin, *Quand dire, c'est vraiment faire* (Fayard: Paris, 2018), p. 15.

12 This is the concept put forward by James Gibson in his *Ecological Approach to Visual Perception* (Paris: Dehors, 2014). He defines 'affordances' as properties that exist in the environment and invite some type of action; 'affordances' are prompts (cf. the way a door handle prompts a human body to turn it, and a cliff ledge prompts the vulture to take flight).

13 Edgar Wind, quoted in Pierre Hadot, *La Philosophie comme éducation des adultes* (Paris: Vrin, 2019), p. 273.

14 Cornelius Osgood, *Contributions to the Ethnology of the Kutchin* (New Haven, CT: Yale University Press, 1936).

15 Eduardo Viveiros de Castro, *The Relative Native* (Chicago: Hau, 2016).

16 This is akin to Deleuze's view of difference. See Gilles Deleuze, *Difference and Repetition*, translated by Paul Patton (New York: Columbia University Press, 1994).

17 Maurice Merleau-Ponty, *La Nature, notes. Cours du Collège de France* (Paris: Seuil, 1995), p. 277.

18 The past tells us who we are, but there is never any essence or foundation in it: according to Foucault's formula, at the origin of a thing lies not its truth or its essence, but 'disparity'. Conceptually, this is Foucauldian logic applied to Darwin. This variant could be called a 'pre-specific singularity', in terms derived from Simondon, but I have to admit this is somewhat obscure. This concept means that the variant has no precise, assignable content; it predates the individuation of a species, of each species, the way it assumes structured form. It is, for example, the ethological fact of being territorial, but that's all – it simply means inheriting a past of territorial practices and logics. There is a pre-specific (pre-individual) singularity of territorial species which is an experience

of space as a geopolitical place, and it exists in parallel among them and among us; each one is a variant without a model.

19 Hence the differences appear, but against the background of an analogy of relationship. We can bring out the decisive differences to imagine controlled investigations: how does our relationship to the coat of arms differ from the wolves' relationship to droppings? How are we to understand the suspension of marking when wolves enter the territory of another pack? How should we understand, in the light of this analogy, the fact that the pack does not leave markings when it is in impassable valleys, but marks all the crossroads as soon as it finds itself on a track taken by other living beings? What other living beings cause it to place its coats of arms and flags? The suspension of marking becomes intriguing.

20 Claude Lévi-Strauss, *The Savage Mind* (London: Weidenfeld and Nicolson, 1966), p. 218.

21 Ibid., p. 220.

22 Friedrich Nietzsche, *Fragments posthumes (1882–1884)* (Paris: Gallimard, 1997), X, 26.

23 Thanks to Alain Damasio, who helped me forge this nuance.

24 Thanks to Jean-Christophe Bailly, who introduced me to the force of this quotation.

25 Adolf Portmann, *Animal Forms and Patterns: A Study of the Appearance of Animals* (New York: Schocken Books, 1967).

26 This is the animist definition of metamorphosis into an animal: see Viveiros de Castro, *The Relative Native*, p. 243.

27 Friedrich Nietzsche, *Ecce Homo*, 'Why I Am So Clever', translated by Anthony M. Ludovici, at: http://www.gutenberg.org/files/52190/52190-h/52190-h.htm.

28 See John Dewey, *How We Think* (Boston, MA: D. C. Heath and Company, 1910).

29 Lévi-Strauss and Éribon, *Conversations with Claude Lévi-Strauss*, p. 139.

30 'The opposition between culture and nature is neither a primitive fact nor an objective aspect of the world order. We should see it as an artificial creation of culture, a defensive work that culture has dug around its periphery because it felt capable of affirming its existence and its originality only by cutting all the passages likely to attest to its original connivance with the other manifestations of life.' Claude Lévi-Strauss, *Les Structures élémentaires de la parenté* (Berlin: De Gruyter-Mouton, 2002), p. xvii.

31 I am here diverting for my own use Latour's powerful idea of 'landing on Earth'. See Bruno Latour, *Down to Earth: Politics in the New Climatic Regime*, translated by Catherine Porter (Cambridge: Polity, 2018). (This is the translation of the book whose title in French is *Où atterrir?*, which literally means 'Where to land?' or 'Where to come down to earth?' – Translator's note.)

Notes to Chapter Two

1 See Peter Godfrey-Smith, *Other Minds: The Octopus and the Evolution of Intelligent Life* (London: William Collins, 2018).

2 See Jean Goedert et al., 'Euryhaline Ecology of Early Tetrapods Revealed by Stable Isotopes', *Nature*, vol. 558, 2018, pp. 68–72.

3 It should be remembered that the degree of salinity of the internal metabolic water is not identical to that of the salt water of the original environment; it is lower, even in present-day teleost fish.

4 See Lori Marino et al., 'Neuroanatomy of the Killer Whale (*Orcinus orca*) from Magnetic Resonance Images', *Anatomical Record*, vol. 281A, no. 2, 2004, pp. 1256–63; Lori Marino et al., 'Cetaceans Have Complex Brains for Complex Cognition', PLOS/*Biology*, May 2007.

5   Richard G. Delisle, *Les Philosophies du néo-darwinisme* (Paris: PUF, 2009).

6   See Joël Bockaert, *La Communication du vivant* (Paris: Odile Jacob, 2017).

7   See Stephen Jay Gould, *Wonderful Life: The Burgess Shale and the Nature of History* (New York: W. W. Norton & Co., 1989), and Virginie Orgogozo, 'Replaying the Tape of Life in the Twenty-First Century', *Interface Focus*, December 2015.

8   See Virginie Orgogozo, Baptiste Morizot and Arnaud Martin, 'The Differential View of Genotype-Phenotype Relationships', *Frontiers in Genetics*, 19 May 2015, at: https://www.frontiersin.org/articles/10.3389/fgene.2015.00179/full.

9   See Gould, *Wonderful Life*; Simon Conway Morris, *The Crucible of Creation: The Burgess Shale and the Rise of Animals* (Oxford: Oxford University Press, 1998).

10   See Simon Conway Morris, *Life's Solution: Inevitable Humans in a Lonely Universe* (Cambridge: Cambridge University Press, 2003).

11   See Jennifer Ackerman, *The Genius of Birds* (London: Penguin, 2015).

12   See Godfrey-Smith, *Other Minds*.

13   See S. A. Ramesh et al., 'GABA Signalling Modulates Plant Growth by Directly Regulating the Activity of Plant-Specific Anion Transporters', *Nature Communications*, vol. 6, 2015.

14   See Frans de Waal, 'Le comportement moral des animaux', lecture, TEDxPeachtree, November 2011, at: www.ted.com/talks/frans_de_waal_do_animals_have_morals?language=fr#t-211873.

15   Pierre Legagneux et al., 'Our House Is Burning: Discrepancy in Climate Change vs Biodiversity Coverage in the Media as Compared to Scientific Literature', *Frontiers in Ecology and Evolution*, January 2018.

16   Only partly, because we also need a cellular machinery and an

environment to express and modify them: each secret can be translated differently depending on the environmental 'code' used.

17 See Peter Singer, *Ethics into Action: Henry Spira and the Animal Rights Movement* (Lanham, MD: Rowman and Littlefield, 1998).

Notes to Chapter Three

1 Plato, *The Republic*, 430e–432b.

2 Peter Sloterdijk, *You Must Change Your Life*, translated by Wieland Hoban (Cambridge: Polity Press, 2013).

3 René Descartes, *Les Passions de l'âme* (1649) (Paris: Garnier-Flammarion, 1998), Part I, first article.

4 Baruch Spinoza, *Ethics*, part III, prop. 11.

5 Strictly speaking, it is a matter of equality, following the distinction drawn in Chantal Jacquet, *L'Unité du corps et de l'esprit. Affects, actions et passions chez Spinoza* (Paris: PUF, 2004).

6 The difference between joy and pleasure is that pleasure is the joy of part of one's being, whereas joy concerns the whole of the soul: see Spinoza, *Ethics*, Part III, scholia 11.

7 See the work of the Capuchin Yves de Paris (1588–1678), *Les Vaines Excuses du pécheur*, Book II (Paris: Veuve Thierry, 1662), p. 417.

8 See Pierre Le Moyne, S.J. (1602–1672), *Les Peintures morales*, Book IV (Paris: Sébastien Cramoisy, 1645), p. 424.

9 See René de Ceriziers, S.J. (1603–1662), *Les Consolations de la philosophie et de la théologie* (Paris: Michel Soly, 1640), p. 4.

10 Nicolas Coëffeteau (1574–1623), *Tableau des passions humaines*, Book III (Paris: Sébastien Cramoisy, 1625), p. 69.

11 André-Georges Haudricourt, 'Domestication des animaux, culture des plantes et traitement d'autrui', *L'Homme*, vol. II, no. 1, 1962, pp. 40–50.

12 The domestication of sheep, goats and then cattle and horses is characteristic of the Neolithic developments that took place between eleven thousand and eight thousand years ago, accompanied by sedentarization and the invention of agriculture. See Olivier Aurenche and Stefan Kozlowski, *La Naissance du Néolithique au Proche-Orient* (Paris: CNRS Éditions, 2015); Jacques Cauvin, *Naissance des divinités, naissance de l'agriculture* (Paris: CNRS Éditions, 2013).

13 'As if nature, having emerged undisciplined from the hands of God, needed training to become perfected.' The words are those of John Baird Callicott, describing the relations between the Judeo-Christianity of Genesis and nature, in *Pensées de la terre*, translated by Pierre Madelin (Marseilles: Wildproject, 2010), p. 47.

14 Stépanoff, 'Human-Animal "Joint Commitment" in a Reindeer Herding System'.

15 Spinoza, *Ethics*, Part III, 'Definition of emotions', 1.

16 It is this point, among others, that the neurobiologist Antonio Damasio rediscovers in *Looking for Spinoza: Joy, Sorrow, and the Feeling Brain* (New York: Harcourt, 2003).

17 The idea of diplomacy applies primarily to relations with the living world outside of us (nature or biodiversity); it is developed in line with this dimension of the philosophy of ecology in my book *Les Diplomates. Cohabiter avec les loups sur une autre carte du vivant* (Marseille: Wildproject, 2016).

18 '*Hic sunt dracones*' (in Latin, literally 'Here be dragons') is a phrase appearing in medieval cartography and used to designate as yet unknown territories, mimicking a common practice of placing sea snakes and other mythological creatures in the blank areas of a map.

19 Internal flows (coded as passions, drives, emotions, feelings, etc.) are, before they are heteronomized by the morals of the charioteer, like a wild animal before overdomestication: its behaviour is more subtle,

its sociality more balanced, its displays more delicate. It only becomes gross when it is simplified, reduced so as to be controllable.

20 See Philippe Descola, *Beyond Nature and Culture*, translated by Janet Lloyd (Chicago: University of Chicago Press, 2014).

21 See Gilles Deleuze, *Spinoza: Practical Philosophy*, translated by Robert Hurley (San Francisco: City Lights Books, 1988), chapter 2.

22 Steve Peters, *The Chimp Paradox* (London: Vermilion, 2012), p. 11.

23 Ibid.

24 Ibid.

25 Ibid.

26 Virginia Woolf, *The Voyage Out*, at: https://www.gutenberg.org/files/144/144-h/144-h.htm.

27 '[The Stoics] do not believe that the passionate and irrational faculty is distinct from the rational faculty by a difference in nature, but that it is the same part of the soul, which they call *dianoia* and *hegemonikon* (faculty of reflection and guiding principle), which changes and is totally transformed in the passions and in the transformations it undergoes, either in its state or in its dispositions, and that it becomes vice or virtue; in itself, this faculty has nothing irrational about it, but it is said to be irrational when, by the excess of the impulse, it becomes very strong and triumphant and is led to something improper, contrary to the choice of reason. Passion is thus reason, but vicious and depraved – reason which, through the effect of a bad and perverted judgment, has acquired strength and vigour.' Plutarch, quoted in Pierre Hadot, *La Citadelle intérieure* (Fayard: Paris, 1992), p. 154.

28 See Ferhat Taylan, *Mésopolitique. Connaître, théoriser et gouverner les milieux de vie (1750–1900)* (Paris: Éditions de la Sorbonne, 2018).

29 'It is a matter of refreshing, rekindling, and constantly awakening an inner state that is constantly in danger of dozing off and fading away. It is always a question of putting in order an internal discourse which

is dispersed and diluted in futility and routine. In writing his thoughts, Marcus Aurelius therefore practices Stoic spiritual exercises, that is to say he uses a technique, a process, writing, to influence himself, to transform his inner discourse by meditating on the dogmas and rules of life of Stoicism' (Hadot, *La Citadelle Intérieure*, p. 95).

30 Ryan Holiday, *The Daily Stoic: 366 Meditations on Wisdom, Perseverance and the Art of Living* (New York: Portfolio, 2016).

31 Permaculture appeals to similar models of action. Traditional agriculture was labour intensive, industrial agriculture was energy intensive, and permaculture systems are information and design intensive. See David Holmgren, *Permaculture: Principles and Pathways Beyond Sustainability* (London: Permanent Publications, 2011).

32 *Ethics*, Part IV, prop. 4, corollary.

33 Ludwig Wittgenstein, *Remarques mêlées (1914–1951)*, translated by Gérard Granel (Paris: Flammarion, 2002).

34 Spinoza, *Ethics*, Part IV, prop. 7.

35 I am drawing here on Balthasar Thomass, *Être heureux avec Spinoza* (Paris: Eyrolles, 2008).

36 Friedrich Nietzsche, *Beyond Good and Evil*, translated by Helen Zimmern, IV, § 117, at: https://www.gutenberg.org/files/4363/4363-h/4363-h.htm.

37 See Robert Musil, *The Enthusiasts*, translated by Andrea Simon (New York: Performing Arts Journal Publications, 1983).

38 Sloterdijk, *You Must Change Your Life*, p. 165. Sloterdijk's mistake here comes down to the fact that, by rather uneasily taking up the metaphor of training in his 'asceticology', he confuses all anthropotechnics with those resulting from human resources training, with its rhetoric of domestication applied to inner life. He does not go as far as to examine the precise and practical modalities of such an exercise: how to exercise not against oneself, but with oneself. This is in fact what all true ascetics

do, those who are not resentful, life-denying ascetics. What he lacks is a map of the relationships with the living world within us that would stop seeing as natural those we have established since the Neolithic.

39 Davi Kopenawa and Bruce Albert, *La Chute du ciel* (2010) (Paris: Pocket, 'Terre humaine', 2014).

Notes to Chapter Four

1 'Fellow traveller' because this collaboration induces an incessant dialogue on the project and its method. 'Volunteer' because it's a matter of going out into the field to 'work' like the others and with the others, by engaging in the practice – a different figure from the researcher who observes the practitioners from the outside with a notepad. Also, volunteering helps maintain total independence. 'Researcher', finally, because – as we shall see – this immersion in practice makes it possible to record, in the experimental laboratory that we become, philosophical experiences.

2 The expression is taken from Jean-Marc Landry. See the CanOvis website (a portmanteau that merges Canis and Ovis, and makes the project's position visible): www.ipra-landry.com/nos-projets-de-recherche/projet-CanOvis. Thermal imager videos are available on the site under the 'Resources> CanOvis Videos' tab. See in particular the one entitled 'Événement inattendu à la couchade' ('Unexpected event at bedtime').

3 Ibid.

4 Egyptian proverb.

5 Michael D. Wise, *Producing Predators: Wolves, Work and Conquest in the Northern Rockies* (Lincoln: University of Nebraska Press, 2016).

6 Kurdish proverb.

7 I have explored this in various works: *Les Diplomates. Cohabiter avec les loups sur une autre carte du vivant*; 'Nouvelles alliances avec la terre. Une

cohabitation diplomatique avec le vivant', *Tracés*, no. 33, 2017, at: journals.openedition.org/traces/7001; *On the Trail of Animals*, translated by Andrew Brown (Cambridge: Polity Press, 2021).

8   As I read her book, after writing this text, I realized that in some ways this idea has something in common with Donna Haraway's beautiful slogan, 'staying with the trouble'. What interests me here, however, is something different – the idea, which will emerge later, that moral turmoil and contradictory empathies do not depoliticize, but politicize *better*. Staying with the trouble is here a moment, an initial phase, in a metamorphosis that allows us to act differently. See Donna Haraway, *Staying with the Trouble: Making Kin in the Chthulucene* (Durham, NC: Duke University Press, 2016).

9   Minus the grandeur, this is similar to what Nelson Mandela felt about his Black brothers when, in 1995, he proposed the Truth and Reconciliation Commission.

10 The despicable character, in the light of this moral philosophy, is paradoxically not necessarily the least empathetic person: rather, you can tell him from the fact that he *never* feels he has lacked empathy or generosity.

11 This formula was developed by the anthropologist Eduardo Viveiros de Castro to describe the perspectivist ontology: in the latter, it is your position in the field of the relationships you have with others that constitutes your most real identity, and not any intrinsic and independent 'essence' you might have. See Viveiros de Castro, *The Relative Native*, p. 258.

12 The name of this organization, PastoraLoup, is based on *'pasteur'* meaning shepherd and *'loup'* meaning wolf. See https://www.ferus.fr/benevolat/pastoraloup. (Translator's note.)

13 One might ask what interdependences exist between wolves and shepherding. First, even when the wolf is not actually present, his reflection

is inscribed in the flesh of the sheep due to millions of years of coevolution. Indeed, the vigour, vitality and vigilance which animate sheep (despite our efforts to make them more manageable) are a gift from the wolf. Predatory pressure helped create sheep, with their virtues and powers, and we now take advantage of this by domesticating them. The constitutive relationships are very clear. Interdependences are woven into evolutionary history, but also into political history: French shepherding has never been so well understood and represented, it has never had such political leverage as it has since the return of the wolf (it is an objective alliance). We need to face up to the paradox that the living conditions of the shepherds were in many respects improved by the return of the wolf: huts built in the pastures, sheep dogs and fences paid for, lavish compensation . . . An intriguing potential interdependence between wolves and shepherding was pointed out to me by one researcher: because of the return of the wolf, the shepherds benefit from fully funded helpers. For sociological reasons that are not clear, these are often women. According to this researcher (and I have not found any hard data on the question), this creates the conditions for love affairs that start in the mountain pastures. The hut becomes a different place in the middle of a storm, depending on whether you're alone with your dog or with a human partner for a few summer months. Does the wolf help to repopulate the mountains by triggering love affairs? This is a question to be explored.

14 Aldo Leopold, *A Sand County Almanac* (London: Penguin, 2020).

15 This embodiment is not a personification, because it is often acephalous, produced by collectives, nebulae, or even multispecific groups, as we will see below.

16 Josiah Royce, *The Philosophy of Loyalty* (Nashville, TN: Vanderbilt University Press, 1995).

17 I am here following Scott Pratt's magisterial interpretation of Royce

in 'Philosophy in the "Middle Ground": A Reply to My Critics', in *Transactions of the Charles S. Peirce Society*, vol. 39, no. 4, 2003, pp. 591–616. It is in his critical dialogue with the 'logic of relations' of the pragmatist Charles Sanders Peirce that Royce makes the break-through that interests us here. His thesis takes on its full meaning in light of the central concepts of his political philosophy: 'loyalty' to a community, as a place of historical and constructed belonging, is for Royce the constitutive force of the human world. Loyalty is thought of as a framework for interpreting experience, a framework common to a collective, one that enables us to understand ourselves and the world. So we always come from a certain side. But once this postu-late has been made, we need to think about establishing relationships *between* communities loyal to themselves: it is in the difficulty that he raises for himself, by placing the focus on loyalty, that Royce can take seriously the *relation* with otherness. For without otherness, loy-alty is at best solipsistic, and at worst meaningless. Otherness is what communities and loyalties are transformed by. There is therefore a second, centrifugal force which he calls 'interpretation', centred on the emergence of meaning. In *The Philosophy of Loyalty*, he concludes that if we are to go beyond ourselves and find meaning in association, we need a network of interpretive connections with others, in the terms of which actions and judgments can be questioned and constructed. But this interaction, for Royce, must have a particular form: it often requires an intercessor precisely because, without an intercessor, the logics of loyalty reduce otherness to a pure self (in amorous fusion, for example) or to a pure other (as the enemy absolutized). Dyadic relationships are unstable and prone to conflict. This dyad without outside is, in Royce's view, an essentially dangerous community. The relationship must then be mediated by a process of interpretation, defended by an intercessor.

18 Josiah Royce, *War and Insurance. An Address* (New York: Macmillan Press, 1914). The date of publication is obviously rich with meaning.

19 Pratt, 'Philosophy in the "Middle Ground"', p. 606.

20 Royce, *War and Insurance*, p. 52 (my emphasis).

21 Pratt lucidly adds that, from the point of view of each side, the intercessor seems to live in contradiction; his judgments seem erratic and his goals confused: but this is precisely because the latter are judged according to the community of interpretation of a single side.

22 Pratt, 'Philosophy in the "Middle Ground"', p. 606 (my emphasis).

23 It is not strictly speaking the type of spokesperson defended by Bruno Latour. In order to become established, this character needs an original network of institutions; see the discussion in Bruno Latour, *Politics of Nature: How to Bring the Sciences Into Democracy*, translated by Catherine Porter (Cambridge, MA and London: Harvard University Press, 2008). In reality, the spokespersons of the wolves or the sheep have little to do with Latour's conceptual figure, since they fit into the pre-existing traditional representational institutions.

24 For example, in the Groupe National Loup (National Wolf Group) sponsored by the French state, the Associations for the Protection of Nature (APN) present themselves, legitimately in my opinion, as the spokespersons of the wolf; the representatives of the shepherds' union speak on behalf of sheep farmers but also sheep. What is confusing about this institutional form is that it perpetuates the splits and radicalizes them. So when the representatives of the wolf propose a reasonable measure for the benefit of the relationship, this is in all cases rejected on principle by the representatives of shepherds on the grounds that it is the pro-wolf group that is defending it, and the latter inevitably defend the interests of one side to the detriment of the other. The converse also happens, albeit more rarely.

25 We are witnessing this phenomenon today. The more human interests

are threatened by climate change, the more spontaneous morality leaps to their defence: the advances in environmental ethics (biocentrism and ecocentrism) of the last fifty years have been swept away, and 'political ecology' becomes merely the language of sustainable environmental management, intended above all to protect human beings alone in the face of an 'unstable nature'. If the defenders of the living world are identified as representatives of non-humans in a dualistic logic of contradictory interests, these non-humans have no chance of being heard, in the face of interests presented as those of humans in a situation of crisis, distress or danger. This is why climate change needs representatives of interdependences more than representatives of the interests of non-humans envisaged as contradicting those of human beings. This is true from a strategic point of view, but also from a philosophical point of view: to set the representatives of bees or wolves against the representatives of sheep farmers or farmers is to replay by metonymic shift the dualist opposition Humans/Nature – precisely the labyrinth we are trying to get out of.

26 Morizot, *Les Diplomates*, p. 289.

27 The CanOvis project clearly brings creativity of this kind to the fore, mainly through its original position, in contact with sheep farmers and wolves and at the service of both. From this there emerge new initiatives. One of the most promising, in my opinion, is the creation of a decision-support tool, currently being tested, called 'Vigi-prédation'. One of the initiators of the project, Jean-Luc Borelli, working in parallel with the observation of wolves in CanOvis and the management of 'avalanche risk', works in the winter as a tracker-rescuer, and came up with the idea of combining these two questions. His innovative intuition consists in conceiving the risk of attacks by wolves on herds neither as a technical variable that it is possible to fully control, nor as a mere given over which no control is possible, but as a natural hazard,

with the mixture of acceptance of the unforeseen and active room for manoeuvre that this particular type of risk implies. Guided by the deep similarity that he observed between these two types of natural hazards – avalanches, and the act of predation – Jean-Luc Borelli then imagined taking the most innovative initiatives of American and French experts for the management of 'avalanche risk' and transposing it to wolves. What the experts have understood is that the best ways to limit accidents come down to simple and pragmatic decision-support tools, which allow those involved to shape in real time the type of vigilance best suited to the context, while being wary of the 'traps of the unconscious'. The decision-support tool makes it possible to objectify the parameters of the situation in order to have a better understanding of the danger and to react in an adjusted manner. It is a question of adapting one's mode of vigilance in the face of an evolving situation, both to increase the degree of protection in the face of a situation that is becoming critical and to know when to decrease it and return to calm, so as not to exhaust oneself by constant and disproportionate attention. The idea is to offer shepherds a decision-support tool in face of the 'wolf risk' similar to the decision-support tools offered to mountain practitioners to manage the 'avalanche risk'. The originality of this approach therefore comes down to combining new knowledge about wolves as they come into contact with herds, with a risk approach that focuses on the human factor and the vigilance methods to be adopted so as to improve the real-time response to an evolving situation, and thus provide 'the right protection at the right time'. This tool is currently being tested in the field, through dialogue and co-construction with sheep farmers and shepherds.

28 One could object that this approach does not make it possible to protect living beings which do not strictly speaking constitute interdependences, for example redundant species in ecosystems, those which are 'useless' to us or for the healthy and autonomous functioning of

ecosystems – while biocentric environmental ethics defend the intrinsic need to defend *each* form of life in itself. My answer is that this approach does not have a monopolistic aim, it is one language among others – and above all it is a response to a specific situation. Indeed, the new climate situation, weakening our living conditions, will place humans in situations of vulnerability and distress, so that the interests of other living beings will not weigh heavily on our decisions or priorities. It was a luxury of the Thirty Glorious Years of affluence in France (1945–75) that other living beings could be protected in the name of a universal right to exist, grounded in the broadening of ethics proposed by philosophers from rich and developed countries. Indeed, there is an infrastructure of unconscious political economy underneath the biocentric environmental ethics of duty to every life form, and it can be summed up in one sentence: once abundance and security for humans are ensured, we now have the free time, excess energy and money to protect other species, however inconspicuous or seemingly unnecessary to us or to ecosystems. But this luxury is over. The new situation forces us to think differently if we want to make room for other living beings and not run the risk, in the context of a systemic crisis in human societies (climatic, migratory, health, food, etc.), that they will disappear completely off the agenda of priorities. All of us in developed countries will enter into a 'subsistence ecology' which will rule out for the time being luxury cars, private jets and vacations halfway around the world, and the moral and 'selfless' ecology of nature conservation, which relied on the excess calories of rich countries and was based on a plentiful supply of dollars and NGOs. The subsistence ecology that awaits us is neither more nor less than that of all peoples who are aware of their constitutive relationships with their giving environments: what economist Joan Martinez Allier calls 'poor environmentalism'. To put it more bluntly: in the twenty-first century the richest countries will experience a climate migration towards the environmentalism of the poor – towards an ecology of care for giving environments, which no longer sees a split between the environments intended for production (sacrificed to the market) and the microscopic environments cleansed of all human activity, which are viewed as an 'attack' on them (natural parks in the traditional sense of the term). In order not to lose sight of living beings in this conjuncture where the order of priorities will necessarily put human security needs back at the top of the pile, the solution I am proposing here comes down to bringing as many life forms as possible into the Noah's Ark of interdependences, which presents us as woven into them and transfigures our supposedly separated human interests into communities of multispecific importance. It is a way of immediately adjusting ecological thinking to the economic situation that will affect the twenty-first century, when we will no longer have the luxury of devoting energy and funds to the protection of little bustards, for example, for the sole reason that they are beautiful birds and that an environmental ethic states that every species has a sacred right to exist. But this solution goes further: the truth is that we never really know who plays what role in interdependences; and it is in this sense that we must make room for as many living participants in ecosystems as imaginable, while showing consideration for their evolutionary, ecological and human history.

29 Thanks to Charles Stépanoff for his criticism on this point. This reflection was inspired indirectly by his distinction between hierarchical and heterarchical shamanism. See *Voyager dans l'invisible* (Paris: La Découverte, 2019).

30 For some, this may render the decision to call such a person a 'diplomat' obsolete, since the presence of a mandating power and a strict institutional format that gives him his prerogatives and obligations belong to the essence of the character of the diplomat. I don't believe that

this objection is decisive (or that there is anything essential about such words): conceptual creation based on analogy always involves stressing some things and omitting others – emphasizing certain traits of the original character and omitting others, to create something new from the old. Here I am emphasizing certain obvious properties of the original idea of the diplomat, but omitting the existence of a formal institutionalized mandating power (which may exist more informally – it is simply not a necessary condition).

31 Finally, it is important to clarify that this understanding of diplomacy does not involve compromise (this is the classic way that 'radicals' interpret diplomacy). This connotation belongs to the outdated cosmology where the separate terms are primary and fixed: there is only compromise between the pure interests of each of the isolated parts. As soon as the point of view of interdependences emerges, the whole political and moral cartography of interests is changed. The diplomacy in question is uncompromising: it will not compromise on the interests of the relation.

32 Some of these struggles are conducted by beekeeping inter-professionals (Interapi) or federations (the French Federation of Professional Beekeepers, FFAP). But these poles must not obscure less visible and more grassroots forms of mobilization which are taking place all over France.

33 The same fight is being waged by the defenders of a sustainable agro-ecology, who are also diplomats vis-à-vis the life of the soil, when they are obsessed with its point of view as a node of interdependence. One example is the tireless work of the Bourguignon couple, whose microbiological knowledge of the field means they can be great whistle-blowers and great diplomats for the life of the soil. See Claude and Lydia Bourguignon, *Le Sol, la terre et les champs. Pour retrouver une agriculture saine* (Paris: Sang de la Terre, 2015).

34 I have sketched out concepts for thinking about such agonistic,

combative alliances in 'Nouvelles alliances avec la terre'. Lena Balaud and Antoine Chopot have taken up this concept of alliance in their formula of 'sylvan alliances', setting it in another theoretical context, close to Marx and Rancière. Their operation has the important merit of translating this concept more clearly towards the struggles of the radical left, by the use of a conceptual lexicon which comes from the latter. It nevertheless has the weakness of sometimes speaking of alliances with living beings in metaphorical terms, a risk that the concept of 'interspecies alliance' precisely tries to avoid, so as not to fall into the poetic-militant invocation of purely verbal alliances, in which non-human living beings are once again instrumentalized and rendered invisible for interhuman political causes. In their defence, let me say that it is extremely difficult to dodge all metaphors in the conceptual enterprise that I am trying to explore, one which resemantizes the idea of alliance to describe common fronts with entities which do not make contracts with each other and do not speak. Any ecological and ethological imprecision sounds here, to our modern ears, like a metaphor, because it is a forbidden theoretical path, ridiculed by an anthropocentric modernity that hears it only as if it were one of Aesop's fables. See Léna Balaud and Antoine Chopot, 'Nous ne sommes pas seuls. Les alliances sylvestres et la division politique', the text based on a presentation at the Ferme de Lachaud in August 2017, at ladivisionpolitique.toile-libre. org/nous-ne-sommespas-seuls-rencontres-greffer-de-louvert.

35 See Raj Patel and Jason W. Moore, *A History of the World in Seven Cheap Things: A Guide to Capitalism, Nature, and the Future of the Planet* (London: Verso, 2020).

36 Ibid.

37 I am thinking here of the practices defended by the Network for Forest Alternatives (RAF) or, in other respects, by the Pro Silva management.

38 One could object that the idea of interspecific interdependence diplo-

macy, as a transformed political philosophy with regard to the living, is utopian. It seems to me that it is, but 'realistically' so – in a very particular sense, as formulated by John Rawls, who says that political philosophy is realistically utopian when it pushes back what ordinary reflection conceives of as the limits of practical political possibilities (John Rawls, *The Law of Peoples*, new edition (Cambridge, MA: Harvard University Press, 2001)). That is to say, it is its pragmatist capacity to free the theoretical and practical imagination of those concerned for new forms of relations and mobilizations that constitutes its only potential value.

39 Hadot, *La Philosophie comme éducation des adultes*, p. 280.

40 Ibid., p. 261.

41 The contemporary difficulty democratic states have in accepting the idea of limits on growth, production and consumption reveals this aporia. Modern societies view this injunction, necessary today, as a denial of democracy. Liberal theorists see it as a regression with regard to the progressive project (material abundance and freedoms for all); in other words, the architectural political platform of modernity was not compatible with the living world which nevertheless is the basis of democracies. Modernity must rethink itself by accepting limits not as an exogenous constraint of 'Nature' imposing itself on democratic sovereignty from the outside, but as an endogenous condition for human collectives themselves: the independence of a human collective can never be its release or emancipation from the living world on which it is founded. See the illuminating work of Pierre Charbonnier, *Affluence and Freedom: An Environmental History of Political Ideas*, translated by Andrew Brown (Cambridge: Polity Press, 2021).

Notes to Epilogue

1 Free evolution does not mean putting something under a preserving glass, but preserving the evolutionary potential, resilience and spontaneous ecological dynamics that are necessary in themselves and for all around them.

2 According to Immanuel Kant in the *Foundations of Metaphysics of Morals* (1785), the human being alone has an absolute value: 'Beings whose existence depends not on our will but on nature's, have nevertheless, if they are irrational beings, only a relative value as means, and are therefore called *things*; rational beings, on the contrary, are called *persons*, because their very nature points them out as ends in themselves, that is as something which must not be used merely as means, and so far therefore restricts freedom of action (and is an object of respect)' (Immanuel Kant, *Foundations of the Metaphysics of Morals* (1785), at https://courses.lumenlearning.com/suny-classicreadings/chapter/immanuel-kant-on-moral-principles.)

Notes to Afterword

1 On the 'panimal', see above, p. 68 (Translator's note.)

2 Gilbert Simondon (1924–89) was a French philosopher whose work on individuation has influenced Morizot (see above, p. 229, n. 18). (Translator's note.)

3 Adolf Portmann, *Animal Forms and Patterns: A Study of the Appearance of Animals* (New York: Schocken Books, 1967).

4 This quotation is from Gilles Deleuze, *Negotiations, 1972–1990*, translated by Martin Joughin (New York: Columbia University Press, 1995), p. 140.

Credits